Confidence in Public Speaking

Book Team

Editor *Stan Stoga*
Production Editor *Harry Halloran*
Designer *David C. Lansdon*
Art Editor *Gayle A. Salow*
Photo Editor *Michelle Oberhoffer*
Permissions Editor *Karen L. Storlie*
Visuals Processor *Andê Meyer*

WCB **Wm. C. Brown Publishers**

President *G. Franklin Lewis*
Vice President, Publisher *George Wm. Bergquist*
Vice President, Publisher *Thomas E. Doran*
Vice President, Operations and Production *Beverly Kolz*
National Sales Manager *Virginia S. Moffat*
Advertising Manager *Ann M. Knepper*
Marketing Manager *Kathleen Nietzke*
Production Editorial Manager *Colleen A. Yonda*
Production Editorial Manager *Julie A. Kennedy*
Publishing Services Manager *Karen J. Slaght*
Manager of Visuals and Design *Faye M. Schilling*

Cover concept by Geri Wolfe Boesen
Cover illustration and chapter opener illustration by Paul Micich

The credits section for this book begins on page 339, and is
considered an extension of the copyright page.

Library of Congress Catalog Card Number: 89-60782

ISBN 0-697-08618-6

Printed in the United States of America by Wm. C. Brown Publishers,
2460 Kerper Boulevard, Dubuque, IA 52001

10 9 8 7 6 5 4 3 2

Confidence in Public Speaking
Fourth Edition

Paul Edward Nelson
Ohio University, Athens

Judy Cornelia Pearson
Ohio University, Athens

 Wm. C. Brown Publishers

Mid = 1,2,5,7, 9,11, 12
Final = 3,4, 6,8,10,13, 14

Contents

3

The Speaker 35

For the two of our

six children who

have not yet left

the nest:

Benjamin Joseph

Pearson-Nelson, 11

and Rebekah

Kristina Pearson-

Nelson, 8

4

The Audience 55

5

Selecting a Topic and Purpose 77

6

Finding Information   95

7

Speech Organization   119

8

Support Material   141

9

Introducing and Concluding Your Speech   159

10

Language and Your Speech 177

11

Delivery 199

12

Presentational Aids   225

13

Informative Speaking   255

14

Persuasive Speaking   289

Preface

Confidence in Public Speaking was conceived in the late 1970s, born in 1981, and advanced through its childhood with a second edition in 1984 and a third edition in 1987. Having survived the 1980s, this book is ready for its stormy adolescence.

This text is for beginning students whether they are 18 to 21 years old, in mid-career, or retired. This text recognizes that college students continue to change. Once the bastion of affluent youth who had just graduated from high school, today's colleges are populated by people of all ages, colors, creeds, nationalities, and economic levels. The pictures, the illustrations, and the examples recognize the dynamic changes in our college demographics.

What Is the Philosophy behind this Book?

This text was written as a careful blending of traditional rhetoric and social science research. The origins of this field of study extend back to the time of the Romans and Greeks and beyond, but many of the practices are enlightened by twentieth-century social science research.

Besides its blending of ancient and modern streams of knowledge, this book is based on the idea that speakers need to know something before they should say anything. Though the book does teach public speaking skills, those skills are of value only if the speaker has learned to conceptualize, analyze, and criticize the ideas, practices, and polemics that occur in the world.

This text is based on the assumption that human beings learn incrementally; that is, they learn in small bites, not big gulps, especially when they are learning a complex skill such as public speaking. For that reason, the book encourages students and teachers to move from simple to complex, to learn public speaking one small lesson at a time.

Finally, this text is written on the assumption that a textbook ought to be interesting and instructive. We have tried to make this book interesting by telling stories of our students, their fears, their blunders, their successes, and their triumphs. The book is full of examples from their lives and from their speeches. Like many of you, they started the course full of fear and uncertainty and they finished it saying that it was one of the most valuable courses they had ever taken.

What Is New in the Fourth Edition?

Be careful teachers. Two chapters have been switched around. In the fourth edition the chapter on speech organization comes before the chapter on support material. We switched the two chapters in this edition on recommendation of our adopters, who felt students should know the organizational patterns before they found out about the content, ideas, and support material that constitute the body of the speech. Otherwise, the chapters are in the same order as the third edition.

What else is new? Each chapter begins with a simplified outline of inquiries that invite the reader to seek the answers to the questions. We expanded the section on why public speaking is important to learn, added a section on competence, improved the continuity of the confidence theme throughout the book, and highlighted the incremental method more than before.

Some constructivist thought has been woven into the text to emphasize the idea that receivers, inspired by the words of the speaker, compose their own unique messages in their minds. The section on audience analysis has developed beyond demographics to the current idea of psychographics, and the chapter on topic and purpose now includes the statement of central idea or thesis statement so familiar from freshman composition.

The section on oral footnotes has been expanded, as has the section on humor, which now includes wit as well. Also expanded is the section on forecasting organization, and newly introduced is the idea of *mid-speech sag*. The languages of speaking and writing are now conveniently compared in a table that clarifies the differences. And we added a section on computer-generated graphics because of the omnipresence of personal computers.

Finally, the chapter on persuasion has two more types of persuasive speeches, the speech of policy and the speech of values, for a total of six kinds of persuasive speeches.

What Special Features Will You Find?

Each chapter is loaded with features designed to help students understand the content. Each chapter begins with a question outline and ends with application exercises and application assignments that invite students to immediately apply ideas they have just learned. Between the question outline and the application features are lists to summarize the content of each section, graphics to show what is meant, tables to illustrate the content, and even an occasional cartoon. Each chapter includes a vocabulary list, with definitions, of the important concepts.

Perhaps the most important special features are the hundreds of students' speeches, stated in part or in their entirety. You will not find the speeches of Abraham Lincoln or Martin Luther King, Jr. in this book. They were great speakers, but most beginning speakers do not speak as they did. Instead, the text is full of speeches by real students who were in the same position you are in now.

The book begins by inviting you to think of reasons why you should study and practice public speaking. If you are convinced of the rationale for public speaking, then the rest of the book and the course will be both enjoyable and enlightening.

The second chapter is not about speaking but about listening. You will spend about twenty times more time listening to speeches than delivering them in this course. Therefore, it is important to learn how to listen and think analytically about what you hear.

Chapters three and four are about the speaker and the audience, two essential ingredients in the public speaking process. Successful speakers must necessarily be audience-centered because all messages need to be adapted to those who listen.

Next comes a series of eight chapters, the nuts and bolts of public speaking: topic and purpose, finding information, organizing your speech, discovering support material, composing an introduction and conclusion, using the language of public speech, delivery, and presentational aids.

The last two chapters focus on the two most popular forms of public speaking: informative speaking and persuasive speaking.

How Is the Book Organized?

The authors of *Confidence in Public Speaking* are Paul Nelson and Judy Pearson, both of Ohio University in Athens, Ohio.

Paul Nelson and Judy Pearson are a married couple. He is Dean of the College of Communication, and she is a professor in the School of Interpersonal Communication. They have produced many children (six) and many books (eleven), but the basic course in public speaking is their first love. In fact, they even met at a basic course convention.

They have taught public speaking at a variety of schools, big and small, private and public. Judy earned her doctorate at Indiana University and was basic course director—administrator for the public speaking course—at Bradley University, Indiana University-Purdue University at Fort Wayne, and Iowa State University. Paul earned his doctorate at the University of Minnesota and was basic course director at the University of Missouri and chair of the department at Iowa State University before becoming dean at Ohio University.

Some authors of public speaking texts haven't taught the course since they were graduate students. These two authors together have over thirty years experience teaching public speaking and administering public speaking courses. Because they are teachers, they wrote a text that is highly student-centered and very adaptable for the teacher.

Who Wrote this Book?

What Can You Do to Make Future Editions Even Better than this One?

One thing that you can do is to tell us if there are parts of this book—chapters, paragraphs, or even sentences—that need to be improved because you have trouble understanding them. Another thing you can do is to send us examples of your own that you think are as good as or better than the ones in the current book. Your contributions do not have to be entire speeches, although that would be fine. Your contribution could be an alternative to some example, even a couple of sentences, that are in the book.

Send your suggestions or your contributions to:

Paul Nelson and Judy Pearson
483 Radio-TV Communications Building
Ohio University
Athens, OH 45701

Acknowledgements

We would like to thank those faculty members from other colleges and universities who evaluated our work. They include:
Professor Gale Compton,
Eastern Michigan University, Ypsilanti, MI
Professor William Donnelly,
University of Wisconsin—Milwaukee
Professor Robert Jackson,
Ball State University, Muncie, IN
Professor David Kirchner,
Indian Hills Community College, Ottumwa, IA
Professor James Nicholson,
California State University, Los Angeles
Professor Charles Roberts,
McNeese State University, Lake Charles, LA
Professor Ann Scroggi,
Santa Fe Community College, Gainesville, FL
Professor James Stewart,
Tennessee Technical University, Cookeville, TN
Professor Al Teppes,
San Diego City College
Professor Julie Zink,
Spring Hill College, Mobile, AL

Developing Confidence

1

Question Outline

I. What are three reasons why public speaking is an important subject for you to learn?

II. What is the relationship between confidence and competence in public speaking?

III. How does the incremental method develop skills, reduce fear, and increase confidence?

IV. What are the similarities and differences between casual and formal communication?

V. What are the seven components of the communication transaction?

Speech is civilization itself. The word, even the most contradictory word, preserves contact—it is silence which isolates.

THOMAS MANN

Introduction

Confidence in Public Speaking is a college-level textbook for beginning speakers. You may have given speeches in high school, on the job, or even on important occasions, but this book starts at the beginning and carries you through some important types of speeches. Before you begin learning about public speaking, you should first be convinced that this instruction will be of value to you.

Why Should You Learn Public Speaking?

As you sit in your first class in public speaking you might wonder why you should bother to learn how to speak in public. After all, public speaking is frightening to many people and generally we try to avoid doing things that frighten us. So we will start by looking briefly at some of the reasons why you might want to learn from this course.

One reason why you might want to learn how to speak in public is that this activity can give you a high degree of self-satisfaction. Many of the people who are the top public speakers of our time were at one time timid and afraid of other people. Thousands of people in business take the Dale Carnegie course in public speaking. A teacher in that program once told me that he became a teacher in that course because he spent so many years being afraid and inadequate in public situations. He found that conquering his fear and developing his skills were so self-satisfying that he ended up devoting his life to teaching other adults how to do the same thing.

Another reason for learning public speaking is that having something to say and knowing how to say it to others, i.e., communication, can be an invaluable asset in getting ahead in the work world. Studies indicate that people who say little or nothing rarely, if ever, assume positions of leadership. People who are good at encouraging, explaining, motivating, and articulating goals tend to move up to more responsible positions. One of the authors once taught public speaking to union leaders, none of whom had finished college, and found that they needed no encouragement to learn because they had already found that knowing something and being able to communicate it to others moved them up the union hierarchy.

A third reason for learning public speaking is that civilized human beings have been using public speaking as a primary mode of communication since people emerged from caves. The Greeks and Romans venerated people skilled in public speaking, and the people who are best at it still emerge at the top in professions like politics, religion, entertainment, business, education, and even sports. One of the reasons that so many students are still expected to complete a course in public speaking is that even today, in the age of computers and high technology communication, the ability to speak to others is regarded as one of the distinguishing characteristics of an educated person.

Public speaking, then, is something that you want to learn because it gives you satisfaction to be able to tell others what you know, because the ability to speak to others—to inform, explain, motivate, and persuade—is an ability that can advance you in your job or profession, and because the capacity to speak to others, to analyze an audience, and to successfully communicate is seen in our society as something that educated people can do.

This book is called "Confidence in Public Speaking" because gaining confidence is a first step in a longer process that will lead to competence in public speaking.

At first you have to overcome fear, learn how to organize thoughts, learn how to best communicate those thoughts to an audience, and how to evaluate your effectiveness. One course in public speaking ordinarily will not be enough to make you into a professional, but it is a necessary first step. This course will be your starting place, enough to give you the tools for future growth. The activities outlined in this book with the careful coaching by your teacher and the encouragement of your classmates can launch you into a lifetime of increasing satisfaction and effectiveness as a public speaker.

You should be careful not to have unrealistic expectations. Everyone does not start from the same place. Our colleges today are populated by people of all ages, cultures, nationalities, and experiences. Some students have been active in the work world for years. Some come to college with half a lifetime or more of experience; others have very little experience and may even be uncertain about their command of the English language.

This book works on building your confidence so you can spend a lifetime working on your competence and your effectiveness with audiences in public speaking situations. With education and experience you will learn more so that you can speak with authority on more subjects. During your lifetime you will occasionally find issues at work, at home, in your neighborhood, and in social and professional organizations that make you want to speak out and influence other people.

Confidence and Competence

Whatever your age, you have been speaking for many years. Your speaking may have been confined to talking to relatives, friends, classmates, or co-workers. You may not have had much experience talking to twenty, fifty, or one hundred people at once. However, you can learn to speak to larger groups just as you have already learned to talk with those who are close to you.

The method of learning advocated in this book is the **incremental method.** An increment is a brief exposure to a larger whole. Taking a step is an increment in learning to walk. Learning to start a computer is a step in learning to use software. Learning to read a stock market report is a step in learning how to invest. In public speaking, the incremental method is based on the idea that a public speech is complex and can best be learned in increments, or small steps, that lead to mastery of a larger whole.

This book encourages the notion of learning public speaking gradually in small, easy-to-master steps that give you encouragement as you learn. Learning to say a few words about yourself to an audience is easier than researching a complex issue. Preparing a one-minute speech is easier than delivering a ten-minute speech. The idea of learning a complex activity gradually, in small steps, is the key to incremental learning.

Along with gradual learning, the incremental method depends heavily on cooperative support from your teacher and classmates. Teachers and fellow students who reinforce what you did well are inviting you to do more of the same. Their constructive comments about what you could improve show support that is necessary for your development as a speaker.

The incremental method of gaining confidence in public speaking then, is based on two ideas: gradual mastery of simple steps toward a complex goal, and continued reinforcement and support as you learn the steps toward effective public communication.

You already speak. You spend many waking hours talking to others. Most of this talk is **casual communication** with people you know well. Sometimes you talk to express yourself: "Wow, it's hot in here."; sometimes you talk to influence others: "Why don't you open that window over there?"; and other times you add to what people know: "The window will open if you reach up and unlock the sash." Generally, our casual communication with others is for the purposes of self-expression, persuading, or informing. These purposes are the same ones you will find in the more formal arena that we call public speaking.

You know the purposes of both casual and formal communication, and daily you practice the skills that are used in both. For example, you arrange your thoughts, adapt them to your listeners, and respond to their reactions.

1. You arrange your thoughts. When you came onto the campus today, someone may have asked you the location of a certain building. Your message may have been something like this: "Do you see that red brick

building over there? Well, the building you are looking for is a three-story building right across the street from the building you see." The arrangement of your thoughts in casual communication is the same as the **organization** of your ideas in formal communication like public speaking. You do it daily.

2. You adapt your thoughts to your listener. In casual communication you might observe that the person who asked you the question appeared to be a campus visitor, not a student. So you avoided using names of buildings and streets that only students and local residents were likely to know. You did not say, without pointing, that the building the visitor sought was "on the other side of Old Main"—a familiar reference that another student might have understood. Adapting your thoughts to the listener is something you practice all the time. Called listener adaptation in casual communication, this becomes **audience adaptation** in formal communication like public speaking.

3. You respond to your listener's reactions. If the stranger on campus says, "I'm sorry; I am color-blind and I do not know which building you mean," then you would, with ease, use another referent: "That is the building over there (pointing) with the statue in front." You adjust your message to your listener in both casual and formal communication. Responding to your listener's reactions is another communication skill that you have been practicing for years. Called responding in casual communication, it is called **audience feedback** in public speaking.

You are already a person with speaking skills. You have been using them since you were a child, and you have probably improved them with experience. You are not coming into your class in public speaking without any background; instead, you have only to learn how to further develop those skills and abilities that you already possess.

Speaking Formally

Although you are already a practiced speaker at the casual level, you need to learn how to build on those skills and abilities for more formal situations like those in public speaking. The purposes—self-expression, informing, and persuading—are essentially the same in casual or formal communication. The skills in arranging, adapting, and responding are the same as organization, audience adaptation, and feedback in the more formal public speaking situation. What, then, are the differences between communicating casually and formally?

Important differences between casual communication and formal communication are improved language, organization, preparation, and delivery. All you have to learn is how to be even more successful at what you already do daily in your casual conversations with other people.

1. *Improved language* In our everyday communication we are careless with language. We might drop an occasional profanity among friends, have little concern about what words we use to express ourselves, and show little regard for the niceties of grammar, syntax, or diction. But the language of the home, the factory, and the street may not be appropriate behind the pulpit, the podium, or the microphone.

Reprinted by permission of NEA, Inc.

Instead, formal communication calls for care in word choice, concern for audience response to the words, and constant editing of our casual talk for the more discerning scrutiny of a larger audience.

2. *Improved organization* Although you may have been fairly careful in the arrangement of your thoughts for the stranger on campus, and you probably tell a story without blowing the punch line, you are going to have to be even more careful in formal communication. You might be able to scribble out a plan for a doghouse with pencil on a tablet, but a building of steel, glass, and concrete takes drafting tools, sharp pencils, and an even sharper mind.

One of the chief ways to clarify your thoughts for an audience is organizing them in ways that they, not you, understand. Empathy—putting yourself in another person's shoes—is an essential element in organizing your thoughts so the audience can understand them.

3. *Improved preparation* You may not prepare for casual communication: your words to friendly fellow employees on the job may be spontaneous. But in formal communication the speaker often prepares by speaking from knowledge reflecting research, by practicing what to say to avoid errors, and by exercising care to stay on the topic being addressed. This preparation is an important part of your college education because through it you will not only learn more about a variety of topics in which you are interested, but you will learn how to communicate those ideas to others.

4. *Improved delivery* In casual communication we are not as careful about how we communicate a message, particularly if it is to someone like our spouse or classmate. We don't care if we are standing or seated, droppin' our g's, or leaving large gaps of silence in our talk. When we speak formally in a public situation, however, we must be aware of how we communicate. How we look and act when we speak may determine whether or not the audience listens. You are already more careful when you talk to someone higher in status, when you are asking a stranger for help, and when you are speaking for others. Generally, the more people you are addressing, the more careful you have to be about how you deliver your message.

Modeling the Transaction

What happens when people communicate? A transaction occurs in which both the speaker and the listener, at the same time, send, receive, and interpret messages. At first you might think that public speaking is predominantly one-way communication, with words going only to the audience. But reflection on the situation reveals that the speaker receives messages from the audience, and that optimally both audience and speaker continually respond to each other. If you doubt that speakers are strongly influenced by the reactions of the audience, consider this example.

While teaching at the University of Missouri one of the authors challenged the honors section of a public speaking class to subtly reinforce some behavior without his catching on. Soon after the challenge they noticed that he stroked his beard. They determined that looking attentive, asking questions, and showing interest were reinforcing to the professor. After a few weeks of rewarding him for stroking his beard, they had increased the number of strokes from one or two per class hour to over twenty.

Communication is thus transactional with speaker and listener simultaneously sending, receiving, and interpreting messages. What else is part of this process called communication? There are seven ingredients in communication transactions: sources or speakers, receivers or listeners, verbal and nonverbal messages, a channel or means of communication, responses or feedback, obstacles or noise, and a situation or context in which communication occurs. Let us examine each of these components of the process in more detail, since they are part of the model of communication on which this book is developed.

Source

The **source** or speaker originates the message. Who the sender is makes a difference in whom, if anyone, will listen. Consider the person who walks down a street in New York City. Blind people clink their cups for contributions, street corner evangelists shake their Bibles in the air, and vendors push everything from bagels to booties. Would you listen to the messages they are sending? Some of the talented singers, dancers, and instrumentalists might attract your attention, but few of the many contenders for your eye and ear would succeed. Sources send messages but no transaction occurs until the source and receiver are conjoined by the messages between them.

Similarly, in the lecture hall you hear some professors who capture your attention and leave you wishing for more. Occasionally you hear others whose ideas put you to sleep. There is no such thing as a source without a receiver or a speaker without an audience, because both are necessary components in the communication transaction.

Receiver

The **receiver,** listener, or audience is the individual or group that hears, and hopefully listens to, the message sent by the source. All individuals are unique. What you have as receivers are individuals who have all inherited certain characteristics and developed others as a result of their families, friends, and education.

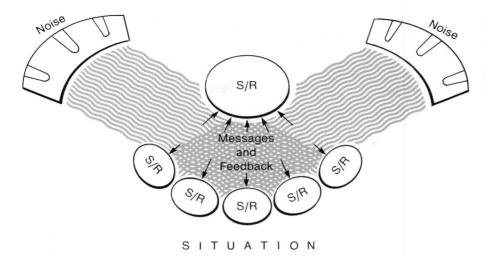

Figure 1.1 A communication transaction with S/R indicating that people serve simultaneously as senders and receivers.

SITUATION

The best speakers can "read" an audience; they can—through analysis or intuition—tell what an audience wants, needs, or responds to. This sort of group empathy allows some speakers to be seen as charismatic: they seem to exhibit what the audience feels.

Even a beginning speaker can learn to see the world through the audience's eyes. Nothing helps more in the classroom than to listen carefully to your classmates' speeches, because every speech will reveal as much about the speaker as it does about the issue being discussed. Few speakers outside the classroom are able to hear everyone in their audience reveal herself or himself through a speech.

Message

Verbal and nonverbal messages are an integral part of the communciation transaction. What else links the source and the receiver? The message is sensed by both the source and the receiver: the facial expressions seen, the words heard, the visual aids illustrated, and the ideas or meanings conveyed simultaneously between source and receiver. **Verbal messages** are the words chosen for the speech. **Nonverbal messages** are the movements, gestures, facial expressions, and paralinguistic features that reinforce or contradict the words, such as pitch or tone that can alter the meaning of the words.

Channel

The **channel** is the means of communciation whether it be coaxial cable, microwave, radio, video, or air. In the public speaking classroom the channel is the air that carries the sound waves from the mouth of the source to the ear of the receiver. The channel might not seem to make very much difference, but messages have decidedly different impact depending on whether they are heard as a rumor or observed on network news.

Messages are both seen and heard.

Some public speaking students discover the differences in channels when their teacher videotapes their speeches. Watching yourself electronically reproduced is not the same as watching a live performance, because different channels are themselves part of the message. As Marshall McLuhan said, "The medium is the message."

Feedback

Feedback can be verbal or nonverbal. During a public speech most of the audience feedback is nonverbal: head nodding, smiling, frowning, complete attention, fiddling with a watch. All of this nonverbal feedback is data for the speaker to interpret.

The question-and-answer session is a good example of verbal feedback in which the audience has an opportunity to seek clarification, verify speaker positions on issues, and challenge the speaker's arguments. In any case, feedback, like the thermostat on a furnace or air conditioner, is the speaker's monitoring device that continuously tells if the message is working.

Another component in the transactional process we call communication is **noise,** a term that means interference or obstacles to communication. Noise is whatever keeps a source from gaining feedback, a receiver from hearing words or seeing facial expressions, etc. Noise can be internal or external. If you are distracted during a speech by the presence of another person whom you find attractive, then you are experiencing internal noise that keeps you from receiving the message. If you are unable to hear the speaker because the door is open and you cannot hear over the hall noise, you are experiencing external noise. Noise is a broad term used to classify anything that is an obstacle to communication, whether it be the wanderings of the mind or someone's radio music interfering with the speaker's words.

Communication occurs in a context called the situation. The **situation** is the time, place, and occasion in which the message sending and receiving occurs. The situation can determine what kind of a message is appropriate. Only certain kinds of messages and speakers are possible at funerals, senate debates, bar mitzvahs, court hearings, and dedications.

In the classroom the situation is a room of a certain size containing a number of people who fill a specified number of seats. The physical setting can mean that you can talk almost conversationally, or that you must shout to be heard.

The process of communication is the dynamic interrelationship of source, receiver, message, channel, feedback, noise, and situation. None of these components can be isolated, nor do any of them have any meaning without the others. They are what occurs in public speaking.

Public speaking is more than just a dynamic interrelationship of source, receiver, message, channel, feedback, noise, and situation. First, this relationship is linear; that is, it makes communication look as if the source or speaker imposes a message on an audience. Instead, speaker and audience influence each other.

For example, let's say that you are trying to convince fellow workers that they should unionize. You argue first that the union will result in higher pay. The audience appears unimpressed. So you argue that the union will bring benefits like better working conditions. They doze. Finally, you argue that the workers could get a better medical plan for their families, reduce their out-of-pocket health expenses, and get a dental plan. This argument gets attentive looks, some questions, and considerable interest. The audience has influenced what the speaker will say.

The speaker does convey a message through words and action, but the audience gives meaning to that message through its own thought processes. An example is George Bush as the presidential candidate who said his political opponent was a "card-carrying ACLU (American Civil Liberties Union) member." Most young people did not attribute much meaning to the statement even if they recognized the ACLU as an organization that attracts people of liberal persuasion. But voters in their forties and older remembered the McCarthy era when accusations of being "a card-carrying communist" were enough to bring disgrace and loss of job. In short, the audience gave the message meaning depending on their age, experience, and knowledge of political history.

Audiences interpret messages, they construct messages of their own from the words that they hear, and they carry with them their own rendition of the message and often, others' analysis of the same message. A good example of the latter is the concept of "spin." Political campaigns these days are full of "spin doctors," that is, media experts who try to tell an audience how to interpret the speaker's message. The expert tells the audience who won the political debate, telling the audience what they were supposed to derive from the words. The idea of "spin" recognizes the notion that audiences construct their idea of the message themselves together with what others tell them the message meant. The process of communication is a transaction between source and receivers that includes mutual influence, interpretation and construction of meaning, and the development of an individualized message that includes how others respond.

Preparing to Speak

You might be asked to speak on your very first day of class. The idea of speaking early in the course is consistent with the incremental method as long as the speech is easy to give, poses little risk, and has a high chance of being rewarding to the speaker.

Many speech communication teachers use "ice breakers," short speeches that help the students in the class know each other better. Sometimes the assignment is to introduce yourself, explain your uniqueness, or discuss some interesting aspect of your work, your family, or your recreation.

These suggestions are designed to help you with that first speaking experience in your public speaking class. Even if you do not accomplish them all, these suggestions may be helpful:

1. Talk about something you care about and the audience is more likely to care, too.
2. Focus on a few aspects of the topic that are most likely to interest the audience instead of revealing everything you know about an issue.
3. Compose your speech as a story about the topic to make it easier for you and the audience to remember.
4. In the few minutes you have to get ready, you should write down a few key words to remind you of what you want to say so you will not worry about forgetting your message.
5. Help the audience get acquainted with you by writing your name on the board, pronouncing it carefully, repeating it occasionally, and revealing yourself through the speech.

6. Try to speak as you would speak to a friend, but loudly enough for all to hear.
7. Try to speak slowly for students who may want to write down some of the information you provide.

Perhaps these few suggestions will assist you in your first classroom speech. Following is a brief example of a speech that a student gave during the first week of class. The assignment was to teach the class your name, reveal some information about yourself, then tell a true story about yourself that would help your classmates understand you. The speech was ungraded, but everyone was instructed to take notes on the speech and to reward the speaker with applause after the presentation. No time limit was given, but the expectation was a relatively brief speech. Here is how one student fulfilled the assignment.

My name is Mary McCarthy (she wrote the name on the board when she came to the front of the room). I am twenty-eight years old, and I am the mother of three small children. I am one of many students here who started college at seventeen, dropped out to get married—actually I dropped out to have more fun—and then realized that I was getting nowhere without a degree.

My story about myself is about my work. For the last six years I have worked at a box factory where we manufacture, fold, and ship boxes all over the country to hold appliances like TVs, video recorders, microwaves, and other middle-sized things. The people I work with at

the factory are like me except that most of them never even went a day to college. They are nice folks, but they never have enough money and they never will. With six years seniority I still earn just a little above the minimum wage, and I get only two weeks off per year when the entire factory closes down in August. I had one year of fun after I dropped out of college, but I regret that now I will take three times as long to get my degree because I have to take these courses at night, have to pay a babysitter to take care of the kids, and have to study when I am already tired from work. Just so you don't get the wrong idea, I do not feel very sorry for myself. I am an upbeat person. I love my kids, tolerate my work, and really like my courses. I am tough, and determined to make a better life for myself and my kids. I am Mary McCarthy and I am proud of it. (Audience applause.)

Summary

The goal of this book is to help you learn confidence in public speaking. The ideas of incremental learning and positive reinforcement are two important aspects of learning confidence. Incremental learning is instruction in small palatable bites that encourages you to feel good about yourself, your message, and your audience. The idea is to move from simple to complex speeches, shorter to longer time limits, and single to multiple ideas—and to do this gradually over the term.

You have already practiced the elements of public speaking even if you have never delivered a speech. Casual conversation, the kind we do with our friends daily, is done for the same **purpose** as formal speaking: for self-expression, information, and persuasion. Casual communication also requires arranging of thoughts (speech organization), adapting to your listener (audience adaptation), and responding to your listener (audience feedback in more formal communication).

There are differences between casual and formal communication, too. Among them are the facts that public speaking often requires improved language and organization, increased preparation, and better delivery than does more casual communication.

The transactional nature of communication is illustrated in the process model showing the interrelationship of source, receiver, message, channel, feedback, noise, and situation. Public speaking is the dynamic relationship among these component parts, none of which function independently of the others. Remember too that the individuals in your audience provide the meaning of your speech. They listen, interpret, and construct their message from your words and actions. Speakers influence audiences, audiences influence speakers, and speakers and audiences together formulate messages.

Next we will turn to the complimentary skill called listening. You will spend more of your life listening than speaking, so you should learn to be successful at it. Listen to your classmates so that you can learn from the content of their speeches. Watch your classmates so that you can learn to imitate the good things they do and avoid the problems they exhibit. And listen to your classmates so that you can learn about each of them, because they will be your audience in this class.

▼▼

Application Exercises

1

Write as many reasons as you can why public speaking could be useful to you now or in the future.

2

Examine the characteristics of casual communication—arranging, adapting, and responding—and reveal which you do best.

3

Examine the characteristics of formal communication—improved language, organization, preparation, and delivery—and speculate about which you believe will cause you the least problems.

4

Mark one column "Conversation with Friend between Classes" and a second column "Speech in Front of Class." Take six of the seven components of a communication transaction—source, receiver, message, channel, feedback, noise, and situation—and after each component write briefly about how the model would work in the two situations.

In order to learn the names of your classmates and some information about them, use the following suggestions.

Application Assignment

1. The instructor could write on the board those items that members of the class want to know about one another—name, major, year in college, marital status, hobbies, job, children, etc.

2. Have the class introduce themselves by talking about whatever items on the board they select.

The class should take notes on the information given because it can be an important part of their audience analysis for later speeches.

▼▼▼

Vocabulary

audience adaptation   Messages should be prepared with the particular audience in mind, a process called audience adaptation.

audience feedback   The speaker's adjustments in the message based on the audience's responses to the speech.

casual communication   Informal conversation in private situations with intimates, friends, co-workers, and relatives. This talk tends to be unpremeditated.

channel   The means by which the message is sent: air, paper, microwave, wire, radio signals, video, etc.

feedback   Verbal and nonverbal messages from an audience to a speaker who must interpret those messages.

incremental method   Learning public speaking in simple steps over time.

language   The use of meaningful sounds to communicate feelings and ideas.

noise   Whatever interferes with the communication process by impeding transmission or reception of messages.

nonverbal messages   The gestures, movements, facial expressions, and nonword sounds (pitch and tone) that communicate meaning.

organization   Called arrangement of thought in casual communication, this careful structure and design of thoughts and arguments is characteristic of formal communication.

purpose   Self-expression, informing, and persuading are the purposes of both casual and formal communication.

receiver   The one to whom a message is sent.

situation   The context in which communication occurs.

source   The message sender or—in public speaking—the speaker.

verbal messages   The words that are chosen for the speech.

Listening

2

It is the province of knowledge to speak and it is the privilege of wisdom to listen.

OLIVER WENDELL HOLMES

Introduction

One of the ways that you will grow in confidence as a public speaker and improve your own skills as a communicator is by learning to be a good listener. Listening is harder for some performance-oriented speakers than speaking. Yet effective listening can increase what you know as you learn from the speeches of others, can teach you to be an effective speaker by becoming an active listener and sensitive observer of others, and can help you become expert at analyzing speakers and audiences.

When you enrolled in the public speaking course, you probably wondered how many speeches you would give, how long each would be, and whether you had to submit an outline with your speeches. In other words, you focused on the speaking function of the course. Ironically, most of your time in public speaking class is spent listening to and evaluating speeches. If you have twenty-five classmates, you spend *twenty-five times* as much time listening to speeches as you do delivering them!

The public speaking classroom provides an opportunity for you to become a better informative and evaluative listener. Your skill as an informative listener brings many benefits. You will learn a great deal about a variety of subjects in the one to two hundred speeches you hear, and you will learn more about public speaking techniques as your classmates and instructor present models of effective and ineffective public speaking skills. As an evaluative speech listener, you will learn standards for appraising public speeches that can be applied outside the classroom, you will learn appropriate skills helpful to your own public speaking, and you will help your fellow students improve their ability as effective public speakers. In order to improve as a listener, you should understand the subject of listening and grow in confidence as an informative and evaluative listener by practicing the component skills. Your effort to understand this subject begins with some of the inaccurate assumptions that people hold about listening.

Three False Assumptions about Listening

Perhaps you are already questioning the value of this chapter. You may believe you are already a good listener, that listening, unlike speaking, is something that cannot be taught, or that your most recent hearing test demonstrates you can listen well. If any of these thoughts have occurred to you, you have one or more of the three most common mistaken notions about listening. These false assumptions are worth considering in more detail.

Assuming that You Listen Well

If you ask a classmate if he or she listens well, the likely answer is yes. Virtually everyone from the beginning kindergarten student to the college sophomore to the graduate professor believes that he or she listens effectively to other people. This assumption is not borne out by research. Ralph Nichols and his associates conducted considerable research at the University of Minnesota on thousands of students and hundreds of business and professional people. They found that people remember only half of what they hear immediately after a message, and only twenty-five percent of what they hear when tested two months later.[1] You may be comforted by these statistics the next time you do poorly on a final exam. After

Reprinted by permission of NEA, Inc.

all, the average person remembers only twenty-five percent of what he or she heard early in the term. Nichols' research and your own experience in recalling information demonstrate that the assumption that you listen well is probably inaccurate.

If you feel that you are already an effective listener, you probably do not attempt to identify ways to improve your listening. If you feel that you are not an effective listener, you may have resigned yourself to being inadequate in this area. One of the reasons you may fail to improve your listening is that there are few alternatives available. Studies show that most of your communication time is spent listening, followed, in order, by speaking, reading, and writing.[2] Curiously, you probably spend an inverse proportion of time in required classes studying these other subjects. You probably spent much of your time in grade school, junior high, and high school studying the two communication skills that we actually use the least: reading and writing. But you have probably never taken a course at any grade level on the communication skill you use the most: listening. Because of the lack of course work and study in listening, we incorrectly assume that listening is a communication skill that cannot be learned.

Assuming You Cannot Be Taught to Listen Better

How many times have you said or had someone say to you, "What do you mean you don't know? I told you!"? People assume that if they say something to someone, the person is listening. For instance, you know how frequently you daydream while hearing a lecturer, how often you are distracted by the person next to you as you hear a student speaker, and how regularly you spend time planning

Assuming that Listening and Hearing are the Same Thing

Listening requires hearing and interpretation of what is heard.

your afternoon while sitting in morning classes. In each case, you can hear the speaker, but you may not do well on an examination of the material. Passing a hearing test is not a sufficient guarantee that you are an effective listener.

Hearing and listening are separate activities. **Hearing** is a physical function you are able to perform unless you suffer from physiological damage or cerebral dysfunction. **Listening,** on the other hand, is a selective activity that involves the reception and interpretation of aural stimuli. You can probably hear if your ears are normal, but you can listen only if you recognize the barriers to effective listening and actively do something to overcome them.

Barriers to Effective Listening

After reading the previous section, you may no longer believe that you naturally listen well, that you cannot learn listening skills, and that your hearing is the same as your listening ability. What are some of the factors that interfere with your ability to listen? Have you ever sat in a lecture and smiled when the lecturer made a joke, nodded when he or she sought affirmation, established eye contact with the lecturer, and still not remembered a single thing that the lecturer said?

As students, it is easy to learn how to fake attention. This is the strategy you use in situations where the most acceptable social behavior is paying attention. It is the strategy you may use in classes, at social gatherings, and in "listening" to fellow students' speeches. You undoubtedly use this strategy when you are bombarded with more messages than you want to hear. Consequently, you may learn the appropriate nonverbal behavior—eye contact, attentive appearance, and apparent note taking—when you are actually wondering if the speaker is as tired as you are as you scribble pictures in your notebook. Faking attention is both a result and cause of poor listening.

Faking Attention

Three additional barriers to effective listening are prejudging the speaker, prejudging the speech, and yielding to distractions. Each of these barriers in turn has subtypes that concern you if you wish to improve your listening skills.

• •

Barriers to Effective Listening

1. Faking attention
2. Prejudging the speaker
3. Prejudging the speech
4. Yielding to distractions

• •

We all make judgments about speakers before they say a word. You might dismiss a speaker because of attire, posture, stance, or unattractiveness.

Prejudging the Speaker

Researchers have found that the speaker's gender appears to be an important variable in our judgment. For instance, when male and female speakers are given the same grade, the male speakers receive fewer positive comments than do the female speakers.[3] Female evaluators give men higher evaluations than women,[4] and male evaluators tend to grade women higher than men.[5] In addition, one of the authors found that sexist teachers grade speeches differently: they do not write as many comments as nonsexist teachers do.[6]

Status and stereotypes are two additional preconceived attitudes that affect our ability to listen to another person. If the speaker has high status, you may tend to accept the message more easily, without listening critically to the message. You may not exercise careful judgment if the speaker is a visiting dignitary, a physician, an attorney, or a distinguished professor. If you perceive the speaker to be low in status—a beginning student, a maintenance worker in the dormitory, or a student who flunked the mid-term—you tend not to listen to his or her message at all, and you are unlikely to remember what the speaker said. Perceived status seems to determine whether you are likely to listen critically or at all.

Stereotypes also affect our ability to listen. If the other person announces that she is a Republican, is opposed to women's rights, or believes a woman's place is in the home, you may prematurely judge her as a reactionary and ignore her speech. When speakers seem to belong to groups for whom you have little regard—rich, poor, jocks, brains, or flirts—you may reject their messages.

Do you dismiss seniors as too pretentious or people who slouch as uninteresting? If you draw such conclusions about speakers before they begin a speech, and then ignore the message as a result of this prejudgment, you are handicapped by a factor that interferes with your listening.

Prejudging the Speech

A second set of factors that may interfere with your ability to listen to a speaker is your tendency to prejudge the speech. The same human tendency that causes you to judge the speaker before a speech causes you to judge the speech before you understand it. The most common conclusions we prematurely draw about a speech are that it is boring, too difficult to understand, irrelevant, or inconsistent with our own beliefs.

You may judge a speech to be boring because you feel you already know the information the speaker is presenting, you have already experienced what the speaker is describing, or the speaker is trying to persuade you to do something that you already do. In other words, your own feelings of superiority—informational, experiential, or attitudinal—interfere with your ability to listen.

You may decide a speech is too difficult to understand and dismiss it because "I wouldn't understand it anyway." You may have the tendency to categorize many topics as too difficult, or you may selectively identify topics that deal with thermonuclear power, quantum mechanics, or Keynesian economics as too complex for your understanding, even though the speaker's purpose is to simplify the concept or to inform you of the basic terminology.

Occasionally you may decide that a speech is irrelevant. For some people nearly all topics may seem unimportant. For others, a few topics are dismissed as soon as they are announced. A business major in the audience may feel that American Indian literature does not affect him; a college sophomore may conclude that a speech on retirement is immaterial; or a black student may show no interest in a description of life in an all-white community.

One of the reasons people dismiss another person's topic as irrelevant is because of simple egocentrism. **Egocentrism** is the tendency to view ourselves as the center of any exchange or activity. People who are egocentric are only concerned with themselves and pay little or no attention to others. Egocentrism may cause a listener to dismiss any speeches by others. Whether you refuse to consider most speeches, or ignore certain topics, you are blocking your ability to become an effective listener. If you listen attentively to the speech beyond the statement of the topic or purpose, you may find information that clearly shows the relevance of the topic for you.

On the chalkboard:

Break Even Point
$R = VC + FC$
$50X = 25X + 20,000$
$50X - 25X = 20,000$
$\dfrac{25X}{25} = \dfrac{20,000}{25}$
$X = 800 \text{ units}$

$X = \#\text{ of units}$
$R = $
$VC = $
$FC = 20,000$

Finally, you may dismiss the speech because you decide that you disagree with the topic or purpose. You may feel that a speaker should not inform you about how to smoke crack, provide information on birth control, show examples of pornography, or persuade you to limit salt or sugar consumption. Your opposition to crack, practicing birth control, seeing nudity, or learning about nutritional findings may block your ability to listen to the speaker. You may conclude that the speaker is "on the other side" of the issue and that your seemingly different attitudes prohibit open communication.

Defensiveness commonly occurs when a speaker's topic or position on an issue is different from your own. You may be threatened by the speaker's position and feel that you must defend your own. You may believe you are being attacked because you champion a specific cause—like women's rights, energy conservation, or the anti-tax movement—that the speaker opposes. You may be standing ready for anyone who dares provoke you on your favorite cause. You may be only too eager to find fault with another person's speech. Try to recognize possible blocks to effective listening that defensiveness and dismissal of the speech through disagreement provide in the speaking-listening process.

| Yielding to | The listener's four most common distractions are factual, semantic, mental, and |
| Distractions | physical. Yielding to **factual distractions** means listening only for the facts in- |

stead of the main ideas or general purpose of the speech. The formal educational experiences you have had in which you were required to listen to teachers in order to successfully pass objective exams may contribute to this tendency. Rather than looking at the entire speech, you may be focusing on some small, isolated facts. You jeopardize your understanding of the speaker's main idea or purpose when you jump from fact to fact rather than attempting to weave the major points into an integrated pattern.

Semantic distractions are specific words or phrases that we allow to emotionally affect us. You may react this way if someone uses a word or phrase in an unusual manner, or you find a particular concept distasteful or inappropriate, or you do not understand the meaning of a term. Regionalisms—words that are used in a way unique to a particular geographical area—provide one example of words used in a different way. If a speaker talks about the harmful qualities of "pop," and you refer to soft drinks as "soda," you may react negatively to "pop." If you feel that "girl" should not be used to designate an adult woman, then you may be distracted in your listening. Finally, unfamiliar words may cause a reaction that interferes with listening to the speaker's message.

Mental distractions include your engaging in daydreaming, counterarguments, recollections, or future planning while listening to a speaker. These mental distractions may originate from something the speaker has stated or from your own preoccupation with other thoughts. Perhaps mental distractions occur because of the difference between the speed at which we can listen and the speed at which we can speak. The average American talks at a rate of 125 words per minute, but can receive about 425 words per minute. This discrepancy allows us to engage in many mental side trips that may be more relevant to us. Unfortunately, we may become lost on a side trip and fail to return to the original path.

Physical distractions include any physical stimuli that interfere with our attention to the speaker. Stimuli that may affect our listening are sounds such as a speaker's lisp, a buzzing neon light, or an air hammer; sights such as a speaker's white socks, a message on the chalkboard, or bright sunlight; smells such as a familiar perfume, baking bread, or freshly popped corn.

In this section we surveyed three sets of barriers to effective listening: prejudging the speaker on the basis of gender, status, or stereotypes; prejudging the subject and dismissing it as boring, too complex, irrelevant, or opposed to our own point of view; and yielding to factual, semantic, mental, or physical distractions. Consider how you can overcome these barriers and become more effective as an informative and evaluative listener.

We have considered three false assumptions about listening and some barriers to effective listening. We will now examine the two types of listening that occur most frequently in the public speaking situation: informative listening and evaluative listening.

Informative listening refers to the kind of listening you engage in when you attend class and listen to an instructor, attend baseball practice and listen to the coach, or attend a lecture and listen to a visiting speaker. Your purpose in informative listening is to understand the information the speaker is presenting. You may try to understand relevant information about the speaker and factors that led to the speech, as well as the central idea of the speech itself. Informative listening requires a high level of involvement in the communication process. What are some of the other factors that contribute to effective informational listening? What can you do to overcome many of the barriers discussed in the previous section?

In order to be successful at informative listening, you can engage in at least ten practices. These practices include (1) suspend judgments about the speaker, (2) focus on the speaker as a source of information, (3) concentrate your attention on the speaker, (4) listen to the entire message, (5) focus on the values or experiences that you share with the speaker, (6) focus on the main ideas the speaker is presenting, (7) recall the arbitrary nature of words, (8) focus on the intent, as well as the content, of the message, (9) be aware of your listening intensity, and (10) remove or ignore physical distractions. Let us consider each of these in more detail.

Informative Listening

Practices for Effective Listening

1. Suspend judgments about the speaker.
2. Focus on the speaker as a source of information.
3. Concentrate your attention on the speaker.
4. Listen to the entire message.
5. Focus on the values or experiences that you share with the speaker.
6. Focus on the main ideas the speaker is presenting.
7. Recall the arbitrary nature of words.
8. Focus on the intent, as well as the content, of the message.
9. Be aware of your listening intensity.
10. Remove or ignore physical distractions.

· ·

Suspend Judgments about the Speaker

Suspend your premature judgments about the speaker so you can listen for information. Instead of concluding that speakers are, or are not, worthy of your attention before you have heard them, wait until you have heard the speakers out.

If you make decisions about people because of their membership in a particular group, you risk serious error. Beer drinkers may be thin, members of fraternities may not be conformists, and artists may be disciplined.

Focus on the Speaker as a Source of Information

If you categorize people, it is easy to dismiss them. When you focus on the speaker as a valuable human resource who can share information, ideas, thoughts, and feelings, you are better able to listen with interest and respect. Every speaker you hear is likely to have some information you do not already know. Try to focus on these opportunities to learn something new.

Concentrate Your Attention on the Speaker

If you find yourself dismissing many of the speeches you hear as boring, consider whether you are overly egocentric. Perhaps your inclination to find your classmates' speeches boring is due to your inability to focus on other people. Egocentrism is a trait that is difficult to overcome. The wisest suggestion, in this case, is to keep in mind one of the direct benefits of concentrating your attention on the speaker: if you focus on the other person while speaking, the person will probably focus on you when you are speaking. Even more important, you will come across better if the speaker perceives you to be a careful listener. Nothing else you can do—including dieting, using makeup, wearing new clothing, or making other improvements—will make you as attractive to others as the ability to listen to someone else.

Do not dismiss the speech after you have heard the topic. More than likely the speaker will add new information, insights, or experiences which will shed additional light on the subject. One professor teaches an upper-division argumentation course to twenty students each quarter. Four speeches are assigned, but every speech is given on the same topic. In a ten-week period, students hear eighty speeches on the same topic, but every speech contains some new information. The class would be dismal if the students dismissed the speeches after hearing that they would all cover the same topic. Instead of considering the speeches boring, the students find them interesting, exciting, and highly creative.

Listen to the Entire Message

If you find you are responding emotionally to the speaker's position on a topic and you directly oppose what he or she is recommending, try to concentrate your attention on those attitudes, beliefs, or values you have in common. Try to identify with specific statements the speaker is making. The speaker might seem to be attacking one of your pet beliefs or attitudes, but, if you listen carefully, you may find that the speaker is actually defending it from a different perspective. Maximizing our shared ideas and minimizing our differences result in improved listening and better communication.

Focus on the Values or Experiences You Share with the Speaker

Keep in mind that you do not have to memorize specific facts the speaker is presenting. Rarely will you be given an objective examination on the material in a student speech. If you want the specific information being presented, ask the speaker after class for a copy of the outline, a bibliography, or other pertinent documentation. Asking the speaker for specific information is flattering. Stating in class that you can recall the specific population figures cited but have no idea of the speaker's purpose may seem offensive.

Focus on the Main Ideas the Speaker Is Presenting

If you find that you sometimes react emotionally to four-letter words or to specific usages of some words, you may be forgetting that words are simply arbitrary symbols people have chosen to represent certain things. Words do not have an inherent, intrinsic, "real" meaning. When a speaker uses a word in an unusual way, or when you are unfamiliar with a certain word, do not hesitate to ask how the word is being used. Asking for such information makes the speaker feel good because you are showing interest in the speech, and the inquiry will contribute to your own knowledge. If you cannot overcome a negative reaction to the speaker's choice of words, recognize that the emotional reaction is yours and not necessarily a feeling shared by the rest of the class or the speaker. Listeners need to be open-minded; speakers need to show responsibility in word choice.

Recall the Arbitrary Nature of Words

Active listening takes concentration.

Focus on the Intent and the Content of the Message

Use the time between your listening to the speech and the speaker's rate of speaking to increase your understanding of the speech. Instead of embarking on mental excursions about other topics, focus on all aspects of the topic the speaker has selected. Consider the speaker's background and his or her motivation for selecting a particular topic. Try to relate the major points the speaker has made to his or her stated intentions. By refusing to consider other unrelated matters, you will greatly increase your understanding of the speaker and the speech.

Be Aware of Your Listening Intensity

You listen with varying degrees of intensity. Sometimes when a spouse or roommate gives you information, you barely listen. However, when your supervisor calls you in for an unexpected conference, your listening will be very intense. Occasionally we trick ourselves into listening less intensely than we should. Everyone knows to take notes when the professor says "This will be on the test," but only the intense listener captures the important content in an apparently boring lecture. You need to become a good judge of how intensely to listen, and to learn ways to alter your own listening intensity. A brisk walk between classes, sitting on the front of the chair, acting very interested, and nodding affirmatively when you agree are some methods that people use to listen with appropriate intensity.

Frequently, you can deal with physical distractions like an unusual odor, bright lights, or a distracting noise by moving the stimulus or yourself. In other words, do not choose a seat near the doorway that allows you to observe people passing by in the hall; do not sit so that the sunlight is in your eyes; and do not sit far away from the speaker and close to maintenance noises in the building. If you cannot remove the distraction by moving your seat or removing the distracting object, try to ignore it. You probably can study with the radio or television on, sleep without having complete darkness, and eat while other people are milling around you. Similarly, you can focus your attention on the speaker when other physical stimuli are in your environment.

Consider whether you would be able to concentrate on the speech if it were, instead, a movie you have been wanting to see, or a musical group you enjoy, or a play that has received a rave review. A friend said that when he had difficulty staying up late to study in graduate school, he would consider whether he would have the same difficulty if he were on a date. If the answer was no, he could then convince himself that the fatigue he felt was a function of the task, not of his sleepiness. The same principle can work for you. Consider whether the distractions are merely an excuse for your lack of desire to listen to the speaker. Generally you will find you can ignore the other physical stimuli in your environment if you wish to do so.

As we observed earlier, two kinds of listening are most common in public speaking situations. We have concluded our discussion of informative listening and turn now to evaluative listening.

Evaluative listening is the kind you engage in when you listen to two opposing political speakers, judge the speaking ability of an author, attorney, or instructor, or listen to students speaking in public speaking class. Your purpose in evaluative listening is to judge the speaker's ability to give an effective speech. Evaluative listening is an essential skill in and out of the classroom. What can you do to become a better evaluative listener?

Evaluative Listening

You can be more effective by following three guidelines. First, establish standards of appraisal. Second, consider the positive, as well as the negative, aspects of the speech. Third, view the speech as a whole entity, rather than as a composite of isolated parts. Let us consider each of these guidelines in more depth.

· ·

Ways to be an Evaluative Listener

1. Establish standards of appraisal.
2. Consider the positive, as well as the negative, aspects of the speech.
3. View the speech as an entire unit.

· ·

Establish Standards of Appraisal

In order to evaluate another person's public speaking ability, you must establish criteria by which you make your judgments. The criteria you establish should reflect your beliefs and attitudes about public speaking. Your instructor may suggest a set of criteria by which to judge your classmates' speeches. Many different sets of standards can be used to provide equally valid evaluations of public speaking. Most will include some consideration of the topic choice, purpose, arguments, organization, vocal and bodily aspects of delivery, audience analysis, and adaptation. The criticism form shown in figure 2.1 is based on the authors' perception of a successful public speech and follows the suggestions offered in this text.

Consider the Positive, as Well as the Negative, Aspects of the Speech

Too often people use the word *evaluation* to mean negative criticism. In other words, if they are to evaluate a speech, a newspaper article, or a television program, they feel they must state every aspect of it that could be improved or did not meet their standards. Evaluation should include both positive and negative judgments of what is being evaluated. As a matter of fact, many speech instructors feel you should begin and end your criticism of a speech with positive comments, and "sandwich" your negative remarks in between. Research shows that students perceive positive comments to be more helpful than negative comments.[7]

View the Speech as an Entire Unit

It is very easy to focus on delivery aspects of the speech, to look only for a recognized organizational plan, or to consider only whether the research is current. Viewing small bits of the speech in isolation, you may be able to justify a low evaluation you give to a classmate. Considering all of the parts that went into the speech may not allow such a judgment.

Speeches are like the people who give them. They are composites of many complex, and sometimes conflicting, messages. In order to be evaluated completely and fairly, they must be examined within a variety of contexts. Do not be distracted by a topic that represents one of your pet peeves, or allow the language choices to overshadow the speaker's creativity, or accept the arguments of a speaker who demonstrates a smooth delivery. In short, consider the entire speech in your evaluation.

Evaluation Form for a Public Speech

Speaker _____

Critic _____

Use this scale to evaluate each of the following:

1	2	3	4	5
Excellent	Good	Average	Fair	Weak

Introduction

_____ The introduction gained and maintained attention.
_____ The introduction related the topic to the audience.
_____ The introduction related the speaker to the topic.
_____ The introduction revealed the organization and development of the speech.

Topic selection and statement of purpose

_____ The topic selected was appropriate for the speaker.
_____ The topic selected was appropriate for the audience.
_____ The topic selected was appropriate for the occasion.
_____ The statement of purpose was clear and appropriate for the speaker, audience, and occasion.
_____ The stated purpose was achieved.

Content

_____ The speaker consulted available sources including personal experience, interviews, and printed materials for information.
_____ The speaker supplied a sufficient amount of evidence and supporting materials.
_____ The speech was organized in a manner that did not distract from the speech.
_____ The main points were clearly identified.
_____ Sufficient transitions were provided.

Source

_____ The speaker described his or her competence.
_____ The speaker demonstrated trustworthiness.
_____ The speaker exhibited dynamism.
_____ The speaker established coorientation.

Delivery

_____ The vocal aspects of delivery—pitch, rate, pause, volume, enunciation, fluency, and vocal variety—added to the message and did not distract from it.
_____ The bodily aspects of delivery—gestures, facial expressions, eye contact, and movement—added to the message and did not distract from it.
_____ Visual aids were used appropriately to clarify the message.

Audience analysis

_____ The speaker demonstrated his or her sensitivity to the interests of the audience.
_____ The speaker adapted the message to the knowledge level of the audience on the particular topic.
_____ The speaker adapted the message to the demographic variables of the audience.
_____ The speaker adapted the message to the attitudes of the audience.

Conclusion

_____ The conclusion forewarned the audience that the speaker was about to stop.
_____ The conclusion reminded the audience of the central idea or the main points of the speech.
_____ The conclusion specified precisely what the audience was to think or do in response to the speech.
_____ The conclusion ended the speech in an upbeat manner that caused the audience members to think or do as the speaker intended.

Figure 2.1 Evaluation form for a public speech.

Summary

We have considered informative and evaluative listening in this chapter. You learned the role of listening in the public speaking classroom. You learned to identify three false assumptions about listening: most people assume that they listen well, that they cannot be taught how to be better listeners, and that hearing and listening are the same phenomenon. After we dispelled these misconceptions, you learned three sets of barriers to effective listening: prejudging the speaker on the basis of gender, status, stereotype, or another factor; prejudging the subject and dismissing it as boring, too complex, irrelevant, or opposed to your own point of view; and yielding to factual, semantic, mental, or physical distractions. You then considered thirteen practices in which you should engage when you listen for informative and evaluative purposes. These practices are (1) suspend judgments about the speaker, (2) focus on the speaker as a source of information, (3) concentrate your attention on the speaker, (4) listen to the entire message, (5) focus on the values or experiences that you share with the speaker, (6) focus on the main ideas the speaker is presenting, (7) recall the arbitrary nature of words, (8) focus on the intent, as well as the content, of the message, (9) be aware of your listening intensity, (10) remove or ignore physical distractions, (11) establish standards of appraisal, (12) consider the positive, as well as the negative, aspects of the speech, and (13) view the speech as an entire unit.

You will spend considerably more time in this course listening than speaking. Use that opportunity to advance yourself as a person who recognizes effective listening as the hard work that it is, who learns from the words and concerns of others, and who at the same time learns the responsibilities of being both a speaker and a listener. Effective listening can help you develop confidence as a communicator.

Application Exercises

1

State which of the barriers to effective listening will be the least, and the greatest, problem for you.

2

Are you an effective, informative listener? After you have listened to a number of speeches in class, select one and complete the following.

Speaker's name _____

Topic _____

Statement of purpose _____

_____

Main points:

1. _____
2. _____

3. _____

4. _____

What are the speaker's qualifications on this topic?

_____

_____

What response is the speaker seeking from the audience?

_____

_____

3

Establish standards of appraisal for evaluating speeches. In order to make judgments about your classmates' speeches, you need standards by which to evaluate them. Create a criticism form including all of the essential elements of effective public speaking. Note exactly what you would include and how you would weigh each aspect. (Does delivery count more for you than content? Is a great deal of evidence more important to you than adaptation to the audience?)

4

Write a speech criticism. Using the criticism form that you created in exercise 3, evaluate three speeches that other students delivered in class. After you have completed your criticism, give each completed form to the speaker. Together discuss how accurately you have assessed the speech. Are you satisfied with the form? Do you believe your form would be useful for others? Does the speaker feel that the form included all the relevant factors? Can he or she suggest items that could or should be included? Is he or she satisfied with your use of the form? What differences of opinion exist between the two of you? Why? Can you resolve these differences? What has the experience demonstrated?

▼▼▼

1

Application Assignments

Using the evaluation form shown in figure 2.1, evaluate one or more speeches delivered by classmates. The form asks you to evaluate the introduction, topic selection, statement of purpose, content, source, delivery, audience analysis, and conclusion. Which aspects of the speech do you find easiest to evaluate? What can you do to strengthen your ability to evaluate those aspects?

2

Using the evaluation form shown in figure 2.1, evaluate a formal speech outside the classroom. Did you notice any particular differences between a classroom speech and a public speech in a different context or situation?

Vocabulary

egocentrism　The tendency to view oneself as the center of any exchange or activity; overconcern with the presentation of oneself to others; a barrier to listening.

evaluative listening　Listening to a speaker for the purpose of evaluating his or her ability to present an effective speech.

factual distractions　Factual information that detracts from our attention to primary ideas; a barrier to listening.

hearing　The physiological process by which sound is received by the ear.

informative listening　Listening to a speaker in order to understand the information that he or she is presenting.

listening　The selective process of receiving and interpreting sounds.

mental distractions　Communication with ourselves while we are engaged in communication with others; a barrier to listening.

physical distractions　Environmental stimuli that interfere with our focus on another person and a message; a barrier to effective listening.

semantic distractions　Bits or units of information in the message that interfere with our understanding of the main ideas or total meaning of the message; a barrier to effective listening.

Endnotes

1. Ralph Nichols and Leonard Stevens, ''Listening to People,'' *Harvard Business Review* 35 (1957): 85–92.
2. See, for example, P. T. Rankin, ''The Measurement of the Ability to Understand Spoken Language,'' *Dissertation Abstracts* 12 (1926): 847; D. Bird, ''Teaching Listening Comprehension,'' *Journal of Communication* 3 (1953): 127–30; Mariam E. Wilt, ''A Study of Teacher Awareness of Listening as a Factor in Elementary Education,'' *Journal of Educational Research* 43 (1950): 626; D. Bird, ''Have You Tried Listening?'' *Journal of the American Dietetic Association* 30 (1954): 225–30; and B. Markgraf, ''An Observational Study Determining the Amount of Time That Students in the Tenth and Twelfth Grades Are Expected to Listen in the Classroom'' (Master's thesis, University of Wisconsin, 1957).
3. Judy C. Pearson, ''The Influence of Sex and Sexism on the Criticism of Classroom Speeches'' (Paper presented at the International Communication Association, Philadelphia, Pa., May 1979); and Jo A. Sprague, ''An Investigation of the Written Critique Behavior of College Communication Instructors,'' (Ph.D. dissertation, Purdue University, 1971), 44–46.
4. Emil R. Pfister, ''A Study of the Influence of Certain Selected Factors on the Ratings of Speech Performances'' (Ed.D. dissertation, Michigan State University, 1955), 88.
5. Pfister, 92.
6. Pearson, 14.
7. Stephen Lee Young, ''Student Perceptions of Helpfulness in Classroom Speech Criticism,'' *Speech Teacher* 23 (1974): 222–34.

The Speaker

3

Question Outline

I. What does "Credibility is in the eye of the beholder" mean?

II. How is the way you see yourself related to how audiences perceive you?

III. What are four dimensions of source credibility in public speaking?

IV. How does speech anxiety affect a speaker's competence?

V. What are some ways to reduce speech anxiety?

VI. How does the Golden Rule apply to public speaking?

Speech is human, silence is divine, yet also brutish and dead; therefore we must learn both acts

THOMAS CARLYLE

Big Jack Johnson strode up to the podium like a person about to announce a lotto winner. His hands gripped the sides of the lectern as he leaned toward his audience, his eyes looking directly into theirs. His words were penetrating, his manner confident, and his voice vigorous. For ten minutes his audience sat there spellbound until he broke it off—leaving them wanting more.

Introduction

This story is the kind of fantasy that many public speaking students would like to experience. The good part about this fantasy is that it is very positive, the speaker as a hero. The bad part is that it is deceptive: this is not the way most communication between speaker and audience really occurs. Instead, we often start public speaking full of uncertainties about ourselves, our message, and our audiences. We need some experience to feel better about ourselves, we need to compose some messages until we get better at organizing our thoughts and ideas, and we need to develop a relationship with an audience until we feel more comfortable communicating with them. What we need to do is grow in confidence by discovering more about ourselves as a source.

The Speaker-Audience Relationship

Chapter 1 described the communication process as transactional; that is, the seven components of the process are interrelated and cannot be isolated. Speaker and audience cannot be separated; they are interdependent. Who the speaker is, what the speaker says, and what the speaker does makes a difference, of course. But what also makes a difference is how the audience, the receivers, respond to the speaker and his or her speech. Speaker and audience are conjoined. This chapter explores the speaker-audience relationship, the idea of ethos or source credibility, the dimensions of credibility, how credibility can be improved in a speech, and how you can affect a speaker's credibility when you introduce a speaker.

Source Credibility

Twenty-three centuries ago Aristotle wrote that a speaker's "character may almost be called the most effective means of persuasion he possesses." That idea is as true today as it was then. Your character goes by many names: reputation, honesty, loyalty, sincerity, faithfulness, and responsibility.

Aristotle called this idea *ethos;* today it is often called **source credibility.** Whatever it is called, the idea focuses on the source's, or speaker's, contribution to the speaker-audience relationship. Source credibility is not something that a speaker possesses like a suit of clothes used to dazzle an audience. Credibility is not something that is in you. Instead, credibility is born of the relationship between the speaker and the audience. It is the audience's judgment or evaluation of a speaker.

MISS PEACH by Mell Lazarus.
Courtesy of Mell Lazarus and
News America Syndicate.

"Credibility is in the eye of the beholder"[1] is a slogan that captures the idea. The audience perceives a speaker at a particular time, place, and occasion talking about a particular topic. The implications for you as a public speaker are:

1. Credibility must be established with every audience you face; it is not readily transferable.
2. You are more credible on some topics than on others; choose topics about which you can establish credibility with an audience.
3. You may be more credible in some situations than in others; many people can relate well to a classroom audience; fewer are seen as credible at board of directors meetings, at American Medical Association conventions, and on the college lecture circuit.
4. You may be more credible with some audiences than with others. Would you be seen as more credible to your classmates, an audience of professors, an organization of quilt makers, or a workshop for automobile mechanics?
5. You may be more credible with one ethnic or cultural group than another. Would you be credible to an audience of black Americans, Hispanics, or new immigrants to this country, or does your own mastery of the English language create problems in influencing others?

Self-Perception

How you see yourself can be how your audience sees you. Since source credibility depends on how your listeners perceive you, you should consider your self-perception, how it is developed, how it can be changed, and why it is important to the public speaker.

Self-perception is how you view yourself, your competencies, your physical self, and your psychological self. The student portrayed in the fantasy at the beginning of the chapter appeared to be high in self-confidence and self-assurance, devoid of anxiety, and determined to communicate.

What is your self-perception? If you were an animal, would you be an eagle or a mouse? Do you see yourself as master of the podium, lord of the lectern, or as a victim of an awesome audience?

A student came to one of the authors because she was shy, and it showed every time she spoke. Her voice was meek, her eyes examined the floor, and the audience felt sorry for her.

Fellow students tried to be supportive: "Don't be afraid of us; we're your friends" said one. "Look at us," said another, "so we can hear what you say. The little that I heard sounded good to me." The student said that her classmates were seeing her exactly as she felt.

To overcome her anxiety, redeem herself in class, and improve her grades, the student decided to try a new approach and act confidently. She practiced her speech over and over in the empty classroom. She sometimes pretended the audience did not believe her. At other times she pretended that they agreed with every word.

Acting confidently made her feel confident.[2] She behaved more boldly than her self-perception would ordinarily permit. But more than ever before, her actions depicted her true feelings about the issue.

The way you see yourself is often the way your audience will see you. Maybe you will have to behave confidently before you feel confident, but working on your own self-perception is the first step toward being confident. And one important way to improve your self-perception is to succeed at every classroom speech.

An audience will judge you as credible depending on what you show and tell them. Why do you dress up when you go for a job interview? Are you trying to deceive the interviewer into thinking you always look this good? No, but you are trying to make a good impression for the purpose of securing a job.

Similarly, audiences quickly judge a speaker—even before the speaker talks. Your perceptions of your fellow students are based on everything you sense about them: the way they look, the way they act, the way they sound. When you speak in front of them, you are trying to make a good impression in order to communicate a message.

You can help determine **audience perceptions** with your own choices. The kind of language you use can tell a great deal about your education. Your vocabulary can reveal how much or how little you know about a subject. Your use of arguments and evidence can demonstrate how logical or reasonable you are. How you dress tells the audience what kind of relationship you want with them. A smooth performance can show that you cared enough to prepare and practice a speech for them.

You earn the right to speak about particular topics. As one petite female student said in the beginning of her speech:

> I am a woman. I am five feet tall. I have spent twenty-five years in a world that seems to be designed for six-foot-tall men. Today I am going to talk about that problem so you can empathize with small people.

You earn the right to talk about children by raising them, about various jobs by doing them, and about your neighborhood by living there. You can also earn the right to talk by interviewing others, reading about an issue, and studying a topic. Ultimately, the audience decides whether you have earned the right to tell them about an issue.

On the basis that good theory breeds good practice, we are going to look at four dimensions of source credibility, four components that seem to affect how audiences perceive speakers. The four components are common ground, dynamism, trustworthiness, and competence.[3]

. . . .

Four Dimensions of Source Credibility

Common Ground
Dynamism
Trustworthiness
Competence

. . . .

Common Ground

Before class began, the speaker, Jack Thomas, had "drawn" a floor plan on the classroom floor with masking tape. The floor plan filled the room so most of the classroom chairs were within the tape boundaries. The speaker pointed out that he lived in married student housing. This housing was a joke on campus because it consisted of World War II-vintage Quonset huts, tin buildings that look like half-buried coffee cans.

The student walked around his floor plan telling his audience the square footage in the kitchen, the bedroom, the living room, and the bathroom. Did the people in class have that much space? He pointed out that his housing cost sixty dollars per month. How much were classmates paying for housing? By the time Jack Thomas finished explaining the facts about married student housing, his audience no longer thought of it as a joke.

Jack Thomas used a dimension of source credibility called **common ground,** a term like communion, communism, and communication that denotes "sharedness." You can share physical space, ideas, political positions, race, religion, organizational membership, gender, age, or ideology with an audience. Introduced early in a speech, common ground becomes a catalyst for other dimensions of source credibility. Why? Because we like familiarity, we like to be affirmed ("I agree with you"), and because agreement and affirmation build rapport with an audience.

Common ground is a very relational dimension of source credibility. It says: "Here are the important ways that I as speaker am just like you as audience members." Common ground is like a verbal handshake; it tells the audience that you want to have a relationship with them.

Dynamism

Have you ever watched evangelist Jimmy Swaggart on television? He moves across the stage pacing back and forth like a lion on a leash. He sweats until his shirt drips. He batters the air with his Bible. He mops his brow, weeps, shouts, beats the piano keys, and sings. He exudes energy like a generator arcing current into thousands of willing cells.

Jimmy Swaggart is an example of one kind of **dynamism,** the kind that exhibits boldness, activity, strength, assertiveness, and energy. Whether this kind of hyperactivity is attractive depends on the culture of the observer and the expectations of the audience. Persons from Southeast Asia, and even American Episcopalians, might find Swaggart's histrionics unattractive. Nonetheless, the speaker's activity level may help hold the attention of an audience that grows weary of watching a stationary speaker. The audience sets the standard of appropriateness for dynamism.

Why is dynamism important to an audience? Audiences seem to prefer action, expression, and power over passiveness, blandness, and weakness. How can you encourage an audience to perceive you as dynamic?

1. *Purposeful movement* Animation can be seen as a sign of the speaker's warmth and affection for the audience. The speaker's genuine enthusiasm for the topic can show his or her sincerity. Instead of

Common ground is what a speaker shares "in common" with the audience.

remaining stationary, the audience may appreciate some motion and emotion about the topic.

2. *Facial expression* Use your eyes, eyebrows, and mouth to denote surprise, pleasure, annoyance, disapproval, or skepticism. Your face does not have to be a composite of emotions; instead, a natural, relaxed appearance may be the most appropriate.

3. *Lively language* Use action verbs and concrete, specific nouns to liven your speech. "He flew through the house like a hornet on fire" is more exciting than "He hurried through the house."

4. *Gestures* Use your arms, hands, head, and neck to help convey your message. Gestures that reinforce the message result in high fidelity communication.

All of these are methods of encouraging the audience to see you as dynamic. But remember that source credibility is an audience perception, so you must be very careful to exhibit dynamism in ways that are appropriate to the audience,

A speaker's reputation can invite trust.

the situation, and the topic. Do not act on this section on dynamism, however, by standing up in front of an audience exuding energy without saying anything. Dynamism may or may not be your strength. Do not worry. There are other dimensions to source credibility that may be to your audience's liking.

Trustworthiness

In class one day David Gold gave what appeared to be an outstanding speech against the censorship of musical videos by church groups seeking to limit the raw lyrics and images on late-night television.

After David's speech, Drew Everts asked for David's sources. The next week he gave a speech revealing that David had made up many of the quotes the class heard in his speech. He had paraphrased the words of the church officials to make them sound more extreme than they actually were. Also the position he took on the issue itself was not supported by some of the groups he cited in his speech.

David Gold had to drop the course because Drew Everts had shown him to be unethical. Would anyone who heard his speech and Drew's rejoinder ever trust anything David said? The consequences for violating trust are severe and long-lasting.

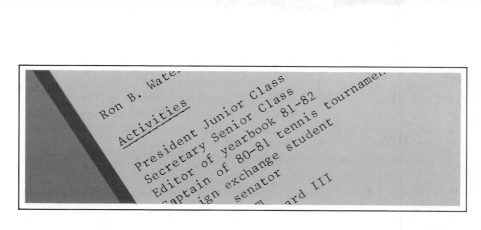

This dramatic event stunned the class and was a vivid demonstration of the importance of trustworthiness. **Trustworthiness** is a dimension of source credibility that refers to the speaker's integrity, honesty, fairness, and sincerity.

Trust is difficult to build, easy to destroy. The person who has been faithful in a relationship for years can falter once and find that trust destroyed. A friend who deceives, betrays a confidence, or lies is usually a friend no longer. The worst of family disputes, terrible working relationships, and long-term feuds are based on a loss of trust.

In public speaking, the audience has expectations that, if violated, lead to a loss of trustworthiness. The audience has the right to expect that you followed the rules in preparing your speech. The expectations may include the following:

1. The speaker has actually spoken to the people interviewed and is quoting or paraphrasing them accurately.
2. The speaker has actually gathered evidence from the sources claimed and is quoting or paraphrasing it accurately.
3. The speaker reveals which parts of the speech are taken directly or indirectly from other sources.
4. The speaker has the best interests of the audience in mind and does not encourage them to do things the speaker knows will be psychologically or physically harmful to them.
5. The speaker is expressing personal beliefs and ideas and is not just putting on a show to impress the audience.

Lest we become too dismal in this discussion of trustworthiness as a dimension of source credibility, we must point out that violations of trust are rare. Nearly all students prepare and deliver their speeches by following the rules. They do not try to trick, deceive, lie, fabricate, exaggerate, or threaten the welfare of their audience.

Competence

A black professor from an Ivy League school gave a lecture at a midwestern university that had once gone to the Supreme Court to keep a black student out of its law school. The white audience was highly skeptical of a black professor since they had never seen one before. The professor spoke for fifty minutes without notes. His speech included long quotes from books which he cited by book, year of publication, and page number. His speech on racism was interesting and novel to the audience, and it overflowed with arguments, evidence, and powerful reasoning. When the speech was completed, the questioning began, and the professor was as adept at debate as he was at public speaking. By the time his lecture was over, the audience was dazzled by his competence.

Competence is the audience's perception of the speaker's expertise, knowledge, and experience on the topic or issue at hand. It is the proof that you know what you are doing.

How do you demonstrate your competence? You might have a résumé or curriculum vitae that shows your age, education, experience, and goals. A résumé is your statement of competence as it appears on paper. Another way to show your competence is by your ability to do things. The technician in the laboratory shows his or her competence by fixing the computers every time they fail. The security person shows competence by a zero property and cash loss in the company served. The financial advisor shows competence by lowering taxes, increasing profit, and decreasing losses.

How do you exhibit competence in a public speech? The professor cited in the preceding true story did it by flashing his photographic mind. You can do it by:

1. Disclosing your relationship to the topic: "Since I am the only Mormon in this class, I would like to explain some of my beliefs so you will understand me and my religion better."
2. Using sources that are not used by everyone else: "According to *Daedalus,* a publication of the National Academy of Arts and Sciences. . . ."
3. Wearing clothing or objects to signal your relationship to the topic: "As this lab coat might indicate, I am a biochemistry senior. My topic? The safety of sugar substitutes."
4. Using live models to illustrate your point: "To help me with my speech on violence in football, I want you to meet my 280-pound, six-foot-six friend Rocky Scaradelli."
5. Revealing experiences related to the topic: "I worked at the bottom of city government for over fifteen years so I have a few stories to tell about inefficiency in government."
6. Demonstrating talent: "These ten watercolors of Wisconsin wildlife are some of the pictures that I completed myself when I was stationed there."
7. Avoid disorganization: A speech that the audience perceives as sloppily organized reduces the speaker's credibility.

You will think of creative ways to signal your own competence without being blatant. You always tread the fine line between arrogance about your competence and simply being open about your knowledge or ability. More speakers fail to establish their competence than overdo it by boasting about their accomplishments.

Now that you know the four dimensions of source credibility, you might think that a credible speaker has to be equally strong on common ground, dynamism, trustworthiness, and competence. Actually, it may be impossible for a speaker to function positively with all four dimensions at once. For example, the more a speaker emphasizes competence or expertise, the less the audience may see the speaker as being like them. The more a speaker emphasizes common ground or similarity, the less the audience may see the speaker as being expert. What you do is emphasize your own strongest dimensions for the audience. If you are not very dynamic, then emphasize your expertise; if you are not very competent, then emphasize your common ground with the audience.

Overcoming **speech anxiety** is an important step in building confidence and in establishing source credibility. You can be trustworthy, dynamic, and find common ground, but you can still be judged less than competent if you appear to be afraid of your audience.

Overcoming
Anxiety

Even with experience in debate, individual events, acting, or talking before groups, you are likely to feel apprehension about giving a public speech. Perhaps it will help you to know that your feelings are shared by practically everyone who performs, that such feelings are perfectly normal, and that anxiety can be reduced until it becomes an asset instead of a liability for you as a speaker.

Speech anxiety is common. One of the authors met a person who organized Dale Carnegie courses for people wanting to learn public speaking. He said that he originally took the course because he was determined to overcome his fear of public speaking. He ended up working for the Carnegie organization. Many people, like this person, are nervous about public speaking, but they learn to master their fear.

Athletes are nervous before a game, singers get worked up prior to a performance, and actors have the jitters before a play. Most normal human beings get a dry mouth, perspiring hands, and shaky knees when they first stand in front of an audience.

At first nervousness may prohibit effective speaking because you are so worried about yourself that you cannot worry about your message or how the audience is receiving it. You were nervous the first time you drove a car too, and maybe you continued to be nervous for a few months, but you conquered it just as you will in public speaking. Increased confidence brings decreased anxiety.

Anxiety is normal. There are some persons who suffer from abnormally high anxiety when they have to perform, but chances are excellent that you are not one of them. Mostly, you feel a lot more anxiety than your audience sees. You think that they know your mouth is dry; they don't. You think they see your hands sticking to your notes; they don't. And you think that your knees must be rattling the room, but they aren't. Increased confidence reduces both physical and mental signs of anxiety.

What is being discussed here comes under the general category of fear, fear of the unknown or a state. Speech anxiety is a trait or fear of a specific thing like test anxiety (the specific fear of taking an exam), telephone anxiety (the specific fear of talking on a telephone), or even authority anxiety (the specific fear of talking to police, professors, and others in positions of authority).

Sometimes our anxiety serves us well, as when it provides us with a readiness to respond so we perform particularly well because of our heightened responsiveness. At other times anxiety can reduce your effectiveness because your arousal is an obstacle to good performance. The speaker who feels no arousal at all before a speech may perform poorly. So will the speaker who feels overly aroused. The goal in this course is to reach the point where you do feel a strong need to perform well but not so aroused that you flounder. The key is to grow in confidence so you control the anxiety without becoming so overconfident that you perform poorly.

Anxiety can be reduced. Among the ways to convert anxiety into the performer's edge are:

1. *Repetition* Repeated exposure to the very thing that is frightening you over time and with repeated positive reinforcement—the incremental method—reduces anxiety. You start with brief speeches that take minimum effort and pose little danger and move gradually to longer, more complex speeches.
2. *Support* Learning in a supportive setting like a public speaking class will help you overcome your anxiety. Everyone in the room can help you become a better speaker. Your fellow students have the same fears, assignments, audience, and teacher, who is experienced at teaching speakers.
3. *Preparation* If you go into your speech aware that you know more about the topic than your classmates, your worries will be reduced.
4. *Practice* If you have rehearsed your speech many times until you know its contents well, then you will feel more confident when you address your classmates.
5. *Audience focus* Focus on your audience and the message you want them to receive, instead of thinking about yourself, your knees, your notes, and your pores.
6. *Start strong* Practice the beginning of your speech so you can deliver it automatically, since much of your anxiety will dissipate after the first couple of minutes.
7. *Self-confidence* Your belief that you can speak well will help you to do it.

Although these seven methods can help you reduce the trait that we call speech anxiety, there are many other standard methods of reducing the state that we call fear. Imaging, systematic desensitization, and relaxation or stress reduction techniques are just three of these other methods.

Practice your speech until you know it well.

Imaging is thinking through in your mind what you are going to say, what you are going to do, and how you are going to respond to the audience. Many people have practiced imaging without necessarily knowing the term. For example, when you have to face an unpleasant meeting with your boss, when you have to meet your future in-laws for the first time, and when you have to try a new play for the first time in a game you might go over and over the impending situation in your mind until you feel more confident that you can do it. That is imaging, and it works in speech making when you imagine over and over exactly what you will say and do in your speech.

Systematic desensitization exposes you to the stimulus that you fear over and over again, associating it each time with something pleasant. You condition yourself to overcome fear by replacing fear with good feelings over a period of time. Programs of systematic desensitization have been developed by psychological counselors and communication experts for the purpose of increasing your confidence by reducing fear.

Relaxation techniques and stress reduction techniques come in many forms, but one example of such a technique is deep breathing exercises before a particularly stressful event. Some people use meditation, other people use aerobics, and still others use forceful physical exercise like running, swimming, or a hard game of basketball to reduce stress and increase their feelings of relaxation before an event that might otherwise arouse fear. You should use whatever methods work for you.

One of the authors carried a small vial of smelling salts to class the first day he taught public speaking. He thought students would faint because they were so filled with anxiety about public speaking. Seventeen years and thousands of students later, he threw away the vial that had never been used. The fact is that in a world threatened by nuclear holocaust, by heart attacks and cancer, automobile accidents and chemical addictions, the fear of public speaking is greatly overrated. This book and your course are designed to reduce your fears and increase your confidence. You are unlikely to find another undergraduate class where you are able to speak so much and the teacher is allowed to speak so little. You will learn to enjoy that feeling, forget about anxiety, and grow in confidence.

Ethics in Public Speaking

Ethics can affect your credibility as a public speaker. Often the words that emerge from someone's mouth are only as good as the person who speaks them. A moral derelict can be an effective speaker, and a fine person can be a totally ineffective speaker. How, then, are we supposed to evaluate the ethical dimension of public speaking?

Obey the Golden Rule

Actually, much has already been written in this chapter about **ethics.** Recall, for example, the student who distorted evidence, dreamed up quotes, and deceived his audience. The simplest guide to ethics in public speaking is the Golden Rule: Do unto others as you would have them do unto you. Would you want someone to lie to you, deceive you? Of course not. But obeying the Golden Rule is as tough in public speaking as it is in life.

It first involves examining the merit of our goal. Most student speeches have highly virtuous goals: stop eating non-nutritious foods, start exercising, avoid chemical dependence, and establish equal pay for men and women. However, many speeches in history have been used to attack people for their race or religion, to start wars or continue them, or to maintain an unjust system. In your speeches, you should be aware of your goal and whether it serves the welfare of your listeners.

. . . .

Ethics of Public Speaking

Obey the Golden Rule: Do unto others as you would have them do unto you.

. . . .

A second area in which the Golden Rule figures is in examining the way you reach your goal, your means of informing or convincing the audience. In 1985, newspapers went to the extreme reporting the number of children abducted each year. Milk cartons, posters, and TV commercials had pictures of children missing for months or years: "Kathy was 4′ 1″ and weighed 55 pounds when this picture was taken in 1978." People taught their children to avoid strangers, schools had workshops on how to break a stranger's instep, and some people who worked regularly with children were regarded as potential molesters.

After six months of this paranoia, newsmagazines reported that the number of abducted children had been greatly exaggerated. Most of the children who disappeared had been taken by a disgruntled parent who was angry about a divorce or separation. The number kidnapped by evil-minded strangers was actually quite small. During the months that newspapers were printing the stories about child abduction that the public seemed anxious to believe, only a cautious few were checking the facts. The newspapers had been trying to convince people to be more careful with their children (a virtuous goal) using inflated figures about the problem (an unethical means).

Observing the Golden Rule in public speaking means that you must strive to speak from your own convictions and beliefs. Accurately cite authentic sources. Avoid falsification, distortion, and exaggeration, and think always "Would I want someone else to do this to me in a speech?"

Fortunately most people still adhere to the time-honored belief in integrity. That is, perhaps, why violations of public trust stand out as such heinous offenses. In the public speaking classroom you and your classmates have an opportunity to practice honesty.

One of the ways you can learn to apply the theory behind common ground, trustworthiness, dynamism, and competence is to introduce another speaker. This is an optional application assignment explained at the end of the chapter, but it is shown here to demonstrate how you can use the ideas presented in this chapter.

Introducing Another Speaker

The assignment given in this case was to interview another student outside class, have both the introducer and the person being introduced stand in front of the room, and have the introducer try to reveal specific details and a general theme about the person. Here is how one student delivered the speech.

On Thursday, campus voters went to the polls to elect senators for the University Student-Apartment Community. Our duty was to elect the most qualified candidates. I am pleased to report that this duty was fulfilled in at least one instance. I am speaking of Sandra Humphry, the new senator for Zone 13.

Sandra has a genuine interest in our school. Her goal is to develop a more cohesive student community. Sandra has lived in University Village for three years, so she has had firsthand experience with typical problems.

A full-time office assistant in the statistics department for two years, Sandra enjoys time with her husband, Bob, and her five-year-old daughter, Lauri. A hard worker, Sandra has experience selling Avon products, installing wallpaper, and investing in livestock.

Her life has always been busy. In high school, Sandra was an active participant in cheerleading, drama, forensics, ski club, and pep club. She was secretary of the Student Council and was elected to the National Honor Society.

Learn to introduce another speaker so the audience wants to hear the message.

She is also smart. Sandra graduated ninth in a class of 325 students. She earned a State of Michigan Scholarship, attended both the University of Michigan and the University of Kentucky, from which she emerged as an honors student.

Sandra's husband is a varsity basketball player. This gives her opportunities that many of us do not have. She is able to meet many dignitaries, including the governor of Kentucky and the president of this university.

With all of these accomplishments as a political activist and an intelligent human being, you might expect Sandra to be quite egotistical. Instead, she appears shy and reserved, a person who refuses to lose her modest, down-to-earth gracefulness. A gregarious person, Sandra is a human dynamo to her friends, and her dedication to family and community is without parallel.

Fellow classmates, I present to you Senator Humphry.[4]

In a very brief speech, Gene Turk, the speaker, communicated an immense amount of information about Sandra. His main themes were her political activities and her intelligence, with subthemes about her work and her family.

Source credibility is a product of the source-audience transaction. Your view of yourself—whether you are confident or not—can be transmitted to an audience, so an upbeat, positive attitude is vital in a speaker. Most important, though, is how the audience evaluates you and your message since the listeners determine your effectiveness as a speaker.

Source credibility is also the audience's perception of the speaker's competence, dynamism, trustworthiness, and common ground. Common ground is whatever you have in common with your audience; trustworthiness is how honest they feel you are; dynamism is determined by how energetic they find you; and competence is how qualified they judge you to be. In all cases the speaker has to display these characteristics if he or she desires the maximum positive response from listeners.

Source anxiety affects source credibility because audiences tend to find speakers incompetent when they appear afraid of the audience. You discovered in this chapter that your anxiety can be reduced through repetition and reinforcement, audience supportiveness, careful preparation, practice, focusing on the message and the audience, a strong introduction, and a belief in your own capability. Some standard methods of reducing fear are imaging, systematic desensitization, and relaxation or stress reduction techniques.

The ethics of public communication can be summarized with the Golden Rule: Do unto others as you would have them do unto you. Goals, and the means of achieving those goals, must be measured against the audience's welfare. Audiences have a right to expect ethical use of arguments, evidence, and espoused positions without distortion, exaggeration, or mendacity. When you introduce another person to an audience you should repeat that person's name occasionally, establish a few themes or subthemes around which you can organize memorable details, and convince the audience of the person's credibility.

Knowing about source credibility can help you grow in confidence as a public speaker especially if you begin by recognizing that speakers earn the right through the knowledge, ideas, and their relationship to the audience.

Summary

Application Exercises

1

How others see you is often influenced by how you see yourself. This exercise should be completed both early and late in the term to see if your public speaking class has altered your self-perception.

Circle the adjectives that best describe the way you perceive yourself. *Underline* the adjectives that best describe the way you think the audience will perceive you as a speaker. Complete the exercise in pencil the first time so that you can repeat it at the end of the term.

Assertive	Exciting	Experienced	Formal	Anxious
Friendly	Humorous	Polite	Bold	Reserved
Talented	Handsome	Bashful	Shy	Thorough
Beautiful	Cautious	Open-minded	Pretty	Scientific
Colorful	Caring	Bright	Daring	Conserva-
Extreme	Energetic	Fast	Slow	tive
Good looking	Gracious	Effective	Casual	Analytical

2

Write down the name of a topic and list three things you could do to signal your competence on that topic. For example, under the topic "Teenage Pregnancies" you might state (a) I went to a high school where four out of every ten young women were pregnant before graduation; (b) I can tell you what has happened to them in the ten years since they were teenage mothers; and (c) I can tell you what I have read about the issue over the last three years.

3

Make a list of all the common ground you share with the majority of persons in your listening audience. Use this list for suggestions when you try to establish common ground with your audience.

Application Assignments

1

Write and deliver an introduction of another person by (a) interviewing a classmate for information; (b) composing a speech from that information revealing at least one theme and one subtheme of their lives; (c) practicing the speech; and (d) delivering it to the class. At the time of the speech write the name of the person being introduced and your own so that the class learns to know both of you. The class should take notes on your introduction since that information is useful in audience analysis.

2

Write an introduction of yourself that could be used by someone introducing you as a speaker.

audience perception   The way the audience assesses the speaker and the message.

common ground   Similarities that the speaker and the audience share in common; used in introductions of others and early in a speech to help establish source credibility.

competence   The audience's perception of the speaker's expertise, knowledge, and experience.

dynamism   The audience's perception of the speaker's boldness, activity, strength, assertiveness, and energy.

ethics   The speaker's behavior is measured against the Golden Rule: Do unto others as you would have them do unto you.

imaging   Practicing a situation (i.e., delivering a speech) in your mind until you feel more confident.

relaxation techniques   Methods of reducing anxiety through mental and physical tranquility.

self-perception   How you view your physical and psychological self, an important consideration in how others perceive you.

source credibility   Called *ethos* by the ancients, this concept refers to the audience's perceptions of a speaker.

speech anxiety   Fear exhibited when in a public speaking situation.

systematic desensitization   The process of reducing anxiety by repeatedly exposing yourself to small doses of whatever your fear along with positive associations.

trustworthiness   The extent to which the audience finds you honest, fair, and sincere—high in integrity.

1. Ralph L. Rosnow and Edward J. Robinson, eds., *Experiments in Persuasion* (New York: Academic Press, 1967), 18.
2. Daryl Bem argues persuasively that attitudes follow behavior, so acting confident can lead you to be confident. See *Beliefs, Attitudes and Human Affairs* (Belmont, Calif.: Brooks/Cole, 1970), 3.
3. The dimension called coorientation in earlier editions has been changed to the more commonly used term "common ground." The justification for treating coorientation as a dimension of source credibility is rooted in Christopher J. S. Tuppen, "Dimensions of Communicator Credibility: An Oblique Solution," *Speech Monographs* 41 (1974): 253–60.
4. The name of the student being introduced has been changed in this speech by Mr. Gene Turk, a student at Iowa State University who delivered this speech in the honors section of public speaking class.

The Audience

Oratory is the art of enchanting the soul, and therefore he who would be an orator has to learn the difference of human souls. . . .

SOCRATES

Introduction

Another step in building your confidence as a public speaker is learning how to relate to an audience. Speakers, messages, and audiences are inextricably related to each other. After you overcome the initial fear of an audience, you need to learn how audiences influence you and your message, you need to learn audience analysis. The story of Don Lambert illustrates the importance of knowing your audience.

Don Lambert loved politics. When the Professional Secretaries International (PSI) invited him to talk to their group, he enthusiastically agreed. They did not give him a topic for his speech, so he decided to promote his favorite candidate, conservative Republican Judge Sanford D. Hodson.

On the night of the speech Don Lambert was startled to see as many men in the group as women. He had expected all females. Nearly all the men were employers who were there for "Boss's Night" as guests of their secretaries; nearly all the women were secretaries.

As Don delivered his speech, he noticed he was getting very little reaction from the members of PSI, but the men were showing unabashed enthusiasm for his message of support for Judge Hodson. After a rather chilly farewell from his hostesses, Don returned home mystified because half of his audience seemed to dislike his speech while the other half loved it.

The next day, a PSI member who heard the speech told Don what had happened. The predominantly male guests were affluent middle or upper management people and owners of companies. They were mostly Republicans and supporters of Judge Hodson. The secretaries who had invited Don to speak were predominantly registered Democrats who strongly rejected Judge Hodson's political position on the issues. Few of them knew Don before the speech, but afterward they disliked him and his message.

Focusing on the Audience

The story of Don Lambert underlines the importance of knowing your audience before you speak. As speakers we too often focus on ourselves. We speak on what we want to talk about, without considering what the audience might want or need to hear. We use language that we understand without considering that the audience might not know what we are talking about.

Don Lambert should have known before his speech that the audience would consist of both men and women, that the men were predominantly Republican, and the women predominantly Democrats. He should have known beforehand that a talk extolling Judge Hodson was inappropriate for the occasion because it offended the very people who had invited him to speak. Don could have given a speech with an important message for everyone if he had only known about audience analysis.

*Know your audience
well if you want your
speech to succeed.*

What is audience analysis? **Audience analysis** is discovering as much as possible about an audience for the purpose of improving communication.

Why should a speaker analyze an audience? Think it over. Is public speaking an egocentric exercise in talking to oneself in front of a group of people? Is it really a monologue with witnesses? Or is public speaking an attempt to communicate a message from one person to many as effectively as possible? The reason why a speaker analyzes an audience is to find out how best to communicate with them.

Let us consider the wide variety of audiences you might face in your lifetime:

Your classmates	Retired people
Fellow workers	A group of friends
Members of a union	A religious group
A civic organization	A board of directors
Fellow parents	A group of children

Would you talk to all of these audiences about the same topic or in the same way? Of course not. Your choice of topic and your approach to that topic are both strongly influenced by the nature of your audience.

We focus on the audience in our speech by learning the nature of that audience.

• •

Audience Analysis

Age	Organizations
Gender	Family
Race	Neighborhood
Education	

• •

Analyzing an Audience

When we talk to individuals, we are relatively careful about what we say and how we say it. We speak differently to strangers than to intimates, differently to high status than to lower status people, and differently to children than to adults. Similarly, we need to be aware of audience characteristics when we choose a topic, and when we decide how we are going to present that topic to the audience.

What are some characteristics of the audience that make a difference to speakers? Some of the more obvious characteristics of an audience are what we call **demographics,** which literally means "characteristics of the people." They include age, gender, race, education, family, peers, neighborhood, and organizational memberships.

Age

Advancing maturity changes people's preferences. While small children seem to love loud noise, fast action, and a relatively high level of confusion and messiness, older people may be bothered by these same characteristics. Look at these topics and decide which are more appropriate for youth, middle age, or elderly.

Placing your kids in college	Selecting a career
Choosing a major	Planning your estate
Health care in hostels	Saving dollars from taxes
Changing careers	Investment opportunities
Dating	Social security reform

The age of your audience will help determine whether a speech about more powerful stereo speakers or cashing in your annuities is an appropriate topic. The age of your audience will also partly determine what the audience knows from its experience: some people will know about the Depression, World War II, and Civil Defense; others will remember the Vietnam War, the Beatles, and the Civil Rights struggles; and today's youth will know the names of the latest rock groups and the newest trends in clothing.

When you give your speech, consider the ages of the individuals in the group and what you need to do to account for that demographic characteristic. How do the ages represented in your audience relate to the topic you selected and the approach you chose to communicate it? Age is part of audience focus and it is a primary ingredient in audience analysis.

Gender

What difference does it make to the speaker whether the audience is composed of men or women, or a mixture of the two? On neutral topics the genders represented in the audience may make no difference at all. With others, the representation may make all the difference in the world.

At the time this book is being written over fifty percent of all women of eligible age are working. Many are providing a second income in a family, many are single heads of family, and many are simply single. National figures continue to indicate that they are commonly in pink-collar jobs—secretarial and clerical—and underrepresented in upper management, ownership, and boards of directors. Their earning power tends to be less than that of men at almost all educational levels.

Women continue to be responsible for more of the nurturing, child care, cooking and cleaning, and housekeeping chores than men. Men continue to have shorter lives, more heart attacks, and more lung cancer, though the gap is narrowing.

Both men and women seem to have problems with gaining weight, stopping smoking and drinking, and gracefully tolerating the inevitable effects of advancing age.

Gender is an audience characteristic that you need to observe in selecting your topic and composing your speech.

Origin

The origin of your audience members is another important part of audience analysis. Family, neighborhood, race, ethnic group, or home town can all be important influences on a person as an audience member.

Coming from a large or small family can affect how well you listen, since people in a large family learn to live with considerably more noise. The neighborhood that helped shape you can be a source of pride or a memory that you would rather erase. Your race can be perceived as either limiting or expanding your potential. Your ethnic group can have communication traditions that affect how you speak and listen. Kids growing up in metropolitan and suburban areas seem to suffer less from communication apprehension, and are therefore more likely to participate in the give and take of a question-and-answer period.

The following story illustrates some of the influences of ethnicity on Sunday morning behavior.

Rev. Clarence Whitlock, a white Presbyterian minister, was asked to exchange pulpits with Rev. Jackson Brown, the pastor of the local African Methodist Episcopal Church. Accustomed to his own flock, kiddingly known about town as "God's frozen people," Rev. Whitlock approached his all-black audience with some newly-discovered stagefright. He did not know what to expect. After some spirited singing by a woman playing a piano, Rev. Whitlock rose to speak. He had said no more than ten words when the air was punctuated by an "Amen" from scattered members of the congregation. A few sentences later, he heard even more "Amens" from the people. He was on a roll! For a man who had rarely heard more than an occasional snore during his sermons, the tonic of having an audience excited by nearly every sentence was almost more than he could handle. Rev. Whitlock left the AME Church that day with an angelic smile on his face.

Race, ethnic background, and religion converge in this story to demonstrate how different a black congregation was to a minister who had previously preached only to white congregations. Origins are a significant part of audience analysis because the origin of people in your audience should be a factor in topic selection and approach.

The educational level of your audience is still another demographic characteristic that you must consider. A person's level of education may tell you very little about his or her intelligence, ambition, sophistication, or status. However, people with more education tend to read and write more, are usually better acquainted with the news, are more likely to have traveled, and are more likely to have higher incomes.

What are some of the implications for how the speaker approaches the audience?

1. People who read and write regularly tend to have more advanced vocabularies, so adjust your language choices to the educational level of your audience.
2. People who are receptive to new information will need less background and explanation on current issues than those who are not.
3. People who have seen more of the world tend to be more sophisticated about differences between people and cultures.

Take your audience's educational level into account as part of your analysis because it may be an important determinant of topics and approaches.

My neighbor, Louis Gerrig, would hate to be thought predictable, but if I know just a few of the organizations to which he belongs, then I can accurately infer a number of his beliefs.

For example, I know that he is an officer in his local union, the member of a small fundamentalist religious sect, and a member of the American Legion. I inferred, based on his membership in these three groups, that he would hold these beliefs:

We should have tariffs to protect our economy.
We should commit more tax dollars to defense.
We should permit prayers in public schools.
We should prohibit abortions.
We should spend less on welfare and Aid to Dependent Children.
We should not have jobs reserved for minorities.
We should not pay women the same as men for similar jobs.

To check my inferences, I went to Louis Gerrig to find out if I was correct. The only one that he disagreed with was reserving some jobs for minorities. He thought that idea was all right when it was limited to tax-supported jobs like police and firefighters. So Louis was not 100% predictable, but six out of seven is not bad.

Your knowledge about group memberships in your audience is valuable information because group membership signals sets of beliefs that people tend to embrace. Every Roman Catholic does not necessarily believe with strong conviction in everything the church represents, but probably they endorse much of it or they would not identify themselves as such.

Organizations typically reflect beliefs about issues, causes, and concerns. People belong to organizations reflecting interlocking clusters of beliefs that help predict their behavior. Few hard-core conservatives read *The New Republic,* and liberals rarely carry a copy of *National Review.* Our memberships in political parties, churches, street gangs, unions, and professional organizations signal our beliefs. The confident speaker knows about audience memberships and how they influence topic and approach.

Psychographics

Psychographics goes beyond demographics to look at the influences of demographics on a person's actual behavior. Psychographics began as a way to measure people's thinking about products, issues, and ideas. It quickly became an applied science when companies found that they could find customers, their "target audience," through these measures.

One of the authors heard a broadcasting consultant tell five hundred radio and television station owners and managers how they could use psychographics in their business. The consultant would be hired by a station, conduct hundreds of telephone interviews, discover people's interests, find out where they shopped, etc. The resulting information helped the station "target" the audience that would be most appealing to their advertisers. The resulting information went well beyond the demographics of race, income, and occupation to reveal what stations they listened to and why, what products they purchased, how much they spent at the mall and through mail order, etc. The psychographic study concluded with types of audiences in the community.

One category of people might belong to the country club, shop at the most expensive shopping mall, buy high-cost clothing, purchase a new car every second year, and drink costly liquor and wines. Another category might hang out at a corner bar, shop at discount stores, eat at fast food outlets, use mass transit, and drink beer. The people who sell products want to know who uses them, where they live, how much they spend, and where they buy.

What does psychographics have to do with public speaking? In the same way that businesses are interested in their "target audience," the public speaker needs to know the audience in order to inform or influence them. Just as businesses need to know more than the demographics, so do speakers.

You do not have to do telephone surveys to discover the psychographic characteristics of your audience. Your demographic analysis might reveal that your audience has a number of races represented in your audience, but a psychographic analysis goes beyond that data to reveal the cultures. The culture could be a category like "yuppies" who are said to crave expensive clothes, houses, and cars, or it could be a racial group like Vietnamese who are struggling with language, status, and jobs.

As an aspect of audience analysis, psychographics is an important feature for you to consider. Psychographics can help you determine what the audience wants to know about in an informative speech and what the audience is willing to do in a persuasive speech. The audience in a $20,000-per-year private school will be markedly different from the audience in an inner-city community college. And within each kind of educational institution, the audience in every public speaking classroom will be truly unique. Demographic and psychographic analysis will help you discover that uniqueness in your audience just as it did when the consultant examined community uniqueness for the broadcasters.

Some examples of questions that can be answered by psychographic analysis of the audience:

What position do my audience members take on issues?
What are their attitudes about information that I could present?
How will their culture invite them to respond to my message?
How does my mesage fit into the audience's aspirations?
What obstacles to my message and me are posed by who and what they
   are?

Using demographic analysis together with psychographic analysis can provide you with useful information. It can also increase your confidence as a public speaker when you have a reasonably good idea how the audience will respond to you and your ideas.

Methods of Audience Analysis

Some speakers seem to be able to analyze an audience intuitively, but most of us have to resort to formal and informal means of gathering information about an audience. The four most common methods are observations, informants, interviews, and questionnaires.

. . . .

Methods of Audience Analysis

Observation
Informants
Interviews
Questionnaires

. . . .

Observation

Watching and listening reveal the most about your audience during your **observations.** Looking at them can easily reveal their age, race, and gender.

More careful observation can reveal marital status with the presence or absence of rings, affluence by wearing furs, expensive jewelry, or costly clothing, and even religious affiliation by wearing symbols like a cross or a Star of David.

Many persons in an audience advertise their membership in a group by exhibiting the symbols of the group to which they belong. Shriners often wear rings and display symbols of their organization on their lapels. Persons who are active in civic groups and clubs tend to reveal those memberships somewhere on their person.

In the classroom, you have the added advantage of listening to everyone in your audience. Your classmate's speeches, their topics, issues, arguments, and evidence all reveal more about them than you could learn in a complex questionnaire.

Your eyes and ears become the most important tools of audience analysis as you train yourself to become a skilled observer.

Informants

When you are invited to give a speech outside the classroom, your best source of information may be the person who invites you. This person can be your inside **informant** who can tell you:

1. what topics are appropriate;
2. what the organization believes or does;
3. how many people are likely to attend;
4. what the setting or occasion will be;
5. how long you should speak; and
6. what the characteristics of the audience are.

A key question to ask is why they invited you to speak, since that information will help establish credibility in your introduction. If they want you because of your expertise on needlepoint, auto mechanics, or macramé, then you will want to stress that in your speech. If they invited you because you are a model citizen, then emphasize that area of your life. In any case, your inside informant should be able to help analyze your audience so there will be no surprises.

Interviews

When you are invited to speak to a group outside the classroom, you can initiate audience analysis by conducting an **interview** with one or more people from the group—either in person or on the phone. The interview for information on the audience should focus on the same questions listed in the preceding section on inside informants.

When you are conducting audience analysis for a classroom speech, you can select a few people to talk with from class. Try to discover their opinion of your topic, how they think the class will respond to it, and any helpful suggestions for best communicating the topic.

The only problem with interviews is that they tend to take time. Nonetheless, if the outcome is important, the interview is a way to discover more about your audience.

Questionnaires

While interviews take more time to execute than to plan, **questionnaires** take more time to plan than to execute. The key to writing a good questionnaire is to be brief. Respondents tend to register their distaste for long questionnaires by not filling them out.

What should you include in your brief questionnaire? It depends, of course, on what you wish to know. Usually you will be trying to discover what an audience knows about a topic and the audience's predisposition toward that topic.

You can ask open-ended questions, yes-or-no questions, degree questions, or a mixture of all three—as long as you do not ask too many questions.

Open-ended questions are like an essay test that asks an opinion. For example:

"What do you think should be done about teenage pregnancies?"
"What policy should govern working men and women when their child is
    born?"
"What punishments would be appropriate for white collar crimes?"

Yes-or-no questions force a decision. For example:

"Should pregnant teenagers be allowed to complete their high school education?
    _____ Yes _____ No."
"Should a man be allowed 'maternity leave' when his child is born?
    _____ Yes _____ No."
"Should embezzlement of over $10,000 be punished by a prison term of one
    to two years?_____ Yes _____ No."

Degree questions ask to what extent a respondent agrees or disagrees with a question:

"I believe that pregnant students should finish high school."

| Very Strongly Agree | Strongly Agree | Agree | Strongly Disagree | Very Strongly Disagree |

Or it may present a continuum of possible answers from which the respondent can choose:

Embezzlement of $5,000 should be punished by which of the following?

| $5,000 fine 1 year jail | $4,000 fine 2 yrs. jail | $3,000 fine 3 yrs. jail | $2,000 fine 4 yrs. jail | $1,000 & 5 yrs. jail |

How much maternity leave do you think men should receive?
None   Three Days   One Week   Two Weeks   One Month   Two Months

These three kinds of questions can be used in a questionnaire to determine audience attitudes about an issue. The illustration at the bottom of this page is a sample questionnaire. Such a questionnaire administered before your speech can provide you with useful information about your audience's feelings and positions on the issue you plan to discuss in your speech. All you have to do is keep it brief, pertinent, and clear.

Teenage Pregnancy

1. I think that pregnant teenagers should finish high school.
   _____ Yes   _____ No
2. I think that pregnant teenagers should complete high school with their class instead of in special sections or places.
   _____ Yes   _____ No
3. At what grade do you think pregnant teenagers should be allowed to continue their education with their class?
   7th   8th   9th   10th   11th   12th
4. To what extent do you agree that our society punishes pregnant teenagers too much at present?

   | Very Strongly Agree | Strongly Agree | Neutral | Strongly Disagree | Very Strongly Disagree |

5. What, if anything, do you think should be done about the males who are responsible for the pregnancies?

Four factors are important in analyzing the situation you face as a speaker: the size of the audience, the occasion, the time, and the importance.

. . . .

Situational Analysis

Size of audience
Occasion
Time
Importance

. . . .

The **size of the audience** is an important situational factor because it can determine the level of formality, the amount of interaction with the audience, the need for amplification systems, and special visual aids. The larger the audience, the more responsibility on the speaker to carry the message. Larger audiences usually call for more formality in tone and language; smaller audiences allow for a more casual approach, a less formal tone, and informal language. Very large audiences reduce the speaker's ability to observe and respond to subtle cues like facial expressions, and they invite the audience to be more passive than they might be in a smaller group. Large audiences often require microphones and podiums that can limit the speaker's movement, and they may require slides or large posters for visual aids.

Speakers need to be flexible enough to adapt to audience size. On the day this chapter was written, one of the authors was supposed to give a speech on leadership to an audience of over 100 students in an auditorium that held 250 people. Only twenty-five students appeared at the conference. Instead of a formal speech to a large group, the author faced a relatively small group in one corner of a large auditorium. Two hours later, the author was supposed to speak to a small group of twelve or fifteen that turned out to be fifty. Do not depend on the planners to be correct about the size of your audience. Instead, be ready to adapt to the size of audience that actually appears.

Size of Audience

The **occasion** is the second situational factor that makes a difference in how a speaker adapts to an audience. The occasion sets up a number of unstated constraints. The speaker is supposed to be upbeat and even funny at an after-dinner speech, sober and serious at a ribbon cutting, full of energy and enthusiasm at a pep rally, and prudent and factual in a court of law. Even in the classroom, there are a number of unstated assumptions about the occasion that you violate at your own peril: you are expected to follow the assignment, deliver the speech extemporaneously, maintain eye contact, keep to the time limit, dress appropriately, and so on.

Occasion

THE FAMILY CIRCUS®   **By Bil Keane**

"Mommy didn't think it was that funny when I
said it this afternoon. I had to
go to my room."

Outside the classroom the confident speaker finds out what the expectations of the occasion are. Consider for a moment the unstated assumptions for these public speaking occasions:

> A high school commencement address
> A testimonial at a retirement party
> A talk with the team before a big game
> An awards ceremony for top employees
> A pep talk to your salespeople
> A keynote address at a conference
> A "shape up" talk to employees
> An announcement of layoffs at the plant

Each of these occasions calls for quite a different kind of speech, the parameters of which are not clearly stated but seem to be widely understood. Our society seems to dictate that you should not exhibit levity at funerals, nor should you be too intellectual at a ribbon cutting. One of the best ways to find out what is expected is to find out from the individual or the organization inviting you.

Time

The third aspect of occasion that makes a difference to a speaker is when the speech is given—the **time.** Time can include the time of day, the time that you speak during the occasion, and the amount of time you are expected to fill. Early morning speeches find an audience that is fresh but not exactly ready for serious topics. After-lunch or after-dinner speeches invite the audience to sleep unless the speaker is particularly stimulating. The best situation occurs when the audience came only to hear you and that is all they expect to do.

The time you give the speech during that occasion can make a big difference in how receptive your audience happens to be. One of the authors was asked to speak to an Alumni Academy, an audience consisting entirely of people who gave a thousand dollars or more per year to the university. Seven deans were supposed to tell the Academy about their colleges in a series of five-minute speeches—each of which lasted seven minutes or more. By the time the author was scheduled to speak, the audience was tired. So instead of giving a five- to seven-minute presentation about the college, the author told the audience they would think more kindly of the college if they were simply allowed to go have dinner. The audience applauded and left, hopefully thinking good thoughts about the speaker who didn't speak because the audience was too exhausted to listen.

Even when you are the last speaker in your class, you will not be allowed to avoid giving the speech as was the previous case. Instead, when you know you will be one of the last speakers for the day, you should do your best to be stimulating, novel, and empathetic with an audience that has grown tired of hearing speeches.

The amount of time you are expected to fill is still another aspect of time. You will probably find, as the authors have, that people are genuinely relieved when a speech is shorter than expected because so many speeches are much longer than anyone wants. It is easy as a speaker to fall in love with the sound of your own voice and to overestimate how thrilled the audience is to hear you. Audiences will be insulted if you give a speech that is far short of expectations—five minutes instead of thirty—but they will often appreciate a forty-five minute speech even when they expect an hour.

The issue of time becomes considerably more serious when you are one of a number of speakers who address an audience. It is a common occurrence for all of the speakers in the series to use more time than they were given. Here again, the speaker who is brief, stimulating, and meaningful can gain an audience's appreciation.

Time, then, refers to the time of day, the time when you speak during an occasion, and the amount of time you speak. Time is a situational factor that you should carefully consider as you plan your speech.

The fourth situational factor is the **importance of the occasion.** Some occasions are fairly low in importance compared to others, but generally the presence of a speaker signals that an event is not routine. As a speaker you need to take the importance of the occasion into account. An occasion of lesser importance must not be treated as if it were of great importance, and an occasion of greater importance should not be treated lightly.

The occasion can determine the formality and content of your speech.

Rituals and ceremonial events are usually perceived as high in importance. The speaker at a university commencement exercise, the speaker at the opening of a new plant, and the speaker for a major lecture are seen as important players in a major event. Speakers at informal gatherings or local routine events are somewhat farther down the scale. Nonetheless, the speaker must carefully gauge the importance of an event, lest the audience be insulted by the speaker's frivolous treatment of what the audience regards as serious business. The importance of the occasion must definitely be taken into account.

The Uniqueness of the Classroom Audience

Students sometimes think of the speeches they deliver in public speaking class as a mere classroom exercise, not a real speech. Nothing could be farther from the truth. Classroom speeches are delivered to real people who are influenced by what they see and hear. In fact, your classmates as an audience might be even more susceptible to your influence because of their **uniqueness.**

1. The classroom audience, because of the educational setting in which the speech occurs, is exposed to messages that they might otherwise avoid.
2. The size of the audience tends to be relatively small (usually twenty to twenty-five students) and constant, so that the class begins to take on some of the characteristics of an organization.

3. The classroom audience is more likely to include a wider range of positions on the issues, including opposition.
4. Classroom audiences include one person—the professor—who is charged with the responsibility for evaluating and grading each speech.
5. Classroom speeches tend to be short in length (five to twelve minutes) but must be informative or persuasive.
6. The classroom speech is nearly always one of a series of speeches in each class period.
7. The speaker has an opportunity to listen to every member of the audience.
8. The classroom speech audience may be allowed to provide written and/or oral commentaries on the speech.
9. The classroom speech situation is unique because the speaker has more than one opportunity to influence or inform the audience.

Your own classmates, as the audience, do not stay the same during the quarter or semester during which you speak to them: they have their own positions on issues, but they change as they listen and learn; they have information about some subjects, but they are learning more in this class and others; and they are changing themselves as they prepare for speeches and learn more about the topics than they knew before. Next we will look at how you can adapt to this unique audience.

Adapting to Your Audience

This chapter has given you some tools—observation, informants, interviews, and questionnaires—to use in analyzing your audience. This chapter has also reviewed some audience characteristics that tend to make a difference in how an audience responds to a speaker: age, gender, education, family, peers, neighborhood, and organizations. But the tools of analysis and audience demographics will do you no good unless you use them for the purpose of **audience adaptation.**

In the case of the informative speech, adapting to the audience means **translating** ideas. Just as a translator at the United Nations explains an idea expressed in English to the representative from Brazil in Portuguese, the speaker who knows about baud rates, Kbytes, and Mbytes must know how to translate those terms for an audience unfamiliar with them. Perhaps you have already met some apparently intelligent professors who know their subject matter well but are unable to translate it for students who do not. An important part of adapting an informative speech to an audience is the skill of translating ideas.

In the case of persuasive speeches, adaptation means adjusting your message both to the knowledge level of the audience and their present position on the issue. Use the tools introduced in this chapter and the audience characteristics to help discern just where you should "place" your message for maximum effect. Too often speakers believe that the audience will simply adopt their point of view on an issue if they explain how they feel about it. Actually, the audience's position on the issue makes a greater difference than the speaker's position, so the speaker has to start from the audience's position on the issue.

Effective speakers adapt the message to the audience.

Two students in one of our public speaking classes provided an excellent example of what happens when the speaker does and does not adapt to the audience. Both speakers selected topics that seemed to have little appeal for the audience because both appeared to be upper-class hobbies. One of the students spoke about raising an exotic breed of dog that only the rich could afford. The entire speech was difficult for the audience to identify with since they could not see themselves in a position of raising dogs for the wealthy. The other student spoke about raising hackney ponies, an equally exclusive business. But this second student started by explaining that he grew up in a poor section of New Haven, Connecticut. His father was an immigrant who never earned much money, even though he spoke six languages. This student came from a large family, and he and his brothers pooled their earnings for many years before they had enough money to buy good breeding stock. They later earned money by selling colts and winning prize money in contests. By first explaining to the audience that he was an unlikely breeder of expensive horses, the speaker improved the chances that the audience could identify with him and his hobby. He adapted his message to the unique audience.

Summary

The best speakers focus their message and their attention on the audience. They know there is much more to giving a speech than familiarity with the topic. They realize that the audience characteristics, the demographics, can be important in determining what an audience wants to know and do. Further, they realize that the audience's psychographics, the psychological characteristics of the audience—its aspirations, motivations, and problems—can also indicate what an audience is willing to learn and to do.

Your message must be aimed at your "target audience." You can conduct your audience analysis through observation, informants, interviews, and questionnaires. Becauses the speech takes place in a particular situation, you must also be aware of factors like size of audience, occasion, time, and importance.

You have discovered too that the classroom audience is unique, that it differs in many ways from other audiences. But the classroom is a learning situation that provides you with practice in audience analysis and application through adaptation. You learn how to translate ideas into ways your audience will understand, and you learn how to position your speech on an issue in ways that invite audience acceptance. We turn next to the selection of topics appropriate for your audience.

▼▼

Application Exercises

1

Given the observations listed here, what do you think would be the audience's probable response to a speech on abortion, inflation, or gun control? This exercise may be done individually or by the entire class.

The audience responded favorably to an earlier informative speech on race relations.

The audience consists mainly of inner-city people from ethnic neighborhoods.

The audience consists of many married persons with families.

The audience members attend night school on earnings from daytime jobs in factories and retail businesses.

The audience members come from large families.

2

Given the following demographic information, what inferences would you draw about each statement? What inferences would you draw if all five statements described the same audience? This exercise may be done individually or by the entire class.

The audience is predominantly female, aged nineteen to fifty-five.

The audience is predominantly Roman Catholic.

The members of the audience are mainly humanities majors.

The audience members do not have jobs outside the home.

Most audience members belong to all-female organizations.

What topics would be appropriate for an audience described by all five of the statements above?

Application Assignments

The Assumptions Paper/Speech

1

Write your name at the top of your paper and list five assumptions about your class as an audience. Based on your own observations and the audience's demographics, you should make an assumption or inference and state the basis for it. For example, one item might look like this:

Assumption: A majority of individuals in my audience are interested in the subject of marital happiness.

Basis: Nearly everyone is between nineteen and forty-six years of age; most of the persons in class are married or have been; five are divorced and remarried; two women are divorced and still single; the majority of people in the class have children, including the two who are now single.

2

In a two-minute speech, share with your class one of your five assumptions without repeating one that has been explained by someone else. State your assumption and the basis for it to see if the class agrees that it is true of the majority of the class members. In one class hour you can share between ten and twenty assumptions that will help everyone better understand the audience.

▼▼▼

Vocabulary

audience adaptation Making the message appropriate for the particular audience by using analysis and applying its results to message creation.

audience analysis Discovering as much as possible about an audience to improve communication in a public speaking situation.

degree question A question used in interviews and in audience analysis questionnaires that invites an explanation, not just a ''yes'' or ''no'' response.

demographics Discovering audience characteristics like age, gender, education, group membership, etc.

importance The degree of significance attached to an occasion that dictates the speaker's seriousness, content, and approach.

informant The person or group inviting you informs you about the nature of your audience and their expectations for your speech.

interview A situation in which information is sought by an interviewer from an interviewee in person or on the telephone.

observation A method of audience analysis based on what you can see or hear about the audience.

occasion A situational factor referring to the event at which a speech is given, and the kinds of speaking behavior appropriate for that event.

open-ended questions Like essay questions, these invite an explanation and discourage yes-or-no responses from the person being questioned.

psychographics Characteristics of the audience that go beyond demographics to culture, aspirations, style of living, attitudes on issues, and acceptable and unacceptable ideas.

questionnaires A method of audience analysis that asks written questions of individuals to discern their knowledge level or attitudes about a topic.

size of audience A characteristic that can determine everything from the loudness of voice to the formality of language.

time The time of day, the specific time when you are scheduled to speak at an event, and the amount of time you are expected to speak.

translating The skill of taking what you know and rendering it into language and concepts the audience can understand.

uniqueness The particular characteristics of the classroom speaking situation that make it different from other speaking events.

yes-or-no question A question used in interviews and in audience analysis questionnaires that invites only a ''yes'' or ''no'' response.

Selecting a Topic and Purpose

5

Question Outline

I. What are some of the six suggestions for selecting a topic?

II. How do each of the systematic methods of topic selection work?

III. What are some criteria you can use to evaluate your topic?

IV. What are some alternative purposes for a speech?

V. What is a statement of purpose?

In all matters, before beginning, a diligent preparation should be made.

CICERO

Introduction

You can increase your confidence as a public speaker by learning how to select a topic that is appropriate for you and your audience. Many students spend too much time searching for a topic and not enough time *re*searching the topic. This chapter is designed to make topic selection less of a chore and more of a constructive, positive first step in speech preparation. Let us begin by considering some methods of finding appropriate topics. Also we will list those methods from easiest to more difficult. If the easy methods work, then you can avoid having to use more difficult ones.

Selecting a Topic and Purpose

Here are some methods of topic selection used successfully by public speaking students:

1. *Speak about topics you already know* What subjects do you know about? Science, cosmetics, mechanics, or child care? Speak about something you already know, and save a lot of research time.
2. *Speak about topics that interest you* What subjects arouse your interest? What do you like to read about? What elective courses do you choose? Selecting a topic that interests you will make your exploration worth the effort.
3. *Speak about topics that are uniquely your own* Have you had jobs or travel experiences that are unusual? Look at your own background for ideas to share with your audience.
4. *Speak about current topics* What are the newspapers, magazines, radio, and TV news covering at the moment? Which of those news items would you like to discuss with a campus expert? Usually people have little background about current news, so items that interest you could be examined more thoroughly in a speech.
5. *Speak about topics your audience finds interesting* What do people in your class enjoy talking and hearing about? Which of their favorite topics could you discuss with some authority? If people tend to talk with you about certain subjects, then you might want to consider a speech about one of those topics.
6. *Speak about a topic that the audience embraces but you do not* Are there any "sacred cows," things that seem to be accepted without question by your audience, but you think could be challenged? Try to convince members of the audience to join your way of thinking on such a topic.

What if none of these six approaches yields a topic for your speech? Following are some methods of generating a topic.

A closer look at a category you like can produce a topic for your speech.

Try a systematic method of discovering topics. Among the systematic methods are listing, monitoring your behavior, conducting a personal inventory, personal brainstorming, current topics, and clustering.

Searching for a Topic

. . . .

Systematic Methods of Topic Selection

Listing
Monitoring behavior
Personal inventory
Personal brainstorming
Current topics
Clustering

. . . .

Listing	**Listing,** a systematic method of finding a topic, can be done in two ways. The first is to take a broad category and narrow it down to specifics. For example:

overpopulation
overpopulation in developing nations
overpopulation in India
religion as a cause of overpopulation in India
the effect of the Hindu religion on overpopulation in India

The broad idea of overpopulation was narrowed until it resulted in a topic.

The second way to use listing is to start with a broad category and then list related ideas under it. For example:

overpopulation
historical overpopulation
sociological effects of overpopulation
control of overpopulation
birth control and overpopulation
overpopulation predictions for the year 2000
the effect of overpopulation on housing

The single term that interests you is used to stimulate thought about a large number of related topics that would make good speech topics for you.

Monitoring Behavior

Another method besides listing is **monitoring your behavior.** You may not be fully aware of some of your own interests, so study yourself to discover them. You might not realize you are more interested than most people in biology until you realize you have taken more courses in that subject than any other. You might not realize that you are a foreign film afficionado until you note that you go to more of them than most people do. Whether it is biology courses or films, your behavior often indicates your main interests. Those interests can suggest topics you will enjoy exploring as you prepare for a speech.

Personal Inventory

Conducting a **personal inventory** is another way of discovering areas of expertise. A personal inventory is a close examination of your choices on particular aspects of your life. For example, an inventory of your newspaper reading would indicate whether you read front page news, the opinion page, comics, sports, birth and wedding announcements, letters to the editor, or reviews of books, music, TV, or theater. Do a personal inventory of the courses you select, the magazines you read, the hobbies and recreation you most enjoy, or any other aspect of your life. Examining your choices helps you to understand areas of interest and expertise, and suggests topics that you might already know about.

A fourth alternative to discovering your own interests is to try **personal brain-storming.** Brainstorming is usually a small-group activity in which the members think of a number of ideas. After gathering a large quantity of ideas, the group reduces the number to a few by assessing their quality. Personal brainstorming is sitting down and giving yourself five minutes to think of as many ideas as you can for speeches. The items do not need to be titles, just ideas. One student who tried this approach came up with the following list:

child abuse	wife abuse	hair styles	apartheid	elections
politics	classes	food	Mexican food	business
education	critics	teachers	marriage	divorce
television	Lorimar	news anchors	CBS	networks
production	salary	Dallas	soaps	radio formats
jobs income	underclass	inflation	recession	economy
metropolitan	suburban	racism	Hispanics	urban
social status	cities	police	quotas	classes
I.Q.	white-collar	crime	testing	standard tests
class rank	GPA	dark glasses	jewelry	cosmetics
automobiles	maintenance	operation	quality	engines
clothing	colors	fabrics	expense	performance
dating	mergers	taxes	defense	custody

The student's list of topics suggested a speech about how cable and satellite television affects the networks. Naturally, the words listed during personal brainstorming need to be evaluated for audience interest and the speaker's ability to gather information. The chosen topic also needs to be narrowed. But clearly, personal brainstorming is a method of finding topics that yields a large number of ideas.

Consulting a list of **current topics** is still another method of finding a topic. An encyclopedia, a dictionary, a book of facts, a card catalog—almost any standard resource index can give you ideas. Or get an idea from a list of topics that have been used recently by other speakers. The following list of topics is from speeches given by students as this book was being written.

The Case for Nuclear Power
The Power of Poetry
Are Professional Athletes Overpaid?
Why You Should Favor Socialized Medicine
Junk Food and Why It Is Good for You
The Future of Social Security
Let's Increase Defense Spending
Some Reforms for Professional Boxing

Are College Athletics Too Big?
Avoiding AIDS
What You Should Know about Financial Aid
What Men Need to Know about Cooking
Choosing Fabrics for Wear
Nursing—A Noble Calling
The Problem with Required Courses
What Does a Mechanical Engineer Do?
The Perils of the Single-Parent Family
The Long-Distance Marriage
How to Get a Loan
Should Students Invest?
Some Tips for Job Interviewing
Our Child Support Laws
What Is Inflation?
Why You Should Consider a Business Major
The Teacher Shortage: An Opportunity
The Problem with Property Tax
Overcoming Shyness
What Can You Do about Stress?
What Is Right about Our Economy?

If you do not find a topic by listing, monitoring your behavior, using personal inventories, personal brainstorming, or checking current topics then you might want to try a new approach to discovering a topic called "clustering."

Clustering

Clustering is a method originally devised for helping students with written compositions;[1] it can work equally well for helping discover speech topics. The method works like this: Think of a concept or an idea you know something about. Write it in the middle of a sheet of paper and circle it. Then for ten minutes let your mind free associate as you write down any other subjects, related to the first or subsequent ideas. Circle them and attach them to the concept from which they originated. If you wish, use capital letters to indicate a particularly good idea for a speech.

Figure 5.1 shows what a student produced after three minutes of instruction on clustering.[2] He came up with eighteen topics related to genetic engineering in ten minutes. Many could be developed into speech topics by narrowing them, selecting them for appropriateness for the audience, and choosing topics that interest the speaker.

Evaluating Your Topic

Once you have arrived at a general topic, the next step is evaluation, deciding if the topic meets the standards of **appropriateness** to the speaker, audience, and occasion.

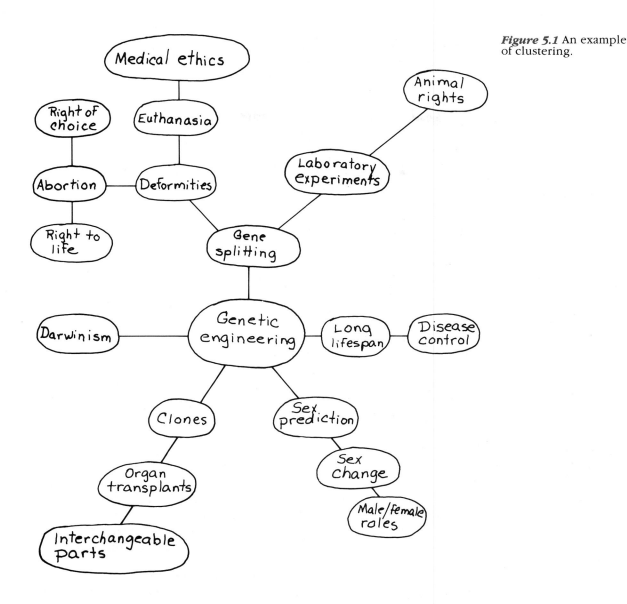

Figure 5.1 An example of clustering.

A speech is appropriate for you as a speaker if you have or can generate interest and knowledge on the topic. Your ability to deliver an interesting speech depends in part on your own interest in the topic. If you are enthusiastic, then the audience is likely to share your feelings. If you are not, the audience will probably know that also. Avoid audience distinterest by selecting a topic that interests you.

Either know something about the topic or have a sincere interest in learning more about it. A speech is appropriate for you as a speaker if you know more about it than most of the people in the audience. This criterion is less difficult

Appropriate to You

than it may first appear. Our knowledge about most topics tends to be superficial, so it is not difficult to learn more about a subject than is generally known to an audience. Then you will have subject matter competence.

Appropriate to the Audience

A speech is appropriate to an audience if it is both interesting and worthwhile to the audience. One of the primary functions of audience analysis is to discern what will interest the audience. The speaker has the responsibility for generating interest in the audience. Let us say that you are very interested in coin collecting, but realize that practically nobody in the class is. You have both interest and knowledge in the topic. You do not have to give up that topic as long as you know you can get the class interested by showing them how easy and profitable coin collecting can be.

Consider also whether a topic is worthwhile for an audience. If the audience is already familiar with a topic, be careful about the information you are presenting. A speech about a topic too familiar to the audience will be highly uninformative. A speech about a topic that is too trivial will not be worth the audience's time. A proper analysis of your audience should reveal both how interesting and worthwhile your topic will be for them.

Appropriate to the Occasion

Finally, consider the topic's appropriateness to the occasion: Is it significant, timely, and tailored? A speech topic is **significant** if it meets the audience's expectations of what should occur on this occasion. In a classroom speech, for example, a common expectation is that the speech should be on a topic of some importance to the class, the campus, the community, or the world. A speech on what you ate for breakfast, how you spent Saturday night, or your most recent fight with your mate may not warrant publicity.

A speech topic is **timely** if it can be linked to the audience's current concerns. A student who gave a speech about a revolution in Liberia did a fine job on the speech, but the revolution had occurred several years before, and the student failed to demonstrate how it related to the present. Ancient history can be timely if the speaker can show how that history speaks to the present.

A speech is **tailored** if the topic is narrowed to fit the time allotted for the speech. It is tough to cover the rise and fall of the Roman Empire in a five-minute speech, but it is quite possible in that amount of time to talk about three ways to avoid osteoporosis through your diet. More speakers err in selecting too large rather than too small a topic. A narrow topic allows you to use research time more effectively: researching too large a topic will result in cutting much of your material to meet the time requirement of the speech.

The purpose of your speech is the overall effect you seek from the audience. Traditionally, speech purposes have been to inform, persuade, and entertain. They could just as well be to convince, actuate, encourage, or celebrate. Fortunately, only two categories are of great interest to students of public speaking: the informative and the persuasive speech.

The **informative purpose** seeks to increase audience understanding or knowledge about some topic: the causes of disease, uses of a tool, places where auto parts can be found, types of plants, the origins of language, or the dangers of drugs.

The **persuasive purpose** tries to modify the audience's behavior by changing their minds about a topic. Its purpose, then, is to alter what the audience knows, how they feel about what they know, and, ultimately, how they behave.

Determining Your Purpose

Just as each class you attend brings you closer to the goal of attaining a degree, each speech brings an audience closer to some ultimate goal. A politician, for instance, delivers single speeches to many audiences. In most cases gaining votes is the goal that lies beyond the immediate speech. One sermon, one lecture, or one speech is only a single bit of information in a larger context of receiving information about a subject.

Let us say you hear a speech in class about avoiding refined sugar. That single persuasive speech is placed in a psychological context that might include a magazine article that you read about the negative effects of sugar, a news clip about obesity, and some comments from a friend about how fat and diabetes are related. The speech, the magazine article, the news item, and the friend's comments are all informative bits that contribute to an ultimate goal of reducing your intake of refined sugar.

Practically every speech has an **ultimate goal,** an objective that is consistent with but lies beyond the immediate speech. If you are aware of that goal, then you can see that your speech is consistent with it. On the other hand, if you aim at nothing, that is exactly what you are likely to hit.

Selecting an Ultimate Goal

• •

Immediate Responses

To read more about the topic
To sign this letter
To complain to officials
To tell others
To listen to other speakers on the topic
To join a group
To vote
To eat
To answer my questions
To state my main arguments

• •

What do you want your audience to do as a result of your speech? The **immediate response** is the audience's realization of the speaker's intention, the audience's increased knowledge, altered feelings, or behavioral change. The immediate response or thesis is different from the ultimate goal but is related to it. If my ultimate goal is to convince you to stop buying a particular product, then the immediate response I seek should be consistent with that goal. For instance, my single speech might get you to remember some reasons why you should exercise, and that is consistent with my ultimate goal of converting you to aerobic exercises like running or swimming.

Immediate responses are easier to assess if you make them behavioral. That is, you try to have an immediate response that allows you to see if your speech had an effect on the audience. If I say that the immediate response I seek is for the audience to state two of the five reasons I mentioned for swimming instead of jogging, then I can measure the effect of my speech by asking a few people to write or say if they know two reasons. **Behavioral responses** call for human behavior: you want the audience to describe, state, list, choose, accept, or reject.

In an informative speech, a behavioral immediate response might be best stated using infinitives like these:

to recognize	to distinguish	to describe	to define
to compare	to contrast	to state	to identify
to differentiate	to learn	to remember	to list

Stated as an immediate response it might look like this:

The immediate response I seek in my speech is to compare the advantages of condominiums and apartments.

or

The immediate response I seek in my speech is to have the audience list the danger signs of cancer.

In both examples the speaker would have the option of finding out how effective the speech was by seeing if the audience remembered the advantages, or could write or recite the list.

In a persuasive speech the immediate response might use infinitives like these:

to sign	to avoid	to discontinue	to accept	to favor
to tell	to convert	to join	to vote	to reject
to agree	to buy	to oppose	to adopt	to object

Table 5.1	Purpose, goal, and response	
Purpose	*Ultimate goal*	*Immediate response*
To inform	To know words used by urban gangs.	To define six words commonly used in the streets.
To persuade	To discourage use of junk food.	To describe the nutritional value of two popular junk foods.

Stated as an immediate response, it might look like this:

> The immediate response that I seek from my audience is for them to oppose the new zoning ordinance.

or

> The immediate response that I seek from my audience is to have them buy baking soda instead of expensive carpet deodorizers.

In both examples the speaker can—at least theoretically—find out if the audience acted on the message. Table 5.1 shows the relationships among the purpose, the ultimate goal, and the immediate response in public speaking.

Often your instructor will ask you to write out the immediate response you seek from your audience. This assignment requires you to explicitly state your objective for the speech. It helps you to focus on the reason why you are giving the speech. One of the better ways to write your immediate response is to:

Writing Your Immediate Responses

1. *Write the response statement as an infinitive phrase.*
   An infinitive is a verbal form that begins with the word *to*. Examples are "to state," "to petition," or "to recommend." An "infinitive phrase" is something less than a sentence with a subject and a verb, and something more than a fragment. It looks like this:

   to state how much shoplifting costs consumers

2. *Include some detail about the expected audience response.*
   Your infinitive phrase should include what you want your audience to do as a result of your speech. If you want them "to eat" (your infinitive) then state what you want them to eat:

   to eat some synthetic foods in class

Look at the examples in table 5.1 for some other ideas on how the statement of audience response can be composed. If your teacher wants you to write your ultimate goal, then use an infinitive phrase along with some single central idea. For instance:

to gain audience acceptance for synthetic foods

Again, table 5.1 shows two more examples of how to compose a statement of ultimate goal.

The Statement of Purpose

Some instructors want their students to state the idea behind speech in a single sentence. This **statement of purpose** is like the central idea or thesis statement expected in many beginning English composition courses. In a public speaking course the statement of purpose is a complete sentence that reveals the purpose of your speech. It might look like one of these examples:

The purpose of my informative speech is to reveal the three main reasons why students drop out of college: grade problems, money problems, and family problems.
The purpose of my speech is to persuade the audience to stop buying products that contain coconut and palm oil among the ingredients.
The purpose of my informative speech is to reveal the ideas behind the Libertarian Party in America.

Notice that the statement of purpose reveals the kind of speech—informative or persuasive—and forecasts the content of the speech. These two ingredients plus the form—a complete sentence—are the necessary characteristics of the statement of purpose.

The chapter ended with some suggestions for writing a statement of immediate response, an ultimate goal, and a statement of purpose. Learning how to find appropriate topics and purposes for you and your audience will help you face your speech with confidence. In the next chapter you will turn to another step in speech preparation: finding and citing written and interviewed sources.

Summary

We began this chapter with suggestions about selecting a topic.

1. Speak about a topic that you already know.
2. Speak about a topic that interests you.
3. Speak about a topic uniquely your own.
4. Speak about a current topic.
5. Speak about a topic that is interesting to your audience.
6. Speak about a topic that the audience embraces but you do not.

We also examined methods of searching for a topic. They included two kinds of listing: using a broad category—like population control—to suggest a series of more specific related topics, and using a broad category to suggest a series of other broad but related topics that could be narrowed for public-speaking topics. Other methods of searching for a topic are as follows. Monitor your own behavior to see what interests you; conduct a personal inventory to bring your choices to a more conscious level; generate a large quantity of topics through personal brainstorming that can be critically analyzed later; consult a list of current topics; and use clustering, or a free association of ideas related to one main concept.

Once chosen, topics need to be evaluated for their appropriateness to you as speaker (interest and knowledge), their appropriateness to your audience (interest and worthwhileness), and their appropriateness for the occasion (significant, timely, and tailored).

The primary purposes of public speaking in the classroom are two: to inform and to persuade. The ultimate goal of a speech is a larger purpose that often goes beyond the single speech. It should be the focal point for the immediate response that the speaker seeks from the audience.

▼▼

Checklist for Topic Appropriateness

Checklist

_____ 1. Do you, as the speaker, have *involvement* with the topic?
_____ 2. Do you, as the speaker, have *competence* in the topic area?
_____ 3. Based on audience analyses, does this topic hold *interest* for your audience?
_____ 4. Based on audience analyses, is the topic *worthwhile* to your audience?
_____ 5. Is the topic *significant* in terms of the speech occasion?
_____ 6. Is the topic *timely* in terms of the speech occasion?
_____ 7. Have you appropriately *narrowed and limited* the topic for the occasion?

• •

▼▼

1
Brainstorming for Topics

Application Exercises

In order to discover the usefulness of brainstorming and to generate a number of possible topics, try this exercise. Take out a pencil and paper, check the time, and allow yourself exactly five minutes to write down as many topics as come to mind. The topics do not have to be stated as specific speech topics: they can be individual words, phrases, or sentences. The range in number of ideas written in this exercise varies from five or six to as many as thirty possible topics.

After you have written down all the topics you can in five minutes, write three more topics in the next three minutes. Most people find it difficult to write down any more ideas, but those who can generally find their best ideas come after they have brainstormed for a period of time.

After you have completed your list of topics, select five that are particularly interesting to you. Finally, from these five, select the one that has the best potential for a public speech. Keep in mind that you should already have or be able to find information about this topic and that you will have to adapt the topic to a specific audience.

2

Brainstorming by Topic Areas

Take out paper and pencil and divide the paper into four to six sections. Write down one of the following topic areas at the top of each section.

Job experiences you have had

Places you have traveled

City, state, or area you are from

People who make you angry

Happy experiences you have had

Unusual experiences you have had

Personal experiences with crime

Your involvement in marriage, divorce, or other family matters

Experiences with members of other groups—the old, the young, other racial or ethnic groups

The effect of the drug culture on your life

Your relationship to local, state, or federal government

Your background in painting, music, sculpture, theater, dance, or other arts

Your feelings about grades, college education, sororities and fraternities, college requirements, student government, or alternatives to a college education

Your reactions to current radio, television, or film practices, policies, or programming

Recent Supreme Court decisions that affect you

Your personal and career goals

Spend approximately three to five minutes jotting down specific topics for each of the four to six topic areas you chose. Underline one topic in each area that is especially interesting to you. From these four to six underlined topics, select the one for which you have the most information or best access to information and which you can adapt to your specific audience.

3

What Magazines You Read

Similarly, individuals' interests are reflected in the magazines they normally read. Complete this exercise to discover your own interests. Consider the magazines you normally purchase or subscribe to and note which ones you read regularly (+), occasionally (0), rarely or never (−).

_____ News Magazines (for example, *Time, Newsweek, U.S. News & World Report*)

_____ Traditional Women's Magazines (for example, *Ladies Home Journal, Good Housekeeping, Redbook*)

_____ Feminist Publications (*Working Woman, Ms., New Woman*)

_____ Political Publications (*Nation, New Republic, National Review*)
_____ Recreational Magazines (*Sports Illustrated, Skiing, RV Travel*)
_____ Hobby Magazines (*Popular Mechanics, The Workbasket*)
_____ Confession Magazines (*True Story, True Confessions, Modern Romances*)
_____ Religious Magazines (*Commonweal, The Watchtower, The Upper Room*)
_____ Sex Emphasis Magazines (*Playboy, Playgirl, Penthouse, Cosmopolitan*)
_____ Professional Journals (*Elementary English, Journal of Abnormal and Social Psychology, American Educational Research Journal*)

4
Topic, Purposes, and Goal

In order to gain experience in formulating general purposes, ultimate goals, and immediate purposes, complete the following exercise. For each of the topics specify the missing information. Remember to write the immediate responses in behavioral terms.

Topic	General Purpose	Immediate Response	Ultimate Goal
Edible plants	To persuade	_____ _____ _____	To convince the audience to eat plants they find in the wild.
Waterbeds	_____	To have the audience list three benefits of sleeping on a waterbed.	_____ _____ _____
Crack	To persuade	_____ _____ _____ _____	_____ _____ _____ _____
Shoplifting	To inform	To have the audience state how much shoplifting costs the consumer.	_____ _____ _____
Selection of the pope	To inform	_____ _____ _____ _____	To give the audience an understanding of how the pope is elected.
Animal abuse	_____	To have the audience distinguish between animal abuse and animal discipline.	_____ _____ _____

5
The Statement of Purpose

To learn how to write a statement of purpose, fill in the blanks with words of your own. The last example should be a complete sentence of your own that states the type of speech—informative or persuasive—and forecasts the content of the speech.

The purpose of my _____ speech is to explain to my audience the meaning of the term *perestroika*.

The purpose of my persuasive speech is to provide five reasons for my audience why they should buy a _____ .

The _____ of my _____ speech is to convince my audience why they should vote for Sam Smith for mayor.

The purpose of my _____ speech is _____

_____ .

▼▼▼

Application Assignment

Topic and Purpose

Select a topic that you found through any of the methods suggested in this chapter. Make sure that the topic is appropriate for you, the audience, and the speech occasion. See that it is interesting and worthwhile to the audience as well as significant, timely, and appropriately narrowed and limited. At the top of your paper write your name and your topic. Then indicate your general purpose, your ultimate goal, and your immediate response for the speech. Your paper should look like this:

Topic: Carver Hall—the Man Behind the Building

General Purpose: to *inform* the audience about a campus building and the person after whom it was named.

Immediate Response: to provide information about Carver Hall and George Washington Carver that my classmates can *tell* roommates and acquaintances, by remembering at least three of the five facts I will relate about the black scientist after whom the building is named.

Ultimate Goal: to encourage classmates *to read* a brief book that tells the stories behind the names of campus buildings.

Make sure that your ultimate goal and immediate response include ways that your audience will behave differently as a result of your speech.

appropriateness   The criterion for evaluating a topic; includes its suitability for you as speaker, for your audience, and for the occasion.

behavioral response   The idea that knowing how you want the audience to act as a result of your speech gives you a way to see its effectiveness.

clustering   A method of topic selection in which you start with a broad topic area and then visually free associate by linking and circling your ideas on a sheet of paper.

current topics   Topics of interest today because they are in the news or on the minds of people in your audience.

immediate response   The effect that you seek in the audience as a result of a single speech.

informative purpose   A purpose in public speaking that seeks to increase the audience's knowledge level about a particular topic.

listing   A systematic method of discovering a topic by either narrowing down a broad topic or starting with a broad category and listing related ideas.

monitoring your behavior   Raising your own actions to consciousness on the assumption that, on your own time, you do what interests you.

personal brainstorming   Assessing your own choices in some specific area of your life; e.g., what you read, what you watch, how you relax, etc.

personal inventory   Discovering your own areas of expertise by surveying your own choices: what do you read, what do you look for, and what do you choose to do?

persuasive purpose   A purpose in public speaking that seeks to change the audience's behavior by changing their minds about a particular topic.

significance   The speech meets the audience's expectations about what should be said by you on this topic and occasion.

statement of purpose   A sentence that reveals the type of speech—informative or persuasive—and forecasts the content.

tailored   The speech topic is narrowed to fit the time allotted for the presentation.

timely   The speech is linked to the audience's current concerns.

ultimate goal   A larger but focused objective that goes beyond the single speech to an effect you want to achieve over time.

1. The idea of clustering comes from Gabriele Lusser Rico, *Writing the Natural Way* (Los Angeles: J. P. Tarcher, Inc., 1983), 35–36. The authors wish to thank Dr. William Miller, Professor in the School of Telecommunications at Ohio University, for bringing this method to their attention.
2. This clustering was designed by Mr. Brad Peters, a student at Ohio University, Athens, Ohio.

Finding Information

6

Question Outline

I. What is the role of your personal experience in providing information for your speech?

II. What should you do before, during, and after an interview?

III. What are some sources of information in the library, and how do you find them?

IV. How should you find sources and record information from them?

V. What is a correct way to cite information from written and interviewed sources?

Order and simplification are the first steps towards mastery of a subject.

THOMAS MANN

Introduction

Suppose you want to give a speech about diets. Perhaps you are a bit overweight yourself and have been on a few diets. If so, then you have the required interest and some knowledge of the topic. But what are you supposed to do beyond that?

This chapter is devoted to helping you flesh out a speech with information gathered from your own personal experience, from interviews with people who know more than you do about the topic, from materials that you get from phone calls or through the mail, and from written resources in the library. The idea behind this chapter is to increase your confidence as a public speaker by helping you discover information.

Personal Experience

One of the richest sources of information is you. You have gone to school for a dozen years or more. You have worked at part-time and full-time jobs. You have gone places and met people who taught you lessons in living. You may have married and returned to school after serving in the armed forces or after raising a family. Whatever your story, it is not exactly like anyone else's. In your own personal experience you can find information that will provide ideas, supporting materials, and arguments for your speeches.

Unfortunately, many students do not see themselves as unique. Sometimes on the first day of class, the authors ask students to identify themselves by name, major, hometown, year in school, age, and any other demographic characteristics they may wish to share. Then each student is asked to state in what way he or she is unique, different from others in the class. If any characteristic is repeated, then that person has to think of another unique feature. The class decides if the characteristic or experience is unique.

How is this exercise related to discovering information for your speech? Your unique experience with a topic should be part of your speech. It demonstrates your interest and involvement with the topic. The person is doing more than simply fulfilling an assignment when he or she talks about alcoholism and its effects on his or her own family. The person who talks about gene transplants is higher in credibility when he reveals his work in the biological sciences.

People are often unaware of their own uniqueness, tending to think that many others have done or experienced what they have. One of the authors spent two years as the chief prelaw advisor for a large university. The biggest difficulty in writing the "Dean's Recommendation" for the prospective law students was getting them to think of how they differed from hundreds of other applicants. Even a twenty-minute interview with each student failed to reveal uniqueness. Often students came back later with second thoughts.

One student came back two days after the interview to ask if it made any difference that she was a concert pianist. How was that related to law school, she inquired. A concert pianist has practiced most of her life. That kind of discipline is exactly what law schools demand. Another student remembered that he had learned the Russian language—in Russia. Still another saw nothing unusual about finishing college in three years with a 4.0 average. Your uniqueness may not be as dramatic as these examples, but the point is that people have difficulty seeing it in themselves even when it clearly exists.

Although personal experience should be a first consideration in looking for speech material, it should be used critically. Your personal experience should:

1. enhance your credibility as a speaker on this topic;
2. provide examples or supporting material; or
3. demonstrate your relationship to the topic.

Ask yourself if the experience you wish to relate in the speech is typical. Is it so typical that it is boring, or so unusual that it was probably a chance occurrence? Will the audience learn from your experience? Does your experience constitute proof or evidence of anything? If your personal experience meets some of these expectations and does not violate the sensibilities of your audience, then it will probably be an asset in your speech.

Interviews

A second important source of ideas and information for your speech is other people. Your campus is a great resource. It is full of faculty and staff, many of whom are experts on some subject or another. Your community likewise is populated with people who have expertise on many issues: government workers on politics; clergy on religion; physicians, psychologists, and nurses on health care; engineers on highways and buildings; and owners and managers on industries and business. The following story illustrates how a speech can be based on an interview.

Norman Donne came to his speech professor's office in despair. He was supposed to give his speech in two days. He had selected a topic but could find nothing on the subject because someone had cut out all of the information from the magazines, newspapers, and books in the library.

Finding Information   **97**

Norman was frustrated and angry. His speech professor recommended that he give his speech on a topic that was of highest interest to him at the moment: the destruction of library resources.

Norman made an appointment to see the associate director of the library. He hit a gold mine. The associate director was part of a national study team investigating the destruction of library resources. He was gratified to find a student interested in this issue who would tell other students how serious the problem was.

After two hours with the associate director, the student knew the average number of pages destroyed in the magazines, the cost of repairing or replacing the damaged books, and the actual amount of damage at his own college. He had more information than he could have found in many days of research. When Norman gave his speech, he supplemented his personal experience with facts and figures that made him more of an authority on library barbarity than anyone in the room.

You may not find all of the information you need in a single interview, but you may discover that interviewing is an efficient way to gather information on your topic. The person you interview can furnish ideas, quotations, and valuable leads to other sources. But first learn when and how to conduct an interview, and how to use the results.

If you can find the information as quickly and easily by looking it up yourself, then do not seek it through an interview. Instead, interview when:

1. The information is not readily available. Maybe the issue is so current that it is not covered in the papers. Perhaps the issue affects such a narrow band of people that it has been overlooked. Interviewing can unearth information that is not in books, magazines, or newspapers.
2. The authority on the subject is available. If you have people on your campus or in your community who have expertise on your topic, then their opinions should be sought.
3. The quotations and ideas are necessary for your speech. Often you can elicit higher-impact quotes from experts for your speech than the press gets because experts learn to be very prudent around reporters. These quotations and ideas can give your speech the sizzle it needs to gain audience interest.

Before your interview determine your purpose, write out your questions, select a person to interview, and arrange an appointment.

Your *purpose* for the interview should be related to the immediate response you seek from the audience and your ultimate goal. For example, your immediate response might be "to learn the Heimlich Maneuver," and your ultimate goal might be for your audience "to save lives by using life-saving techniques on victims." What purpose would be served in having an interview about a maneuver to save victims of choking? Persons in medicine or public health can provide you with authoritative quotations, real-life stories, and reasons for your audience to listen. All of this is possible if you ask the right questions.

Your *questions* should be carefully designed to produce the information you need. Make them specific, clear, and necessary. Some can be "yes or no" questions, but most should call for an opinion. All should be questions that cannot be easily answered by simply looking them up. As much as possible, the questions should be stated without bias, without suggesting an answer, and without threat, anger, or hostility.

Following are some sample questions appropriate for a speech on the Heimlich Maneuver.

How many choking victims are there per year in the USA?
What age groups are most likely to be affected?
Where (in the home, restaurants, etc.) do such incidents usually occur?
How effective is the maneuver in helping victims?
Are there any dangers in having laypersons use the maneuver?
Do you think more people should learn the maneuver?
Have you ever used it to help a victim?
Is there anything related to the Heimlich Maneuver that you think I should
    tell my audience that has not already been mentioned?

Your questions can accompany you to the interview so you will feel confident about your meeting.

Selecting your interviewee is the next important step. Your first consideration is "Who can best answer my questions?" You might want to ask your teacher for an opinion on this issue. Among your criteria for selecting a person for an interview are availability, accessibility, and affability. A person might be on campus or in your community, but may not grant interviews. Or a person may be available and accessible, but unfriendly to interviewers.

The big surprise for many public speaking students is how many important people will submit to an interview for a campus speech. Most people are flattered that others want to know their opinion. If your interview is well planned and implemented, then other students are likely to be welcomed by this same interviewee.

Making an appointment usually involves talking to a secretary or administrative assistant. This person is correctly called a "gatekeeper" because he or she controls the gate, or door, to their employer's office. The way you treat the secretary can determine whether or not you get an appointment, so be polite, clear about your mission, and reasonable about the amount of time that you want and when you want it.

Some guidelines for securing an interview include:

1. Look professional when you ask for the interview. This can help you in gaining an appointment.
2. State your purpose clearly and succinctly. It is best if you can tell the secretary what your mission is, but another alternative is to type a brief note that she can pass on to the interviewee.

3. Ask for an appointment early. Some people will be too heavily scheduled to see you on short notice. The earlier you ask for an appointment, the better your chances of securing an interview.
4. Ask for a brief amount of time. Usually a ten to twenty minute appointment is sufficient. It is better to ask for a brief appointment and let the interviewee extend it, than to ask for a large amount of time that you do not use.
5. Show up for your appointment appropriately dressed and at least five or ten minutes early in case your interviewee wants to take you early. If you are going to be late, call ahead and ask the secretary if you should cancel.

These guidelines will serve you well as you prepare for the interview itself.

During the Interview

One decision you will have to make concerning your interview is whether or not to record it. The advantages of a tape recording are accuracy and completeness. The disadvantages are that some interviewees do not like to be recorded, the presence of a recorder can inhibit disclosures, and sometimes the machine fails, leaving you with a useless tape and no notes. Always ask the person you are interviewing if you can use the tape recorder, and take notes anyway in case modern technology fails.

Interviews rarely start with the first question. Instead, expect the interviewee to express curiosity about you and your project. Be perfectly frank about your purpose, the assignment, and the audience. The interviewee is doing the verbal equivalent of a handshake with the questioning.

During the interview be very careful about the *tone* of your questions and comments. You are not in the role of an investigative reporter interrogating a member of a crime syndicate. Instead, you are a speaker seeking information and cooperation from someone who can help you. Your tone should be friendly and your comments constructive.

During the interview be *flexible*. Even though you have prepared questions, you may find that the responses answer more than one question, and your pre-planned order isn't working as well as you thought. Relax. Check off questions as you ask them or as they are answered. Take a minute at the conclusion of the interview to see if you have covered all of your questions.

Practice *active listening* during your interview. Show an interest in the person's answers. If you hear something that you want to get verbatim, write it down, or ask the interviewee to repeat it if necessary. Do not try to copy every word but do get an accurate rendition of direct quotations.

Make sure that you have accurate *citation information,* your interviewee's name, title, and the name of the company, agency, or department. You will be citing this person's words and using oral footnotes to credit them, so you need correct source information. If the interviewee has time, you may want to read back your direct quotes for verification.

Take notes during your interview.

Finally, remember to *depart*. Give your interviewee an opportunity to stop the interview at the designated time. The interviewee—not you—should extend the interview beyond the designated time. The interviewee will appreciate a gracious good-bye and gratitude for granting the interview. As a parting gesture of good will, the secretary should be thanked as well.

After the Interview

As soon as you can after the interview *review your notes,* write down items that were discussed without complete notes, and make sure you can read your own direct quotes.

If you taped the interview, *listen to your tape* as soon as possible. If you wait even a few hours, you may have difficulty remembering exactly what was said.

The best way to ensure that your interview can be used in your speech is to write the most important material, especially the direct quotations, on *note cards,* each carefully marked with the name of the source and the sequence of cards (see fig. 6.1). With careful preparation before the interview, attentive listening and accurate note taking during the interview, and quick review and note-card composition after the interview, you will increase your confidence as a speaker.

Phone and Mail Requests

Two additional methods of gaining information for your speeches are phone calls and mail requests.

Phone calls are faster than interviews but call for the same kind of decorum. Frequently you have to get through a secretary to talk to your interviewee. Phone calls are a good method if the information you need will take very little time to communicate, if it can be communicated entirely by voice, and if it can be done with a minimum of dialogue.

Figure 6.1 Sample interview note card.

```
Dr. Carson B. Axelrod (M.D. from Stanford U.)
Chair, Dept. of Internal Medicine
Pomeroy Community Hospital

"Laypersons using the Heimlich Maneuver should be wary
about employing the maneuver on infants. An adult can take a
firm, rapid squeeze without fear of fracture, but a small
child could become a dual victim of choking and broken
ribs."



Interviewed 2/24/89
```

One caution about phone call interviews is to make sure that you are available for a return call if the interviewee is unavailable, or make an appointment to call the interviewee back. A busy person is unlikely to make many return calls to an unanswered phone, but a busy person whose secretary has forewarned the interviewee about an impending phone call will be happy to comply. As with interviews, you need to treat the secretary with respect, take accurate notes during the phone conversation, and write the person's name, title or position, and company or department correctly.

Mail inquiries are a good way to get more information. Your librarian can help you locate the addresses of interest groups for everything from alcoholism to zymologists. You will need to request information well in advance of your speech, but special interest organizations will eagerly respond to speakers who are willing to advance their cause. One possible liability is that your one inquiry may place you on the organization's mailing list for life.

You can also write to government agencies. Again, your librarian may have the information if your college is a federal depository for government documents. Or you will learn how to request them from government agencies. In any case, the U.S. Mail is a relatively fast way to secure information about your topic.

Using the Library

The library is the focal point of most colleges and universities. Your public speaking course gives you an opportunity to use this very useful and expensive resource. It will be one of your important sources of information.

Some resources available are:

The librarian; the card catalog or computerized catalog system; general indexes to periodicals; special indexes to periodicals; regular, comprehensive, and specialized dictionaries; general and specialized encyclopedias; yearbooks; and newspapers.

Use your library to find information.

The Librarian

We have been looking at people who can help with your speeches. One of the most important partners for success in your public speaking class is the library staff. These individuals know the library well, and part of their job is to help you use it to your advantage.

If you have not actively used your library, consider a library tour with a member of the library staff. The library should not be a mystery to you; instead, it should be a place that can help you succeed. The more you know about it, the better you can use it.

Start by learning where the following items are located in your library.

The Card Catalog or Computerized Catalog System

The card catalog contains information about every book in the library arranged by author, title, and subject. (Figure 6.2 shows the three basic kinds of cards.) It also indicates what other written resources are available in the library. The card catalog can be hundreds of drawers of alphabetized cards, or it can be computerized so all you have to do is "punch up" the information. The "call number" in the upper left corner of the card reveals where in the library the book or back issues of the periodical are located. You will not be expected, of course, to read a pile of books on every topic about which you speak, but selective reading of available books and back issues of magazines can give you useful information.

General Indexes to Periodicals

The general indexes to periodicals provide you with a guide to magazine articles, book reviews, and even newspaper articles by author and subject. The most popular of these is the *Reader's Guide to Periodical Literature,* which lists by author, title, and subject all of the magazine articles written in the major magazines in

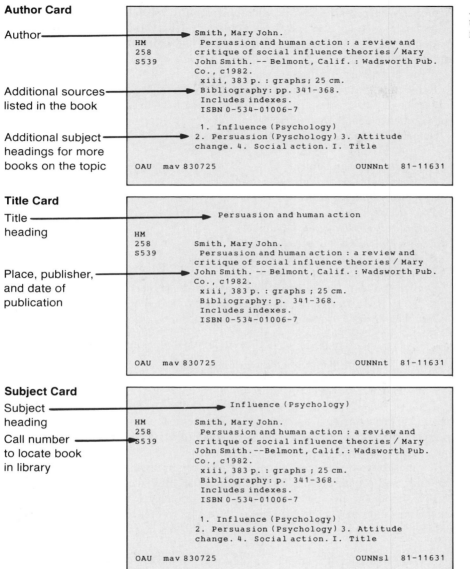

Author Card

Author

Additional sources listed in the book

Additional subject headings for more books on the topic

Title Card

Title heading

Place, publisher, and date of publication

Subject Card

Subject heading

Call number to locate book in library

Smith, Mary John.
HM
258
S539 Persuasion and human action : a review and critique of social influence theories / Mary John Smith. -- Belmont, Calif. : Wadsworth Pub. Co., c1982.
xiii, 383 p. : graphs ; 25 cm.
Bibliography: pp. 341-368.
Includes indexes.
ISBN 0-534-01006-7

1. Influence (Psychology)
2. Persuasion (Pyschology) 3. Attitude change. 4. Social action. I. Title

OAU mav 830725 OUNNnt 81-11631

Persuasion and human action
HM
258
S539 Smith, Mary John.
Persuasion and human action : a review and critique of social influence theories / Mary John Smith. -- Belmont, Calif. : Wadsworth Pub. Co., c1982.
xiii, 383 p. : graphs ; 25 cm.
Bibliography: p. 341-368.
Includes indexes.
ISBN 0-534-01006-7

OAU mav 830725 OUNNnt 81-11631

Influence (Psychology)
HM
258
S539 Smith, Mary John.
Persuasion and human action : a review and critique of social influence theories / Mary John Smith.--Belmont, Calif.: Wadsworth Pub. Co., c1982.
xiii, 383 p. : graphs ; 25 cm.
Bibliography: p. 341-368.
Includes indexes.
ISBN 0-534-01006-7

1. Influence (Psychology)
2. Persuasion (Psychology) 3. Attitude change. 4. Social action. I. Title

OAU mav 830725 OUNNsl 81-11631

Figure 6.2 Author, title, and subject cards for a book.

print. Some of the main general indexes to periodicals and the time period they cover are:

Reader's Guide to Periodical Literature. 1900–. (Author, title, subject)
Book Review Digest. 1905–. (Author, title, subject)
Social Sciences and Humanities Index. 1965–. (Author, subject)
New York Times Index. 1913–. (Author, subject)

**Special Indexes
to Periodicals**

A properly-narrowed topic will sometimes require specialized information. For example, if you decide to attack the grading system, you might find some information in the *Reader's Guide,* but you would find more in the many periodicals and journals that specialize in education. The *Education Index,* for instance, can lead you to articles in 150 magazines and journals.

Remember that specific indexes lead you to specialized periodicals written for professionals and experts. You may find that you have to simplify the articles for your audience's understanding.

Some of the special indexes to periodicals are:

Art Index (author, subject).
Bibliographic Index (subject).
Biography Index (subject).
Book Review Index.
Catholic Periodical Index (subject).
Education Index (author, subject).
Biological and Agricultural Index (subject).
Engineering Index (subject).
Quarterly Cumulative Index Medicus (author, subject).
Index to Book Reviews in the Humanities.
Index to Legal Periodicals (author, subject).
Business Periodicals Index (subject).
Music Index (author, subject).
Public Affairs Information Service (subject).
Technical Book Review Index.

Dictionaries

Need help pronouncing a word? Wonder what some technical term means? Want to know where a word came from? The dictionaries—desktop, comprehensive, and specialized—are the resource to use.

For most of your speeches the collegiate dictionary is sufficient to find spelling, meaning, and pronunciation. But sometimes you may need more. The comprehensive dictionary, like the Oxford English Dictionary, can tell you most of the known meanings and origins of a word. A related reference work, the thesaurus, can provide you with lists of words that mean the same (synonyms) or opposite (antonyms).

Still another kind of dictionary, a dictionary of usage, can tell you how words are used in actual practice. Do you know when to use *affect* and *effect?* A dictionary of usage can tell you. Some examples of these references are:

Black, Henry C. *Law Dictionary.*
Comrie, John Dixon. *Black's Medical Dictionary.*
Fowler, H. W. *A Dictionary of Modern English Usage.*
Partridge, Eric. *Dictionary of Slang and Unconventional English.*
Roget's International Thesaurus.
Webster's New Dictionary of Synonyms.

Encyclopedias are great for finding background information. If you want to give an informative speech about any subject except the most current, you can find some information in the general encyclopedias like *Encyclopaedia Britannica, Encyclopedia Americana,* or a specialized encyclopedia like these:

Buttrick, George A., and Keith R. Crim, eds. *Interpreter's Dictionary of the Bible.*
Dictionary of American History.
Encyclopedia of Philosophy.
Encyclopedia of World Art.
Illing, Robert. *Dictionary of Musicians and Music.*
Mitzel, Harold, ed. *Encyclopedia of Educational Research.*
Munn, Glenn G. *Encyclopedia of Banking and Finance.*
Turner, John, ed. *Encyclopedia of Social Work.*

You can find background information on important people and relatively current facts and figures in yearbooks. For backgrounds on people, reference works like *Who's Who in America* or *The Dictionary of American Biography* are very good. But you are more likely to use the books of facts, statistics, and details available in the other reference works in this list:

Americana Annual.
The Annual Register of World Events.
Economic Almanac.
Facts on File.
Information Please Almanac.
New International Year Book.
Statesman's Year-Book.
Statistical Abstract of the United States.
World Almanac and Book of Facts.

You can find biographies on living women in *Who's Who of American Women,* dead men in the *Dictionary of American Biography,* living news makers in *Current Biography,* famous American women in the *Notable American Women,* and dead historical persons from the British Empire in *Dictionary of National Biography.* You can also find maps *Rand McNally Cosmopolitan World Atlas,* geographical dictionaries *Webster's New Geographical Dictionary,* and indexes for as many as seven newspapers.

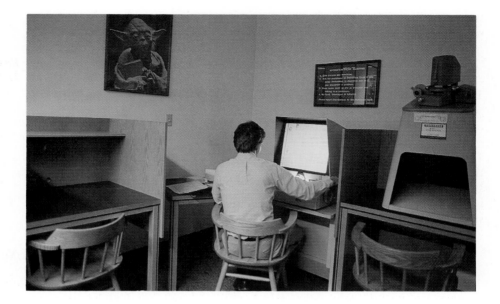

Newspapers

Most newspapers are not indexed so they are somewhat difficult to use for research purposes. Fortunately, some newspapers are indexed by subject so that you can find articles you need. Some of the more important are:

The *Los Angeles Times.*   The *Chicago Tribune.*
The *New York Times.*   The *Wall Street Journal.*
The *Washington Post.*   The *Christian Science Monitor.*

Back issues of newspapers appear in two forms. Your library may have the actual newspaper if it is recent or it will carry back issues on microfilm which requires a microfilm reader available in the library.

If you get confused about these available reference works, then remember only one thing: YOUR LIBRARIAN CAN HELP YOU FIND THE INFORMATION YOU NEED.

Researching Effectively

People like to know more about a subject. A game entitled Trivial Pursuit has been a best seller for several years. The game is based on wide knowledge of many disciplines. The winners are the ones who know the most about the most subjects. The game is popular because people think it is fun to pit one team's knowledge against another's.

You will find that doing research can also be very interesting. At first, you may find it frustrating because you have to learn how to find information, record it, and adapt it for your speech. But you will also find that research can be distracting. As you look for the things you need for your speech other items attract your attention. This section is designed to help you become an effective researcher by providing helpful hints about finding material for your speech.

One of the first principles of research is that research takes time. An earlier chapter on topic selection stressed the importance of finding a topic without delay. Too often students expend most of their time finding a topic and very little time researching it. A more effective pattern is to pick a topic early and leave yourself maximum time for researching it.

Research Takes Time

In addition to finding a topic early, you should narrow it to fit the time allowed. The body of a five-minute speech is rarely more than three minutes long because the introduction and conclusion take about two minutes. The body includes transitions and organizational moves that take time. So you actually have a limited amount of time to present the support material of your speech. Consider the consequences faced by this student.

Patty Richmond was a diligent student. She selected her topic early and gave herself seven days to do the research. The topic she selected was "Clothing." Her first look in the card catalog revealed over two hundred books that dealt in some way or another with the history of clothing; the changing styles; the fabrics in attire; the popular styles of the present; and even the use of clothing around the world. The *Reader's Guide* provided another large pile of note cards with the names of magazine articles about clothing. Patty spent two of her seven days just finding all of the books, magazine articles, and newspaper articles about clothing. She had a huge stack of authors and titles, but she had not read even one article.

Patty was so frustrated that she wanted to drop the course. She did not want to do this for every speech. Her professor suggested that she look through her stack of bibliography cards and find some narrow theme that would interest her and her audience. She decided to speak about clothing and status, and how people's clothing is used in business to indicate status or importance. Only ten of her sources touched on that topic. She saved time by reading only those sources that were directly relevant to her topic, and used nearly all of her note cards in her speech.

The moral of the story is that a topic narrowed to the time limit will save you considerable research time. Too large a topic will leave you with too many sources and too many notes.

An early research step should be to review what you know about the topic. Then set up an interview with one or more persons who can provide information for your speech. Finally, survey the card catalog, the *Reader's Guide to Periodical Literature,* and the indexes that lead you to sources.

Survey Your Sources

Look before you write. You might find, like Patty Richmond did, that there are too many sources for your speech. That indicates that the topic may be too large for a brief speech. Glance over the cards in the card catalog and the subjects in the *Reader's Guide* before you begin listing potential sources. Normally, speakers narrow their topics even further as they discover the amount of information available.

You might wonder how many sources you need for your survey. A good guideline is the "three per minute" rule which says that you will need to find approximately three potential sources for each minute of your speech in order to end up with one per minute for actual use in your speech. Some of your sources—maybe even most—will not yield the kind of information you need. A five-minute speech indicates a need of fifteen sources; the end result is likely to be five that are actually used in the body of the speech.

<table>
<tr><td>

**Recording
Potential Sources**

</td><td>

Your next step in research is to make a *bibliography card* for each book, magazine article, or newspaper article that appears to relate closely to your topic. A bibliography card for a book should list the author, title, place of publication, publisher, date of publication, call number (to locate the book in the library), and any notes you might want to make about the specific information in the book or its importance. A bibliography card for a book would look like figure 6.3 on page 111.

</td></tr>
</table>

Notice that the name of the author is written in normal order and that the title of the book is underlined. Underlining with a typewriter or in handwritten copy is a way of indicating that it appears in italics when printed.

A bibliography card for a periodical or magazine has slightly different information. It should include the name of the author, the title of the article, the name of the periodical (underlined), the volume if indicated, the date of publication in parentheses, and the pages on which the article appears in the periodical.

A bibliography card for a newspaper includes the name of the reporter (if available), the headline, the name of the newspaper (underlined), the exact date, the section, and the page number.

A final suggestion concerns the survey of sources and the gathering of a potential bibliography for your speech. You should have more sources in your potential bibliography than you can use but not so many that you have wasted time writing them. With a potential bibliography of ten sources, only about half are likely to yield material that you can use in your speech. In short, survey with your eyes a large number of potential sources, record on note cards the bibliographic information for those you think will be relevant for your speech topic, and record information only from the ones that prove related to the immediate response and ultimate goal you seek from your audience.

Alison Lure, *The Language of Clothes* (New York: Random House, 1981).

Nearly 300 pages, illustrated, with historical information on clothing.

Call #

Figure 6.3
Bibliography card for a book.

George Bush and Perry London, "On the Disappearance of Knickers: Hypotheses for the Functional Analysis of the Psychology of Clothing," *Journal of Social Psychology*, Vol. 51 (May 1960), pp. 359-366.

Look for a good quote from this academic journal about the importance of clothing in our society.

Call #

Figure 6.4
Bibliography card for a periodical.

Making Index Cards

Your first temptation might be to take a notebook to the library, start writing down the bibliographic information, and enter all the information from that source in your notebook. Doing that would be a serious mistake.

Writing your sources and information in a book will make the information difficult to retrieve. Writing them on index cards is like entering them in a computer where they can be easily rearranged, organized, and discarded.

Figure 6.5
Bibliography card for a
newspaper article.

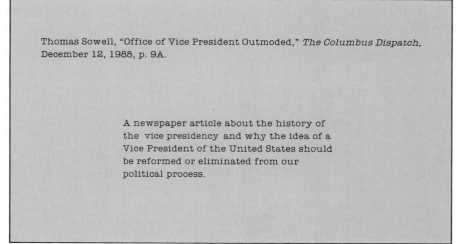

Thomas Sowell, "Office of Vice President Outmoded," *The Columbus Dispatch*,
December 12, 1988, p. 9A.

A newspaper article about the history of
the vice presidency and why the idea of a
Vice President of the United States should
be reformed or eliminated from our
political process.

The recommended method of recording ideas, quotations, and information from
both interviewed and written sources is index cards. Buy 3" × 5" or 4" × 6"
index cards with or without lines. Use them to record the potential sources and
to record the information you find in them. Following are some hints about writing
notes on index cards:

1. Exercise extreme care to record your sources and write your notes
   legibly. Nothing is more irritating than being unable to decipher your
   own notes when you need them for the speech.
2. Write one idea, quotation, or bit of information on each card. Do not
   try to write as much as possible on each card because you will have
   difficulty retrieving and reorganizing the information.
3. Get in the habit of recording the subject, author, title, and page on the
   top of each card so you do not forget where you found your information
   (see fig. 6.6).
4. Take more notes than you need but not so many that you have wasted
   time. If some information looks relevant and interesting, write it on a
   card. But do not try to write down everything you see or you will have
   to discard much of what you wrote.

Notice that the index card in figure 6.6 is a direct quotation limited to a single
idea: how female clothing continues to be a burdensome signal of social standing.
Notice also that the direct quotation has three spaced dots called an ellipsis, indicating that words were edited out to save space on the card and time in the
speech.

An index card from a telephone interview might resemble figure 6.7.

Figure 6.6 Index card with a direct quotation.

```
                   Fashion and Status

Lure, The Language of Clothes, p. 145.

"Certain concessions have been made to female emancipation
 . . . , but any woman who is honest will admit that the full-
length mink coat that advertises her husband's wealth is
heavier and harder to manage than the down jacket she wears
in the country, and that her diamonds and gold jewelry are a
constant invitation to mugging and murder."
```

Figure 6.7 Index card from a telephone interview with paraphrased content.

```
              Topic: Men's Clothing
                   and Status

Dr. Emily Williams
Director, School of Home Economics
Cortlander Community College

Dr. Williams told me that men's clothing changes less
radically than does women's clothing, but that in recent
years shirt and collar colors and designs along with collar
bars, tie tacks, watch chains, and even braces and bow ties
have joined the three piece suit in the executive suite.

Telephone interview 1/12/89
```

The lack of quotation marks indicates that this index card contains a paraphrase rather than a direct quotation from the source.

Learn as You Look

Every person who prepares a speech by doing research learns that it is good to keep an open mind about your topic. Your early notions about the topic may change as you learn more about the subject. It is appropriate to:

1. Narrow your topic as you discover its true scope.
2. Modify your own position on an issue consistent with what you now know about the topic.

". . . yet how is it these vital facts are virtually unknown in this country today?"

3. Pursue new directions on the topic that you did not know when you began your research.

Doing research is learning; let it make you more intelligent, more informed, and more confident.

Oral Footnotes

Two incidents illustrate the importance of oral footnotes. A U.S. presidential candidate dropped out of the race in 1987 when primary opponents from his own party reported that he had lifted, without authorization, part of his speech from that of a British politician. The network news directors had great fun running the videotape of the British politician and the American politician saying virtually the same words. Then the same candidate was found to have received a failing grade in law school because he plagiarized on a class paper. The disclosures about the candidate's dishonesty destroyed his chances for the presidency.

Another person hit the news in the same year when he tried to move from acting president of the largest single-campus university in this country to the president of another university in an adjoining state. In his speech to the faculty at the university where he was a candidate, the aspiring president used sections from a written publication. Someone recognized the words and reported the misdeed to the press. Although he was not dropped as a candidate, the man did not gain the position.

Table 6.1 Oral Footnotes for Public Speaking

Citing a source for paraphrased information:
According to the March 16, 1989, *US* magazine, entertainment celebrities do not necessarily have an easy time finding a dating companion in Los Angeles.

Citing a source for a direct quotation:
Theodore White in his book entitled *In Search of History* states, "What I learned was that people accept government only if the government accepts its first duty—which is to protect them."

Citing a magazine, a reference work, and a speech:
In his speech on campus one month ago, Andrew Young. . . .

Last week's *Time* magazine reported. . . .

According to *World Almanac,* the number of people in. . . .

Both of these unfortunate candidates would have kept out of trouble if they had understood, as you will now, the concept of *oral footnotes*. If they would have revealed their sources by simply telling the audience who they were using as their source, then they could not have been accused of dishonesty in public speaking.

What is an oral footnote, and when should you use one? A footnote is used in written works to indicate where information was found. Usually it includes the name of the author, the name of the article, the name of the magazine or paper, the date of publication, and the page on which the quotation or idea was found. In public speaking an oral footnote is much briefer but equally important. It may be just the name of the person or the publication or speech that is being quoted or paraphrased, or it might include the year or date of publication or the place where the speech was delivered. However brief the citation, the important thing is that the audience understands that the words or ideas came from some source other than the speaker.

What needs to be cited by an oral footnote? Anything that is taken from a source. It could be a direct quotation where you state the exact words of another person from print or a speech. It could be a paraphrase, that is, the words of a source not directly quoted but put in your own words. The candidate for President of the United States did not use the British candidate's exact words, but he followed the same idea so closely that he practically filled in the blanks with his own information. That he took the idea from someone else was indisputable.

What do oral footnotes look like? In table 6.1, you will find the proper form for oral footnotes.

Before leaving the subject of oral footnotes, you should be aware of the connection between oral footnotes and the ethics of public speaking. At the end of Chapter 3, you found that following the Golden Rule—"Do unto others as you would have them do unto you"—is an ethical guide for public speakers. Would you want someone to use something you wrote or said as if it were their own? In our society, using the words of another person, whether those words were in a speech or a newspaper article, is regarded as a serious offense, so serious that people's careers and opportunities have floundered on that single charge of plagiarism. In citing sources it is much better to be too careful than to be careless, because the consequences are rough and avoidance is easy. Part of gaining confidence as a public speaker is the certainty that you have avoided plagiarism by using oral footnotes.

Summary

This chapter on finding information stressed the importance of using your personal experience as a resource—as long as it is directly related to the topic or shows your relationship to the topic. The interview is a valuable means of securing information for your speeches, especially if the interview is well planned, executed, and followed up with accurate notes and quotes. Mentioned also was the possibility of gaining information through phone calls and mail requests.

A third place to find information—besides yourself and other people—is the library. The librarian should be a partner in your plan to produce superior speeches. The library section surveyed the resources available in card catalogs, indexes, dictionaries, encyclopedias, yearbooks, and newspapers.

Effective research requires careful planning. Start your research as soon as you select and narrow a topic, leave time for interviews and surveying library sources, record your sources and the information in them, and modify your plan as you learn more and more about your chosen subject.

Finally, this chapter revealed the importance of citing your sources with oral footnotes. Some colleges and universities expel students who use the words of others without citation. Some others give a failing mark in the course or on the assignment. All educational institutions require as a rule of scholarship that the words and ideas of another person be attributed to the original author. Anything less is regarded as a breach of ethics.

Next, you will work on building your confidence as a public speaker by learning another step in speech preparation: organizing your speech.

▼▼

Application Exercises

1

Evaluating Personal Experience

Write the name of your topic in the top blank and list below it three aspects of your personal life or experience that could be used to enhance your credibility or to provide supporting materials for your speech.

Topic _____

Personal Experience

    1. _____

       _____

2. _____
   _____
3. _____
   _____

Evaluate your personal experience by checking off each item as you use it to examine the experience.

_____ Was your experience typical?

_____ Was your experience so typical that it will be boring or so unusual that it was a chance occurrence?

_____ Was your experience one that this audience will appreciate or from which the audience can learn?

_____ Does your experience constitute proof or evidence of anything?

2
Library Scavenger Hunt

You are much more likely to use reference works if you know where they are in the library and if you know what kind of information is in them. The following exercise is designed to better acquaint you with the library and its reference works.

1. From the card catalog find the author and title of one book that deals with your topic.

   Author _____ Title _____
   _____

2. From the *Reader's Guide to Periodical Literature* find the title and author of one article on your topic.

   Author _____ Title _____
   _____

3. Using the *Education Index* or other specialized index, give the author, title, and name of publication for an article on the topic you have selected.

   Author _____ Title _____
   _____ Publication _____

4. Using an encyclopedia or a yearbook, find specific information about your topic. In one sentence explain what kind of information you found.

   _____
   _____

   Source _____

5. Using *Facts on File* or *The Vertical File* cite one correctly composed fact about your topic on an index card.

6. Using an almanac or a government publication state some information about a topic in correct form on an index card.

3
Bibliographical Form

See if you can state your sources accurately by placing these sources in proper form for a bibliographical entry.

Source A: The name of the book is *Eye to Eye: How People Interact*. The book was published in 1988. The author is Peter Marsh. The place of publication is Topsfield, Massachusetts. The publisher is Salem House Publishers.

Source B: The name of the periodical is *Educational Record: The Magazine of Higher Education*. The date of publication is Spring 1988. The article runs from page 26 through page 31. The author is George B. Vaughan. The name of the article is "Scholarship in Community Colleges: The Path to Respect."

Source C: The name of the reporter is Natalie Bernow. The name of the newspaper is *The Post*. The article appears on page 1. The title of the article is "Women's studies defies tradition."

To check your answers compare them to the examples in this chapter.

Speech Organization

7

Order is Heav'n's first law; and, this confest,

Some are and must be greater than the rest.

ALEXANDER POPE

119

Which of these two statements do you find easier to read and understand?

Statement A

Pakistan is able to produce 15 kilograms of uranium per year, enough to make an adequate nuclear device, according to Senator Alan Cranston. The government feels this pace is necessary. Reports believed to be accurate say that China is giving Pakistan designs for nuclear weapons. Since 1974, the United States and the Soviet Union have not ratified a significant treaty. India and Pakistan appear to be on the verge of a nuclear arms race.

Statement B

The government feels this pace is necessary for two reasons: the first is that India and Pakistan appear to be on the verge of a nuclear arms race; the second is that the United States and the Soviet Union have not ratified a significant treaty since 1974. Senator Alan Cranston says that Pakistan is able to produce 15 kilograms of uranium per year, enough to make an adequate nuclear device. Further, reports indicate that China is giving Pakistan designs for nuclear weapons.

Probably you found statement B easier to read and understand than statement A. Since the content of the two statements is almost identical, the easier understanding must have come from the statement's organization. A look at Statement C indicates all of the organizational moves that were included to give the statement structure.

Statement C

The government feels this pace is necessary *for two reasons: one* is that India and Pakistan appear to be on the verge of a nuclear arms race; the *second* is that the United States and the Soviet Union have not ratified a significant treaty since 1974. Senator Alan Cranston says that Pakistan is able to produce 15 kilograms of uranium per year, enough to make an adequate nuclear device. Reports believed to be accurate say that China is giving Pakistan designs for nuclear weapons.

Also, the sentences in statement B had been arranged in a logical order to improve your comprehension.

In this chapter on speech organization, you will look briefly at how to organize ideas in sentences, paragraphs, and entire speeches. You will also explore the outline as a method of organization that is easy to understand and use. And you will survey six of the patterns of organization most commonly used in public speaking.

Think carefully about how much you can cover in your speech.

Whether you are writing an essay in English class or a speech for public speaking class, you are employing principles of composition. Let us first review some of those principles for similarities between the essay and the speech, and then discuss some differences between the written essay and the speech.

Principles of Composition

1. *The introduction of a speech should reveal the thesis of the speech, unless that would make the speech less persuasive.* Informative speeches nearly always reveal exactly what the speaker intends to cover. The introduction includes a forecast, a statement of what will be revealed in the speech. Some examples follow.

Example A

Why will the social security system have increasing difficulty supporting the population? One reason we will find is the increasing number of older people; another is the decreasing number of younger people who, as wage earners, contribute to the social security system.

Example B

The cost of insurance is driving day-care programs out of existence. This afternoon we will look at some of the reasons why insurance has skyrocketed, and we will discover what some of the local day-care organizations plan to do about the problem.

When do you disclose your purpose and when do you avoid disclosure? In most cases reveal your thesis in informative and persuasive speeches. When you are asking for a big change in the audience, either leave the purpose unstated or wait until the end of the speech to reveal the purpose.

For example, you should not tell a Republican audience you are going to convert them to Democrats. You may push them in that direction during the speech, but to announce your intention at the outset might invite the audience not to listen.

2. *The first sentence in a paragraph should state the central idea for that paragraph.* Ordinarily, the first sentence in a paragraph announces the central idea for that paragraph. The **central idea** is the theme for that paragraph, the idea to which the remainder of the sentences will refer. Observe how this speaker organized a paragraph with the central idea first and the related ideas following.

Now I will tell you what you can do to help stop the nuclear arms race. First, donate money to or join organizations such as Freeze (voters who want a nuclear freeze), SANE, the Council for a Livable World, PeacePac, WAND (Women Action for Nuclear Disarmament), and Earth. Second, you can write to your congressperson expressing your opinion, or join lobbying groups when the nuclear issue is before Congress.

Learn to express yourself clearly by composing your speech with central ideas leading the charge into your support materials, so your listeners will never be in doubt about intentions.

3. *Unite paragraphs with a single idea.* If your speech has three main points, then the speech should be divided into three approximately equal divisions consisting of those three ideas and the paragraphs used

to support them. For instance, if the topic of your speech favors nuclear armaments, your thesis statement for the speech might be:

The United States must maintain its nuclear first-strike capability as a deterrent to the country's enemies, as a means of destroying an enemy obviously preparing for an attack, and as a symbol of democracy's determination to prevail against military foes. The content of the speech would be divided roughly like this:

Example A
The United States must maintain first-strike capability as a deterrent. (⅓ of speech body)

Example B
The United States must have a means of destroying an enemy preparing for attack. (⅓ of speech body)

Example C
The U.S. nuclear force must symbolize our democracy's determination to prevail against military foes. (⅓ of speech body)

The main divisions of a speech do not have to be absolutely equal, but neither should one point be disproportionately longer or shorter than another.

4. *The conclusion of a speech should review the main ideas expressed in the speech.* Even in a five-minute speech an audience can forget the main ideas. Therefore, it is a good idea at the end of the speech to remind the audience exactly what those main points were and how they relate to the thesis of the speech. The review might look like this:

> What I have been trying to explain to you today is that the school levy should be passed if we want teachers' salaries to be competitive, if we want our schools to be in suitable condition for instruction, and if we want laboratories with current equipment.

A speech consists of an introduction that states the thesis of the speech and previews the main ideas. The body is divided into sections consisting of paragraphs, each with a central idea stated early and related to one of the main ideas. The conclusion contains a review or summary of the thesis and main ideas expressed in the speech.

Differences between Speech and Essay Composition

Speech Composition	Essay Composition
usually heard once	can be read often
more attention gainers	fewer attention gainers
shorter sentences	longer sentences
more repetition	less repetition
invites simplification	allows complexities
sounds spontaneous	obviously premeditated

5. *Observe the differences between essay and speech composition.* So far, you have learned a number of similarities between composing an essay and composing a speech. In this section you will discover some differences between the two forms.

Remember that one of the important differences between an essay and a speech is that readers can return to an essay again and again, but a speech is a one-time event. That important difference is why a speech has attention-getters to keep the audience focused on the speech. The sentences tend to be shorter than in a written essay and the speaker often gives overt indications of organization in the speech ("Now, my second point is. . . ."). Also, the speaker often repeats main ideas and has to work harder than the essayist to simplify for audience understanding.

An essay is not delivered. A speech is. But the speech should not sound like an essay being read. Indeed, first-rate speakers work hard to sound spontaneous even though they practice. Using outlines instead of manuscripts encourages such spontaneity. The best speakers are careful not to read a manuscript or to sound overly rehearsed when they deliver their speech.

Next, we consider the conceptual benefits of outlining and some principles of composing an outline for your speech.

Principles of Composition

1. The introduction should reveal the thesis of the speech.
2. The first sentence in a paragraph should state the central idea for that paragraph.
3. Unite paragraphs with a single idea.
4. The conclusion of a speech should review the main ideas expressed in the speech.
5. Observe the differences between essay and speech composition.

Do not read your speech from a manuscript but use an outline instead.

The Outline

Outlining is useful. You can use outlining in speech class to keep your speech spontaneous. An outline can save you time: it takes less time to compose a speech in the form of an outline than it takes to compose a complete manuscript for a speech. An outline is good because it forces you to organize your thoughts.

Your outline is a visual display of your speech organization. It shows your main points, your subpoints, and the amount and kind of support materials. An outline can help when you are gathering your thoughts for a visit to the boss, going to say a few words to fellow employees about an upcoming meeting, or planning what you are going to say to a customer. The outline is a highly useful organizational tool you can employ in a wide variety of situations.

Outlining is relatively easy to learn. There are three principles that govern the writing of an outline—subordination, division, and parallelism. The next section is devoted to helping you understand these three principles so you can learn how to compose an outline.

Principles of Outlining

1. Subordination
2. Division
3. Parallelism

***Figure* 7.1** Symbols and margins indicating subordination.

Symbols and Margins Indicating Subordination

  I. Generalization, conclusion, or argument is a main point.
     A. The first subpoint consists of illustration, evidence, or other supporting material.
     B. The second subpoint consists of similar supporting material for the main point.
       1. The first sub-subpoint provides additional support for the subpoint stated in "B."
       2. The second sub-subpoint also supports subpoint "B."
  II. The second generalization, conclusion, or argument is another main point in the speech.

Subordination

If you follow the **principle of subordination,** your outline will indicate which material is more important and which is less important. More important materials usually consist of generalizations, arguments, or conclusions. Less important materials consist of the supporting evidence for your generalizations, arguments, or conclusions. In the outline Roman numerals indicate the main points, capital letters indicate the subpoints under the Roman numeral statements, and Arabic numbers indicate sub-subpoints under the subpoints. Figure 7.1 shows a typical outline format. Notice, too, that the less important the material, the greater the indention from the left-hand margin.

The principle of subordination is based not only on the symbols (numbers and letters) and indentions, but also on the content of the statements. The subpoints are subordinate to the main points, the sub-subpoints are subordinate to the subpoints, and so on. Therefore, you need to evaluate the content of each statement to determine if it is broader or narrower, more important or less important than the statements above and below it. The student outline in figure 7.1 illustrates how the content of the statements indicates levels of importance.

Division

The second principle of outlining is the **principle of division,** which states that if a point is to be divided it must necessarily have at least two subpoints. For example, the outline illustrated in figure 7.2 contains two main points (I, II), two subpoints (A, B) under main point I, and three sub-subpoints (1, 2, 3) under

Figure 7.2 Content
should reflect
subordination.

Content Subordination

I. Jumping rope is a cardiovascular (CV) activity.
  A. A cardiovascular activity is defined by three main requirements.
    1. Large muscles must be employed in rhythmic, continuous motions.
    2. The heart beat per minute must be elevated to an intensity that is approximately 85% of a person's maximum rate.
    3. The elevated heart rate must be maintained for twenty to thirty minutes to achieve a CV "training effect."
  B. Other CV activities include running, swimming, and handball.
II. Jumping rope requires simple, inexpensive equipment.

subpoint A. All items are either undivided (II) or divided into two or more parts. The principle of division can, however, be applied too rigidly: sometimes a main point will be followed by a single example, a solo clarification, or an amplification. Such cases can be regarded as exceptions to the general rule: points, if divided, must be separated into two or more items of approximately equal importance.

The third principle of outlining is the **principle of parallelism,** which states that main points, subpoints, and sub-subpoints must use the same grammatical and syntactical forms. For instance, the student outline in figure 7.2 includes complete sentences for all divisions. An outline can also be composed of single words, phrases, or clauses as long as they are used consistently throughout. A sentence outline usually gives the most information, but for an extemporaneous speech a word or phrase outline might be sufficient to remind you of what you are going to say.

    To illustrate how the principles of subordination, division, and parallelism work together, look at the complete outline, on the topic of macramé, as shown in figure 7.3. Figure 7.4 summarizes this discussion of outlining.

Parallelism

Form and Content Unite Through Subordination, Division, and Parallelism

AN INFORMATIVE SPEECH ON MACRAMÉ

Statement of purpose: My purpose is to inform the audience about the art of macramé. At the conclusion of my speech the audience should be able to name the two basic knots used in a hanger and to list at least two uses for macramé.

I. Macramé is an ancient art that is gaining modern acceptance.
   A. Macramé was first used by medieval Arabian weavers to finish the edges of fabric.
   B. In the 1800s, sailors passed their time at sea by doing macramé.
   C. Macramé is a fast-growing hobby in the twentieth century.
II. Macramé can be learned in two basic ways.
   A. Macramé can be learned from a book obtained at a local craft shop.
   B. Macramé can be learned by attending classes offered by various organizations.
III. Macramé consists of two basic knots.
   A. The square knot is the fundamental macramé knot.
      1. The square knot consists of four cords, two holding cords and two working cords.
      2. The square knot is constructed in four simple steps.
   B. The half knot is a variation of the square knot involving only the first two steps.
IV. Macramé is a hobby with many uses.
   A. Macramé's most prominent use is as plant hangers and wall hangings.
   B. Macramé can also be used to make many accessories and unusual home furnishings.

Outlining: Principles of Subordination, Division, and Parallelism

Subordination	Division	Parallelism
I. _____ .	Every "A" must have	Each entry must be a
A. _____ .	at least a "B."	complete sentence, a
B. _____ .	Every "1" must have	phrase, or a single
1. _____ .	at least a "2."	word; entries may not
2. _____ .	Every "a" must have	be a mixture of
a. _____ .	at least a "b."	sentences, phrases,
b. _____ .	Every "i" must have at	and words.
i. ____ .	least a "ii."	
ii. ____ .		
II. _____ .		

The introduction, body, and conclusion are the three main component parts of any speech. Within those three main divisions appear smaller subdivisions such as main ideas that support the thesis of the speech, the support material that backs the main ideas, and the visual aids that illustrate your words. Transitions and signposts are the mortar that hold all of these parts together.

Transitions and Signposts

Transitions are statements throughout the speech that relate back to what has already been said and forward to what will be said. For instance, a transition might look like this:

Transitions

> Now that you have seen the consequences of smoking, consider some methods of kicking that habit.

This transition might well appear in the middle of a speech about lung cancer, heart trouble, and high blood pressure in the first half, and "cold turkey," behavioral modification, and substitutions in the second half of the speech.

Transitions also move the speech and the speaker toward, then away from visual aids.

> We know that cancer is a vicious consequence of smoking; just how vicious cancer is can be seen on this graph that indicates how likely you are to contract the disease if you smoke.

After explaining the figures on the visual aid, another transition moves you back into the speech:

> The graphs are grim evidence of how smoking is correlated with cancer, but cancer is not the only terrible consequence: pulmonary emphysema affects smokers more than any other group.

As with all transitions, the statement reflects back to what was said and foward to what will be said. Such transitional statements appear throughout the speech as you move from main point to main point and into and out of support material.

Signposts

Signposts are often briefer than transitions because they do not have to point backward and forward; they have only to tell the listener where the speaker is in the speech. Some examples include:

> My first point is that . . .
> Another reason why you should . . .
> One of the best examples is . . .
> To illustrate this point I will . . .
> Let us look at this picture . . .
> A second, and even more convincing, argument is . . .
> One last illustration will show . . .

Transitions and signposts are the guides that help the audience follow your movement through the speech. Skillful use of transitions and signposts will clarify your organization and help you to become a confident speaker.

Patterns of Organization

Among the possible organizational patterns for your speech are the time-sequence and the spatial-relations patterns—commonly employed in informative speaking—and the problem-solution, cause-effect, and climactic or anticlimactic patterns—frequently used in persuasive speaking. Another pattern of organization, the topical-sequence pattern, may be used in either informative or persuasive speeches. Let's look at each of these in detail.

Time-Sequence Organization

Immediate purpose: To instruct class members about registration procedures for the next session so that they can complete the process without difficulty.

Introduction	I. Registration for classes is a process that can be completed without difficulty by following certain steps.
Body	II. The steps for completing registration include selecting forms, securing signatures, and turning in papers at the correct place.
	A. Go to Central Administration to pick up your registration forms.
	B. Complete your own registration forms including all of the classes you wish to take.
	C. Find your advisor for a signature.
	D. Turn in your registration packet at Window 3 in the Central Administration Building.
Conclusion	III. After you follow the appropriate steps cited above, you must wait for two weeks until the computer sorts out all of the class requests.

Figure 7.5 An example of the time-sequence pattern of organization.

• •

Patterns of Organization

1. Time-sequence
2. Spatial-relations
3. Problem-solution
4. Cause-effect
5. Climactic and anticlimactic
6. Topical-sequence

• •

Time-Sequence

The **time-sequence pattern** is chronological; that is, it states in what order events occur over time. This pattern, obviously, is most appropriate for time-oriented topics. For instance, stating the steps in constructing a cedar chest, in making French bread, or in the development of a blue spruce from seed to maturity would all be appropriate topics for a time-sequence pattern.

An example of a speech outline employing the time-sequence pattern would look like the one shown in figure 7.5. The organization of most "how-to" speeches of this type is crucial because the audience will be unable to "do it" unless all steps are noted in the correct order.

Spatial-Relations

The **spatial-relations pattern** indicates how things are related in space. Topics that lend themselves to a spatial pattern include how to arrange furniture on a stage set, how to design a lighting board, or where to place plants when landscaping. A spatial-relations pattern of organization is shown in figure 7.6.

Problem-Solution

The **problem-solution pattern** is employed more often in persuasive than informative speeches because it is difficult to speak either on problems or solutions without supporting a position on the issue. The problem-solution pattern raises one serious question for the speaker: how much should you say about the problem or the solution? Usually you can work out a proper ratio based on what the audience knows about the issue. If the audience is unaware that a problem exists, you may have to spend time telling them about it. On the other hand, if the problem is well known to all, you can spend most of your time on the solution. This pattern lends itself nicely to outlining, with the problem being one main head and the solution the other. A problem-solution pattern of organization is shown in figure 7.7.

Cause-Effect

The **cause-effect pattern** of organization describes or explains a problem and its ramifications. Some examples include the cause of Parkinson's Disease and the effects that it has on the body; the causes of urban blight and one local government's solution; or the causes of low- and high-pressure systems and their effect on ground temperature. As with the problem-solution pattern, this one lets you decide how much time you should spend on the cause(s) and how much on the effect(s). A cause-effect pattern of organization is shown in figure 7.8. This outline suggests that the speaker will spend about two-thirds of the allotted time talking about the "causes" for high-income occupations (education and family background) and about one-third talking about the effect of those factors.

Climactic and Anticlimactic

The **climactic** and **anticlimactic patterns** hinge on the placement of your strongest arguments or best evidence. If you place your strongest or best material early in your speech and your weaker material at the end, you are using anticlimactic order. If you place the strongest and best material late in the speech, you are using climactic order, because the speech builds to a more dramatic conclusion. A recent study indicates that with a one-sided persuasive message, climactic order is superior to anticlimactic order in securing positive audience evaluation. In the climactic organizational pattern shown in figure 7.9,[1] the speaker moves from the least striking to the most impressive information on the role of women in the future.

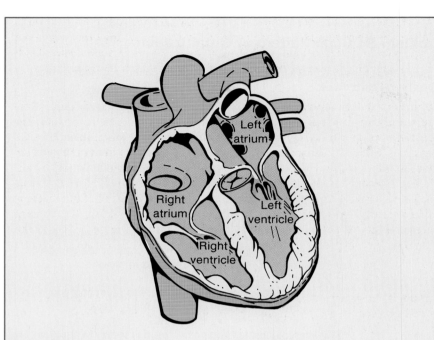

Figure 7.6 An example of the spatial-relations pattern of organization.

Spatial Relations Pattern of Organization

Immediate purpose: To teach my audience to recognize the form and function of the human heart.

Introduction
  I. The human heart is the part of the body that fails or falters in more than a million people per year.

  II. Learning about how your heart is structured and how it functions can help you keep it healthy.

Body
  III. As shown on the visual aid, the heart consists of four chambers, the right and left atrium and the left and right ventricle.

  IV. The atria and the ventricles have different functions.

    A. The right atrium and left atrium are thin-walled receiving chambers for blood.

    B. The right and left ventricles are thick-walled pumping chambers that pump eighteen million gallons of blood in seventy years.

Conclusion
  V. The heart's structure and functions are simple, but heart failure ends life.

  VI. Name the parts and the functions of the heart as a first step in guarding your own health.

Figure 7.7 An example of the problem-solution pattern of organization.

Problem-Solution Pattern of Organization

Immediate purpose: To convince my audience to discontinue practices that invite credit card fraud.

Introduction	I. Thousands of credit card holders are bilked each year by thieves.
	II. Today, you will find out more about the problem of credit card fraud and some solutions to the problem.
Body	III. The problem of credit card fraud is stolen cards, unauthorized copies, and telephone phonies.
	A. When your credit card is taken by a pickpocket or robber, you may be charged for a spending spree by the thief.
	B. When you pay with a credit card, an employee might keep an unauthorized copy of the carbon so your number can be used for phone purchases.
	C. Telephone crooks trick you into revealing your credit card number on the phone to use it themselves for purchases.
Solution	IV. The solution to credit card fraud is to follow the rules on stolen cards, take carbons, and avoid revealing your number to strangers.
	A. Report stolen cards immediately by keeping phone numbers for your cards in a list off your person.
	B. You should take your customer's copy and any full-length carbons or copies at the time of purchase.
	C. Never tell someone your credit card number on the phone unless you placed the call for a purchase.
Conclusion	V. You can avoid credit card fraud by being a cautious customer.
	A. Treat your plastic as if it were worth your line of credit because that is what you can lose—and more.
	B. Watch, guard, and protect your credit card with vigilance and maybe even insurance.
	VI. Your credit card may be worth a fortune to you and those who would prey on you: use it defensively.

Figure 7.8 An example
of the cause-effect
pattern of
organization.

Cause-Effect Pattern of Organization

Immediate purpose: To persuade the class that social drinking leads to alcoholism.

Introduction
 I. Jobs, school, and families bring stress which many of us try to reduce with alcohol.
 II. But for some the social drinking will become problem drinking which will become alcoholism.

Body
 III. Why an individual becomes chemically dependent on alcohol remains a mystery but the reasons seem rooted in nature and nurture.
   A. Children of the chemically dependent have a much greater chance of becoming chemically dependent themselves.
   B. Persons who drink at all risk becoming chemically dependent.
 IV. Social drinking can become problem drinking.
   A. The person who cannot seem to stop drinking is already a problem drinker.
   B. The person who passes out, blacks out, or cannot remember what occurred has a serious drinking problem.
   C. The person whose relationships with others began to fail with regularity has turned from people to alcohol.
 V. The problem drinker becomes an alcoholic.
   A. The person who is unable to stop drinking has become chemically dependent.
   B. The person who is alcoholic must usually be helped by others to stop.
   C. The most common way to avoid reoccurrence is to never drink again.

Conclusion
 VI. The best illustration that social drinking leads to alcoholism is that a nondrinker will never become an alcoholic.
   A. Persons with a family history of chemical dependence can protect themselves by abstinence.
   B. Persons whose families see a person becoming dependent might want to encourage nondrinking before the problem becomes worse.

Figure 7.9 An example of the climactic pattern of organization.

A Climactic Pattern of Organization

Immediate purpose: To have classmates recognize the difference between media-perpetuated views of the attitudes of college students and the actual attitudes shown in a recent study.

Introduction

I. Our elders often think that college students are seeking high-paying jobs and the life of single bliss.
   A. The press headlines stories about the materialistic goals of youth.
   B. Books and magazines emphasize the lives of the swinging singles.

II. A new study indicates that these views of today's youth may be incorrect.

Body

III. A national survey of first-year students indicates that their top goals focus on relationships.
   A. The Institute for Social Research at the University of Michigan finds that eighty percent of the students sought a good marriage and family life.
   B. Seventy percent of the first-year students cite strong friendships as a top goal.

IV. The Michigan study shows that nearly 100% of the first year students want to marry and have children.

V. The study reveals at least one possible contradiction in student attitudes toward top goals.
   A. Two-thirds of the students say the mother of preschool children should be at home with them.
   B. Only four percent of the women expect to be full-time homemakers at age thirty.

Conclusion

VI. First-year students seek good marriages and strong friendships as their top goals in life.

VII. First-year students do not live up to the stereotype portrayed in the media.

Topical Sequence

The **topical-sequence pattern** is employed when you want to divide your topic into a number of parts, such as advantages and disadvantages, different qualities, or various types. Examples of such speeches might be the pros and cons of capital punishment, four qualities necessary in a leader, or three types of local transportation. This pattern is equally useful in informative and persuasive speeches. A topical-sequence pattern of organization is shown in figure 7.10. The speaker who uses this particular topical-sequence is asking each person in the audience to decide whether he or she meets the criteria for becoming an honors student.

We have surveyed six organizational patterns you can use in your public speeches. The one you select for your own speech should be determined largely by the topic you select, how much the audience knows about the topic, and which arguments or evidence the *audience* will perceive as strongest or best.

A Topical-Sequence Pattern of Organization

Immediate purpose: To invite prospective students to measure themselves against the criteria for being a communication major by stating whether or not they qualify on their evaluation of the speech.

Introduction	I. Crowded conditions and shortage of faculty have resulted in new admission standards.
	A. The College of Communication has 2300 majors.
	B. The College of Communication has fifty faculty members.
	II. The new admission standards are more rigorous than those of the past.
Body	III. Direct admission to the College of Communication depends on class rank and SAT scores.
	A. Direct admission students must be in the top half of their high school graduating class.
	B. Direct admission students must have SAT scores of at least 1000, combined verbal and quantitative.
	IV. Transfer students must have a 2.5 cumulative grade point average after forty-five quarter credits for admission.
Conclusion	V. Use your evaluation form to indicate whether or not you qualify for direct or indirect admission to the College of Communication.

Figure 7.10a An example of the topical sequence pattern of organization.

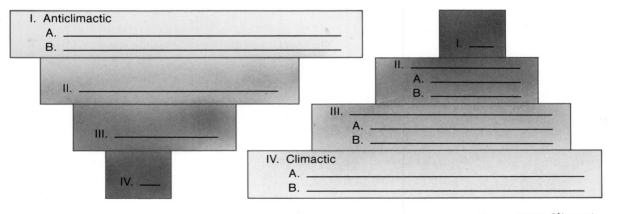

Figure 7.10b Climactic or anticlimactic patterns depend on where you place your best or most important material.

Do not conclude from this discussion that these are the only ways to organize a speech. A recent article in a speech journal tells how storytelling is used in criminal trials by lawyers who need to convince jurors to make sophisticated judgments about complex information.[2] In another case, a student delivered a highly effective speech by telling a series of five stories about himself, interspersed with a refrain that was his main point. His organization was effective, but the speech defied the principles of outlining. The number of ways in which you can organize your speech is limited only by your imagination.

Summary

This chapter on organization began with four principles of composition with special application to public speaking. They were (1) stating the central idea first in a paragraph; (2) organizing paragraphs into larger units related to a single idea; (3) revealing the speech's thesis in the introduction; and (4) reviewing the main ideas in the speech's conclusion.

Next, you learned three principles of outlining: the principles of subordination, which employs margins and symbols to indicate importance; the principle of division, which determines how many points may be discussed under each heading; and the principle of parallelism, which calls for similar form throughout an outline.

Transitions and signposts bind the parts of a speech together and give the audience clues about your progress. The transition relates back to what was said and forward to what you will say. The signpost points to where the speaker is in the speech; e.g., "My first point is. . . ."

Finally, you examined six patterns of organization: time-sequence, spatial-relations, problem-solution, cause-effect, climactic, and topical-sequence. Next we will look at the modes of proof and clarification that constitute the content of your speech, the material that you just have learned to organize.

▼▼

Application Exercises

1

Think of a speech topic not mentioned in this chapter that would be best organized into each of the following patterns. Write the topic in the appropriate blank.

Time-Sequence Pattern	Topic: _____
Spatial-Relations	Topic: _____
Problem-Solution	Topic: _____
Cause-Effect	Topic: _____
Climactic and Anti-Climactic	Topic: _____
Topical-Sequence	Topic: _____

Can you explain why each pattern is most appropriate for each topic?

Go to the library and find the publication called *Vital Speeches of the Day,* which is a collection of current speeches. Make a copy of a speech of your own choosing and highlight the transitions and signposts.

▼▼

Sentence Outline

On a separate paper write your name, the title of your speech, and your immediate purpose. Then compose a sentence outline with at least three main points (generalizations, conclusions, or arguments) introduced with Roman numerals. Develop at least one of these main points by including subpoints and sub-subpoints.

▼▼

anticlimactic pattern An organizational arrangement in which the strongest arguments and supporting materials are presented first and then descend in order of importance.

cause-effect pattern An organizational arrangement in which part of the speech deals with the cause(s) of some problem or issue, and part of it deals with the effect(s) of the problem or issue.

central idea The theme for a paragraph; the idea to which the remainder of the sentences refer.

climactic pattern An organizational arrangement in which the arguments and supporting materials are presented in increasing order of importance with the strongest arguments and evidence presented last.

principle of division An outlining principle that states that every point divided into subordinate parts must be divided into two or more parts.

principle of parallelism An outlining principle that states that all points must be stated in the same grammatical form.

principle of subordination An outlining principle that states that importance is signaled by symbols and indentation.

problem-solution pattern An organizational arrangement in which part of the speech is concerned with the problem(s) and part with the solution(s) to problem(s).

signposts Direct indicators of the speaker's progress; usually an enumeration of the main points: "A second cause is. . . ."

spatial-relations pattern An organizational arrangement in which events or steps are presented according to how they are related in space.

time-sequence pattern An organizational arrangement in which events or steps are presented in the order in which they occur.

topical-sequence pattern An organizational arrangement in which the topic is divided into reasonable parts, such as advantages and disadvantages, or various qualities or types.

transitions The links in a speech that connect the introduction, body, and conclusion, as well as main points and subpoints. They provide previews and reviews, and lead into and away from visual aids.

Endnotes

1. The information about the national survey of freshmen came from Jerald G. Bachman and Lloyd D. Johnston, "The Freshmen, 1979," *Psychology Today* 13 (September 1979): 79–87.
2. W. Lance Bennet, "Storytelling in Criminal Trials: A Model of Social Judgment," *Quarterly Journal of Speech* 64 (February 1978): 1–22.

Support Material

8

Truth is the most valuable thing we have. Let us economize it.

MARK TWAIN

Prosecuting attorney: This person must have committed the crime! Fingerprints place him at the scene, two witnesses saw him enter and leave the apartment building, and he was apprehended carrying items from the victim's jewelry case.

Defense attorney: Does the existence of fingerprints in the apartment prove that the defendant was there at the time of the crime?

Detective: No.

Defense attorney: Did you see the defendant enter and leave the building on the afternoon of December 19?

Witness 1: Yes.

Defense attorney: Did you see the defendant enter the victim's apartment at any time that afternoon?

Witness 1: No.

Defense attorney: Did you see the defendant enter and leave the building on the afternoon of December 19?

Witness 2: Yes.

Defense attorney: Did you see the defendant enter the victim's apartment at any time that afternoon?

Witness 2: No.

Defense attorney: Is it possible that the items found on the defendant's person when he was apprehended had been given to him by the victim to take to the jewelry store for repair?

Detective: No. . . . Well, I don't know. The watch did not work and the ring had a loose stone.

And so it goes in the courtrooms of America as lawyers, prosecuting attorneys, and defense lawyers try to rally evidence to prove their case. What appears at first to be a solid case against the defendant unravels as the defense attorney starts to demonstrate that no one really knows if the defendant committed the crime.

Public speakers have a similar task. Just as the lawyer must present evidence acceptable to the judge and jury, the public speaker must provide proof and clarification to the audience. You will grow in confidence as a public speaker when you learn in this chapter about the content of public speeches—the **modes of proof** and **modes of clarification.**

Modes of Proof

Facts
Examples
Testimony
Statistics

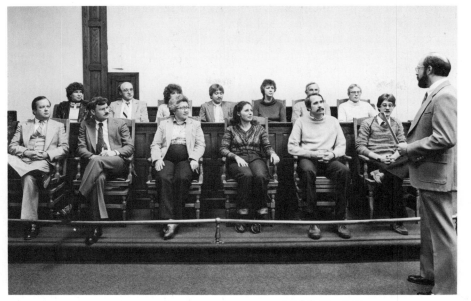

The public speaker, like a lawyer, proves and clarifies for the audience.

Modes of Proof

Of the various modes of proof that can be used in speeches, we will examine four: facts, examples, testimony, and statistics. These are called modes of proof because they function as evidence. They provide backing or support for your ideas.

Facts

A **fact** is a statement about which people agree because it is verifiable. Some facts are based on the laws of nature: "In the presence of gravity, what goes up must come down." This law of nature can be proved by demonstration. Some facts are based on people's perceptions. Did this car hit the pedestrian? Yes, three witnesses will testify under oath that this particular car hit the pedestrian.

In Black's *Law Dictionary* a fact is described as "a circumstance, event, or occurrence as it actually takes or took place; a physical object or appearance, as it actually exists or existed. An actual and absolute reality, as distinguished from mere supposition or opinion; a truth, as distinguished from fiction or error."[1] This definition underlines the notion that a fact, actual or real, is also verifiable, and—unlike testimony or opinion—does not require interpretation or the making of inferences.

Sometimes facts are statements of being that describe some present condition; sometimes they are statements about numbers or statistics. Two of the most useful sources of facts are *Facts on File*, which reveals facts about current issues, and the *Statistical Abstract of the United States*, published by the Census Bureau. Other places to find facts include:

General and specialized encyclopedias.
The Annual Register of World Events.
Economic Almanac.
Facts on File.
Information Please Almanac.
New International Year Book.
Statesman's Year-Book.
World Almanac and Book of Facts.

They are also available in newspapers, magazines, and professional journals.

Facts can be strong support material in your speech as long as you have satisfactory answers to these questions:

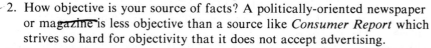

1. Where did you find your facts? Some sources are more reliable than others. The preceding sources are considered more reliable than "facts" found in advertisements or political speeches, for instance.
2. How objective is your source of facts? A politically-oriented newspaper or magazine is less objective than a source like *Consumer Report* which strives so hard for objectivity that it does not accept advertising.
3. Are your facts verifiable? See if you can back your facts with other data. For example, a speaker who uses these facts can support them with the 1984 *Statistical Abstract:*

A baby born in 1982 can expect to live to age 75; a baby born in 1960 could expect to live only to age 70.

Deaths per 100,000,000 motor vehicle miles were 5.3 in 1965, but were down to 2.8 in 1982.

In the fall of 1970, 7.3 million students were in college; in the fall of 1982 over 12 million students were in college.

In 1977, 1.5 billion books were sold; in 1981, 1.7 billion books were sold.

Facts that come from a reliable, objective source and that support the fact with reasonable data are readily usable in a public speech.

Another mode of proof used as support material is the example. An **example** is a specimen, an instance that represents a larger group. In a speech about the need for insurance to cover catastrophic illness, an example about a specific family that lost its home, car, and savings account to pay for a terminally ill child helps make the point. In a speech about credit card fraud, an example of how a clerk used a customer's credit card number for a one-week spree serves as an example of many such fraud cases.

Why do speakers use examples? Audiences have difficulty getting excited about common problems that are stated generically. In the following example, speaker A is stating a problem generically. Speaker B is stating the same problem using an example. Which statement gets you involved in the issue?

Speaker A

Some college students find that being away from the support of their family and friends results in behavior foreign to their nature.

Speaker B

Mary had been an excellent student in high school. She was accustomed to earning As and Bs, but she had to work for them. When she went to college she joined a sorority. Few of the women in her particular sorority tried for high grades. Mary found herself with a highly active social life and depressingly poor grades. Toward the end of her first term, she realized she was going to receive the worst grades ever. She knew that her family, her main financial support, would be angry and disappointed. Just before final exams she was hospitalized with a nervous breakdown.

An example is a powerful way to get your audience involved in the topic of your speech.

Examples may be brief or extended, actual or hypothetical. A **brief example** may be a couple of sentences about something familiar to the audience:

You have all heard by now of the apartment fire near campus last week, but you may not have heard that it was started by a student smoking in bed.

Or you may present a series of related brief examples to heighten the impact, as this student did in a speech on campus law and order:

> Last week a female student was being harassed by a teaching assistant and chose to leave school rather than continue being bothered by him. Last week another student left school because of a racial incident in which he was assaulted, then threatened with future attacks. Finally, last week a student quit college because his roommates refused to let him study or sleep.

These three examples—all of which were true and known to many in the audience—gave the idea additional force.

Extended Examples

An **extended example** is longer than three sentences. The extended example contains more details about a particular case. Following is an extended example detailing the experience of one desperate student:

> Two days before final exams Fred learned why he should keep his dormitory door locked when he was out. He was known in his classes as a great note taker, and he never cut classes. In fact, Fred boasted to others in the dorm that he had taken over 75 pages of notes in some of his classes. One evening, Fred stepped out of his room for a few minutes to get water for his coffee pot, lingering when he stopped to talk to some friends about the finals. When he got back to his room his psychology and his history book were missing—and so were the notes for those two courses. Naturally, he reported them missing and even dug through several dumpsters near the building, but he never got them back. Fred was a victim of campus crime.

The speaker was discussing campus crimes, crimes that are often unreported but always hard on the victim. The extended example about Fred helped the audience to visualize how a simple defensive measure like locking the door could help reduce campus crime.

Actual Examples

An **actual example** is based on fact or reality—it actually occurred. The stories about Mary and Fred really happened so they are actual examples.

Hypothetical Examples

A **hypothetical example** is one that is plausible but created by the speaker to make a point. A student used the following hypothetical example in a classroom speech:

> You have left the children at home with a babysitter from the neighborhood. You know that she is young—15 years old—but the babysitter's mother is "on call" in case of any trouble. While you are away, a friend of the babysitter's—also 15 years old—drops in to visit.

Your kids know that no one is allowed in the home while you are away, and so does the babysitter. The babysitter's friend, a person you have never seen before, is on parole. She finds your car keys, goes to the garage, and takes your car. The babysitter is too afraid to report the theft because she knows that she has broken the rule about allowing others in the house. You come home to find that your kids are OK, but your car is stolen.

The speaker used a hypothetical example to illustrate that you cannot be too careful about babysitters, that criminals are often young people, and they are not necessarily strangers to those present when the crime is committed.

Here are some questions to ask about the examples you use and those you hear in the speeches by others.

Questions about Examples

1. Is the example actual or hypothetical? Actual examples tend to have greater impact than hypothetical examples, but both can increase audience involvement in the issue. Also, speakers can increase the impact of the example by revealing which are actual.
2. Is the example typical or unusual? The more typical an example, the greater its impact. If an example is unlikely, or even unfair, then it will be less convincing. One instance of rude service at a local bank is a poor example if such rudeness is highly unusual. However, if many people have had similar experiences, the example will work.
3. Is the example relevant to the claim it supports? Examples need to be strongly linked to the argument or claim you are making. An example is not a good one unless it serves as support or proof of your point.

Called **testimony,** opinions are used as evidence or support when they reinforce or back up the speaker's claims.

Testimony

There is nothing wrong with using your own opinions in a speech, but often you will find your audience is more impressed when an expert supports what you say. A student who was trying to convince the audience that trucks are rapidly replacing cars and station wagons as vehicles of choice supported his claim with these opinions:[2]

L. R. Windecker, a Ford analyst, said that compact trucks are the fastest selling vehicles in the automotive market.

Duncan Brodie, GMC general director of truck sales, claims that trucks account for three of every ten new vehicles purchased.

The speaker used opinions by Windecker and Brodie because they are in a better position than the speaker to know about truck sales. Speakers use the opinions of others, then, to show an audience that the experts agree with their position.

Most people have an area of expertise about which they know more than others.

Paraphrased Opinions

Opinions come in two forms: paraphrased statements and direct quotations. **Paraphrased statements** occur when you state the expert's opinion in your own words. The expert may have said

> In an increasingly competitive international market, the micro- and mini-vans, sporty pickups, four-wheel-drive utility trucks, and compact pickups have become the hottest items in the automotive market.

Your paraphrase of that same statement might be

> Compact trucks are the fastest-selling vehicles according to L. R. Windecker, a Ford analyst.

Speakers paraphrase to state the opinion in fewer words, and to declare it in a language the particular audience will understand.

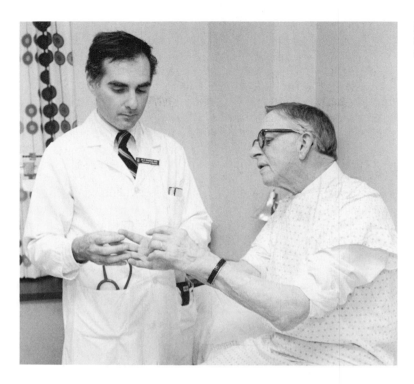

Quote experts about their own area of expertise.

A direct quotation is an opinion stated in the same words used by the expert. For example:

> According to Dr. Bradley Greenberg, professor of communication at Michigan State University, "The combination of sex on TV and in the movies provides a tantalizing aura of a sexually oriented society that's difficult for teen girls to resist or demean."[3]

A speaker uses a direct quotation when the language and length of the expert's words are appropriate for the audience.

Direct Quotations

What questions should you ask about opinions used in your own speech or in the speeches of others?

Questions about Testimony

1. Is the person you quote an expert? Consider whether the person whose opinion you use is qualified by education or experience to be credible to your audience. Most entertainers and sports figures who give testimonials in advertising are not experts on the products they endorse.

2. Is the person being quoted within his or her area of expertise? Physicians render opinions about almost anything; so do politicians. A physician may not be an expert on cancer. You need to check closely to discover who is in a position to give an opinion.
3. Is the person you quote an objective source? Finding an objective source is as difficult as finding an expert source. An objective source has nothing to gain or lose by giving an opinion. Do you think that the Ford analyst and the director of truck sales are objective sources to consult about truck sales? Who would you trust to give sales figures?

Statistics

A fourth mode of proof used in speeches is statistics. **Statistics** are numerical shorthand: they summarize large quantities of information for easier understanding. Unfortunately, statistics can also muddle the obvious unless you use them wisely.

A speaker should use statistics to help the audience understand, not to confuse the listener or make the audience think the speaker is a numbers whiz. For example, someone talking about the high price of food could simply say that food prices have been climbing for the last forty years. But a more impressive way to demonstrate the increase is to show it with statistics.

	1945	1965	1985
1 pound of hamburger	$ .27	$ .51	$1.26
1 pound of pork chops	.37	.97	2.32
1 pound of coffee	.31	.83	2.60
½ gallon milk	.29	.47	1.14
1 loaf of white bread	.09	.21	.55

The figures are average U.S. prices from the U.S. Department of Agriculture. The speaker uses the average price of these items to demonstrate that food prices have risen dramatically.

Statistics are never as simple as they seem. Although it would be difficult to quarrel with the specific figures, one could argue that food prices are not that bad because our total income has also risen dramatically. In fact, Americans spend a smaller portion of their income for food than nearly anyone in the world. To understand statistics, you have to understand the language of statistics and realize that statistics occur in an ever-changing context.

Advice about Statistics

Before you learn more about statistics, note the following guidelines for public speech usage.

1. Provide a context for your statistics. The figures about food costs are deceptive unless you note that income increased at the same time.
2. Simplify your statistics. Maybe the increase in sales is 24.6354%, but your audience will better understand the statistic if you round it off and call it a twenty-five percent increase.

3. Translate your statistics. Stating your statistics in another way may help the audience understand your point. A 500% increase in sales may be more comprehensible if you say the dealer sold one car last year and five this year.
4. Check your statistical sources. A statistic from an unreliable source is of no more value than a lie. Make sure the source of your statistics is expert, unbiased, and in a position to know.
5. Check for consistency. Are your statistics consistent with other known numbers and facts? If only one source says that seventy-five percent of abducted children are taken by strangers and the other sources are considerably lower, then be cautious.
6. Show your statistics. Statistics are difficult to communicate orally. Showing them on visual aids can help your audience understand them more clearly. They will not prove or clarify anything if the audience does not understand them.
7. Use few statistics. An audience is easily inundated with numbers. Unless your audience consists of accountants and statisticians, you should use statistics only when necessary to clarify or prove a point.

Remember that statistics are no more or less trustworthy than opinions. Both must be based on accurate methods of reasoning, which can render the results worthy or worthless.

The Language of Statistics

The most common terms used in statistics are range, mean (or average), mode, and percentage.

The **range** is the difference between the highest and lowest number in a series. In this series of numbers

7   9   13   23   46   53   61   73   82   94

the lowest number is 7 and the highest is 94; the range or difference is 87.

The **mean** or *average* is the result of adding all the numbers in the series and dividing by the number of items. The individual items add up to 461; the number of items is 10. Divide 461 by 10 and you will get 46.1 or an average of 46. Often there will be no average score, just as no one has 2.3 children.

The **mode** is the most commonly recurring score. In this case no number is repeated so there is no mode, but in the list of grades below, the mode would be a C because that score occurs most often in the list.

A = 1
B = 3
C = 6
D = 2
F = 1

The **percentage** is a number expressed as a part of 100. If something occurs .50 or 50% of the time, then it occurs half the time. The price of hamburger has increased more than 400% since 1945 (.27 goes into 1.26 4.6

times $\times$ 100 = 460%) while the price of pork chops has increased more than 800% (.31 goes into 2.60 8.39 times $\times$ 100 = 839%).

<table>
<tr><td>Questions about
Statistics</td><td>Here are some questions to ask about the statistics in your own speech and those of others whose speeches you hear:</td></tr>
</table>

1. Have the statistics been simplified, translated, and placed in context so that you and your audience understand them?
2. Have you gathered your statistics from reliable, unbiased, expert sources?
3. Have you shown the audience your statistics so they can decide their believability for themselves?

Statistics can be a highly economical way to present information to an audience. Because they are easy to distort and often difficult to interpret, the burden of using them to enlighten instead of baffle is the speaker's responsibility.

Modes of Clarification

The modes we have examined so far—facts, examples, opinions, and statistics—are modes of proof because speakers use them to demonstrate the truth of their claims. The **modes of clarification** that we examine in this section are forms of support that are more often used to clarify than to prove a case. The modes of clarification we will explore are explanations, analogies, comparisons, and narratives.

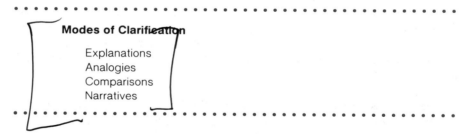

Modes of Clarification

Explanations
Analogies
Comparisons
Narratives

Explanations

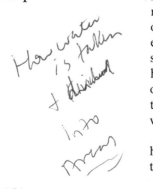

A student who knew about electricity delivered a speech about how electricity moves from the power plant to the light bulb in your home. She drew a picture of a huge power plant with big stacks on one end of the blackboard; on the other end, she drew a house with a single naked bulb inside (figure 8.1). During her speech she moved from the power plant with its steam-driven generators along high voltage power lines with long glass insulators; then to large transformers outside heavily inhabited areas to small transformers in the neighborhood; next to the electrical box in the home, to the interior wiring, and finally to the tiny wire that lights up the bulb.

The student's speech was an **explanation,** an illustration of how electricity is harnessed, transferred, and controlled as it moves from the giant power plant to the tiny light bulb.

How power gets to your home

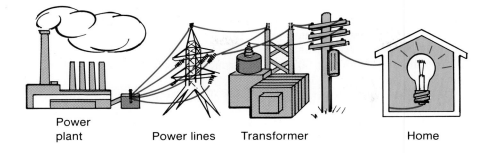

Power
plant Power lines Transformer Home

Figure 8.1 How power gets to your home.

We use explanations every day. The four year old wants to know where rain comes from; the father wants to know why the thirteen year old was late getting home; and the mother wants to know why nobody picks up his or her clothing. All of us do a lot of explaining.

An explanation in a speech is a little different because the speaker must anticipate what the audience does not know. The speaker has to be ready to explain before there is a question. The best speakers have an uncanny sense of when to explain and when not to. To overexplain makes your audience see you as condescending; to underexplain may make your audience see you as haughty, superior.

Analogies

An **analogy** is a relationship between two things that are basically unalike. An analogy used in public speaking usually tries to explain the unfamiliar by comparing it to something the audience finds more familiar. A student used this example to explain why people who have much in common still fight with each other.

> The disputes in the Middle East may seem ridiculous to the outside observer. After all, the people in those countries live side by side on adjoining lands. But their continuing disputes might be easier to understand if you compare those people to your own family. You probably fight more with your parents and brothers and sisters than with neighbors. And you probably have more disputes with neighbors than with people in another block. Similarly the people in the Middle East fight with those who are closest to them.

The speaker was trying to explain a less-familiar concept—disputes in the Middle East—by comparing them with a basically unlike but more familiar concept—the family.

Analogies are good clarifiers. They can make a situation easier to understand. However, they are poor as proof because comparisons of unlike things quickly break down as the differences become obvious. Following is an example.

> The spread of Communism is like a game of dominos. As soon as one country falls under its influence, the country next to it surrenders, and so on like dominos.

A row of dominos and a region of adjoining countries are two fundamentally different things. However, thinking of countries as dominos might help someone conceptualize the notion of regional dominance. But countries are not dominos and they do not literally fall.

The student who gave the speech about electricity moving from the power plant to the light bulb used an analogy for clarification. The speaker correctly assumed that more people understood water than electricity, so she compared the flow of electricity to the flow of water. Both water and electricity need to be controlled, one in pipes and the other in insulated wires. Both water and electricity must be diminished in force before they can be used, the water in smaller and smaller pipes and the electricity in smaller and smaller conductors. Both water and electricity can be very dangerous if they become unleashed, the water by flooding and the electricity by shorting. The analogy used the familiar water to explain the unfamiliar electricity. Figure 8.2 graphically shows an example of another analogy.

Comparison

While an analogy points out similarities between two basically unlike things, a **comparison** points out similarities between two basically similar things.

As with analogies, comparisons work best when they clarify a relationship to the audience. They explain the unfamiliar by comparing it with the familiar. This student from Ohio University correctly assumed that the audience knew more about that university than about Miami University of Ohio, another educational institution in the same state.

> Ohio University and Miami are both residential campuses located in relatively small towns. The number of students on each campus is about the same; the kinds of programs are similar; and the number of students and faculty with cars is about the same. Both campuses have serious parking problems. What you probably did not know is that Miami University has developed an amazingly effective parking policy that I think will work for us.

The comparison of the two universities looks at what the two have in common. The speaker can then argue that because of all the similarities, what worked for one university is likely to work for the other.

More often, comparisons are used to clarify, as in this student speech:

> Going to school is very much like most white-collar jobs. You are expected to be present, you are expected to please the person in charge, and you are expected to do your best if you want to be rewarded. Too many students think that jobs are different from school, but both demand ambition, drive, and the desire to succeed.

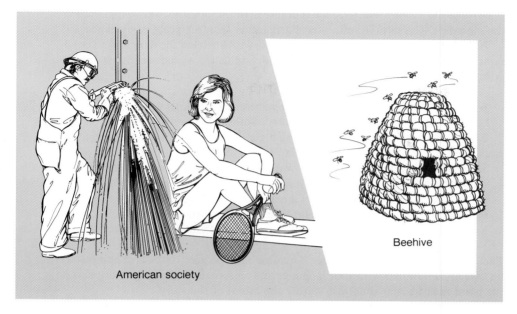

American society

Beehive

Figure 8.2 An analogy finds similarities between two things that are basically different: "American society is like a beehive—both have their worker bees who produce and the drones who do not. Both also have their queen bee who occasionally produces but mainly is pampered."

Figure 8.3 A comparison shows similarities between things that are basically similar: "Sue looks a lot like Sally—both have dark hair, both are thin, both are light-skinned, and both wear the same clothing styles."

An audience that was more familiar with the work world would simply reverse the comparison and state that school is in many ways like work. In any case, the comparison works by explaining the less familiar idea with a more familiar one. Figure 8.3 provides an example of another comparison.

Narratives

A **narrative** is a story told to make a point. Like the other modes in this section, the narrative is used more often for clarification than for proof or evidence.

A Chinese professor told the following story to illustrate the dangers of stereotypical thinking, especially the idea that individuals from other countries are linguistically handicapped.

> A British gentleman attending a reception was seated next to a small and unassuming man whose appearance and clothing suggested he was Chinese. Somewhat uneasy, the British gentleman broke a long silence at the beginning of the dinner by saying to the Chinese man "Goodee Soupee?" The man did not answer. Much later the master of ceremonies said "Tonight we are honored to have with us the ambassador from China, Dr. Willafred Koo." The Chinese man stood up and delivered a stirring speech in flawless English. When he returned to the table, Dr. Koo leaned over to his British neighbor and said "Goodee Speechee?"

The story makes a good point: don't assume that people from other nations are necessarily unfamiliar with your language and culture. But telling the story makes the point much better than just stating the moral of the story.

Most professional speakers have a large repertoire of stories; so do good teachers, preachers, and professors. At his retirement, a distinguished professor told how forty years earlier he had prepared diligently for his classes—and how he used up all of his material in the first two weeks. In despair, he turned to a more experienced professor in the department, who told the newly-appointed professor that he did not have lore, stories to tell that would bring his lectures to life.

Questions about Narratives

There are two questions to ask about stories used to clarify ideas in a speech:

1. Is your story relevant to the point you are trying to make?
2. Is your story long enough to make the point but not so long that it wastes the audience's time?

The narrative will be best if it is detailed and specific, if it involves people or animals, and if it includes some drama or emotion.

Summary

This chapter on support material presents four modes of proof—facts, examples, testimony, and statistics—and four modes of clarification—explanations, analogies, comparisons, and narratives. The chapter also includes questions you should ask about each mode of proof or clarification, questions that you should ask of yourself, and of those persons whose speeches you hear. Now that you know more about the ingredients for a speech, the content, you should face your speech preparation with a new degree of confidence.

1

Write *F* in the blank to indicate you think the item is a statement of fact; write *T* in the blank if you think the item is a statement of testimony or opinion.

_____ 1. Water freezes at 32 degrees Fahrenheit.

_____ 2. Spending money for defense leads to war.

_____ 3. Few people in America die from either malaria or polio.

_____ 4. Only five percent of people with cancer of the esophagus survive.

_____ 5. Prayer in school is the only way to revive religion.

Answers: 1. F; 2. T; 3. F; 4. F; 5. T.

2

A speaker in your class was angry about the way she was treated by an employee in the financial aid office. The speaker built her entire case, "the lousy way students are treated by the people who are supposed to serve them," around the example of her own experience. As a critical listener who knows the questions to ask about examples, how would you evaluate this speaker's use of support material?

3

Either individually or as a class, discuss the following instances of testimonial or opinion evidence in a public speech. Use the "Questions about Opinions" as a guide for evaluating these testimonials.

A. A famous actor is quoted on why you should buy a particular brand of automobile.

B. A study by a national television network indicates that more people watch and trust television news and fewer trust newspapers and magazines.

C. A professor of political science with a speciality in China is quoted about the impact of a recent change in government in that country.

D. A politician running for national office provides testimony about how his legislation on workfare will keep families together.

E. A government study shows which automobiles have the shortest stopping distances.

Give a two-minute speech in which you use one of the four modes of proof and one of the four modes of clarification in support of a claim of your own choosing. For example, you might claim that mandatory helmet laws reduce the number of motorcycle deaths. You could back that claim with one mode of proof, such as statistics from a government document, and one mode of clarification, such as a comparison of one state with the law and another without it.

Vocabulary

actual example An incident or situation that actually occurred which is used as evidence in a speech.

analogies A mode of clarification that compares two fundamentally different things, but because one item in the comparison is familiar to the audience the analogy helps the audience understand.

brief example An example that can be cited in a sentence or two either because it takes few words to say it or because the audience is already familiar with the example.

comparisons A mode of clarification that observes similarities between two things fundamentally alike, but because one item in the comparison is more familiar to the audience the comparison helps the audience to understand.

examples Brief or extended, hypothetical or real, an example is a specimen that illustrates a larger group for an audience.

explanations An expansion, restatement, or further clarification of an idea that otherwise might be only partly understood.

extended example An example that takes three or more sentences to explain because of its complexity or details.

facts Actual instances or things that exist that are verifiable and can be agreed upon by objective observers.

hypothetical example An example created by the speaker, usually plausible but identified as an event that never really occurred.

mean An average derived by adding all the numbers in a series and dividing by the number of items.

mode The number in a series that occurs most often.

modes of clarification Some methods of making an idea clearer to an audience without necessarily providing additional proof.

modes of proof Some methods of providing evidence that the audience will see as support for an argument or claim.

narratives Stories told to clarify an idea, a detailed account with some dramatic qualities.

paraphrased statements An expert's opinion restated in your own words.

percentage A number expressed as part of 100: 15% is the same as .15 which is the same as fifteen times out of one hundred.

range The lowest and the highest number in a series.

statistics The collecting, organizing, and interpreting of numerical information.

testimony Opinion from some person on an issue or idea.

Endnotes

1. J. Burrill. "Circumstantial Evidence," section 218 in Henry C. Black. *Law Dictionary* (St. Paul: West Publishing, 1957), 706.
2. "Light Trucks Go Chic." *Consumers Digest* (December 1985), 22.
3. Greenberg's quotation appears in Bill Mandel, "Media Stir Teen Appetite for Destruction," *The Columbus Dispatch,* 12 December 1988, p. 9A.

Introducing and Concluding Your Speech

9

It is with eloquence as with a flame; it requires fuel to feed it, motion to excite it, and it brightens as it burns.

TACITUS

No one is taking care of our children.

Seven million children are "latchkey" kids who are under 13 and who care for themselves for at least part of every workday.

No one is taking care of our children.

The turnover rate in child care centers was 42 percent because of low pay, poor benefits, and stressful working conditions.

No one is taking care of our children.[1]

Mothers and fathers both have to work these days just to have the standard of living the last generation enjoyed with one wage earner.

Today we are going to explore the issue of day care to see why no one is taking care of our children.

This introduction grabbed the audience's attention. The audience was full of working men and women, all of whom felt that they took care of their children. Most of them also knew that their children had to take care of themselves while they worked.

You have learned audience analysis, topic selection, research skills, and even organizational principles, but nearly everything you have learned so far has been about the body of the speech. In this chapter you will find out how to begin and end your speech.

We will begin with the introduction, the first couple of minutes into a speech. Why is your introduction so crucial to an effective speech? The answer is that much of the sizing-up occurs in the first fifteen seconds of the speech.[2] To learn how to develop an introduction, we will examine the four functions of an introduction, review some strategies that you can use in your introduction, and see an example of an introduction from a student speech. Later in the chapter, we will look at some of the same aspects in the conclusion of your speech.

The beginning of a speech is where most speakers feel the most stress, and the ending often determines whether or not the audience responds as you wish. Hopefully, this chapter will help you grow so you will start and finish your speeches with confidence.

Introducing Your Speech: Four Functions of an Introduction

Outside the classroom you may be introduced by someone else. In the classroom you will probably introduce yourself and your topic to the audience in that part of the speech called the introduction. An introduction serves four functions. You will examine these along with examples from student speeches. The four functions are to (1) gain and maintain attention, (2) relate your topic to your audience, (3) relate yourself as speaker to the topic, and (4) reveal the organization and development of your speech.

Effective speakers gain and maintain attention.

· ·

Introductory Functions

1. Gain and maintain attention
2. Relate topic to the audience
3. Relate speaker to the topic
4. Forecast organization

· ·

Let us consider the first function of an introduction, gaining and maintaining attention. Have you ever watched someone try to teach a group of very small children? As the teacher talks, the children turn around and look at each other. Sometimes they start talking to each other. Occasionally they touch someone. Getting children to pay attention is a very difficult job. Adults are no different. True, adults have learned to look as if they are listening. Their eyes are correctly directed, and their bodies may not move as much as children's bodies do. But the adults have replaced their overt physical activities with mental activities. When you speak to your classmates, their minds will be flitting from your speech to plans for the weekend, to the test the next hour, to the attractive person in the next seat. You will have to gain and maintain their attention.

Gaining and Maintaining Attention

Spend some time planning your introduction. Often students spend too much time thinking of a topic. Chapter 5 should have helped with this problem. After you have chosen your topic, you must take the time to develop your main points. As the class hour approaches, you may find you have little time left to prepare your introduction and conclusion. This is a mistake, however, because your introduction often determines whether the audience listens to your message. The introduction and conclusion are the bookends of your speech. If either or both fall, then the core of the speech may very well fall, too.

There are ten ways you can gain and maintain attention. As you read through them, you may feel overwhelmed. Which method should you select? How will you decide the way you will use to gain and maintain the attention of your audience? It is critical at this point that you understand the principles of audience analysis and adaptation discussed in chapter 4. If everyone in your class has used facts and statistics, for instance, you may want to choose a different method. If your class meets near lunch time, you may want to consider bringing some object of food that they can eat. You may wish to review chapter 4 before you determine the specific method you will use in gaining and maintaining the attention of your audience.

- -

Methods of Gaining and Maintaining Attention

1. Present person or object
2. Invite audience participation
3. Imagine a situation
4. Employ audio equipment
5. Arouse audience suspense
6. Use slides or film
7. Read a quotation
8. State striking facts or figures
9. Tell a story
10. Use humor

- -

Present a Person or Object

This method is used more often for informative speeches than for persuasive ones, but it can be used for both. A student speaking on health food may give everyone a granola bar to eat while listening to the speech. A student who works at a bank may begin a speech about the dangers of a checking account by distributing one blank counter check to each member of the audience. Or, a student who informs the audience about classical ballet may bring a ballerina to class to demonstrate a few turns on point during the speech. All of these are effective ways to gain and maintain attention.

Inviting audience participation early in your speech attracts their attention and interest in your topic. One student who was speaking about some of the problems of poverty asked his audience to sit crowded elbow-to-elbow during his presentation. Another asked the audience three questions about energy and requested they indicate by a show of hands whether they knew the answers. Because most members of the audience were unable to answer the questions, they listened carefully for the answers. One energetic student wrote a draft notice for every person in class, which summoned each one to meet with his or her selective service board. As the student began his speech, each person in the audience opened up a plain white envelope with the unwanted message inside. Such audience participation gained and maintained their attention.

Invite Audience Participation

You might have the audience imagine that they are standing on a ski slope, flying through the air, burrowing underground, and so on. As one student wrote in her plan for an introduction: "In order to gain audience attention, I will ask them to picture in their minds a hospital scene in which each of them is the patient on the operating table. They must watch their own death and subsequent resuscitation. This picture will prepare them for my topic on a second existence and raise the question in their minds of what actually happens in the interim." Inviting the audience to imagine a hypothetical situation is an effective method of gaining and maintaining attention.

Imagine a Situation

A student who was delivering a speech on classical music began with a one-minute excerpt from a famous work. Another, speaking against illegal abortions, played an actual tape of a woman being interviewed on her deathbed by a county sheriff. Both students immediately gained the audience's attention through the use of sound.

Employ Audio Equipment

One student began his speech by saying, "A new sport has hit this state, yet it is a national tradition. It is held in the spring of the year in some of our most beautiful timbered areas. It is open to men and women alike, with women having the same chance of success as men. It is for responsible adults only and requires common sense and patience. This sport of our ancestors is. . . ." Arousing curiosity captures the audience's attention.

Arouse Audience Suspense

A student who was speaking on big city slums began with a rapid series of twelve slides showing trash heaps, crowded rooms, rundown buildings, and rats. An international student from the Philippines showed attractive photographs of her native land. A varsity football player, who was speaking on intentional violence in the sport, showed a film of two kickoff returns in which he and others were deliberately trying to maim their opponents with their face guards. The audience—seeing the slums, the tropical beaches, and football violence—was attentive.

Use Slides or Film

Read a Quotation

The reading can be hypothetical, literary, poetic, dramatic, or real. It can even be an inspirational passage from a speech delivered by a famous person. One student who was giving a speech about some of the delights of being middle aged quoted President Reagan's speech to the Washington Press Club dinner when he turned seventy. "Middle age," Reagan told the Press Club, "is when you're faced with two temptations and you choose the one that will get you home at 9 o'clock."[3] You can find quotations in newspapers, newsmagazines, and collections of speeches like *Vital Speeches of the Day*. The important thing to remember is that quotations need to be directly related to the topic being discussed in your speech.

State Striking Facts or Figures

We use almost nineteen million barrels of oil in this country every day.

In 1930, twenty-five percent of the population were farmers; today, farmers make up only two percent of the population.

Such statements are like headlines. They are designed to grab the eye or ear for attention. Most topics you explore will have such facts and statistics that you can use as "headlines."

Tell a Story

Telling a story to gain the audience's attention is one of the oldest and most commonly used methods. Often the story can be humorous. This story is an analogy from the introduction of a student speech:

> I'd like to share with you a story about a man who, every morning, took his horse and wagon out into the woods to gather firewood. He would later take the wood to a nearby town and sell it for his only income. He was by no means wealthy, yet he lived a comfortable life. One day, in his greed, the man found that if he doubled his load of wood each day, he could earn twice as much money. He also found that if he spent half as much on feed for his horse, he could save even more money. This worked fine until one day the extra loads and the reduced food proved too much for the horse, and it collapsed from exhaustion and hunger.

The student revealed in his speech that the man represented farmers who find that they are expected to produce more and more goods despite government controls limiting their capacity to do so. The analogy got the audience involved in a speech that might have drawn less attention if it had been an openly-announced speech on government control of farmers.

Use Humor

Often overused, the use of jokes or humor to gain and maintain attention can be effective, especially if the humor is related to the topic. Too often, jokes are told for their own sake, whether they have anything to do with the subject of the speech or not. Another word of caution: if you are not good at telling jokes, then you ought to practice someplace before your speech in front of the class. On the other hand, if you are quite good at telling jokes or using humor in conversation, then humor related to your topic might be a good option for you.

Some speakers are not good at telling jokes, but they are witty. When you think of humor in public speaking, you should think of the term *humor* in its broadest sense to include wit and cleverness.

An example of a speaker who shocked her audience with her wit is Dr. Johnetta Cole, who is president of Atlanta's Spelman College. She was invited to address the National Press Club, a group that probably had never heard from a black female college president because there are only about a dozen in the nation. Dr. Cole won over her audience by proposing a toast in black English: "We bees fur 'lowin difurnce an' 'spectin difrunce til difrunce don make no mo difrunce," a toast that she translated for the crowd: "We are for allowing difference and expecting difference until difference doesn't make any more difference."[4] That toast was a clever way for Dr. Cole to say I am black and I can speak the language of the streets, but I am also a woman who is a college president, which I would like to become so common that it is not unusual.

These ten methods of gaining and maintaining attention in the introductory portion of a speech are not the only ones. There are dozens of other ways. Just think of imaginative ways to involve the audience. You can start by stating a problem for which your speech is the solution. You can create dramatic conflict between seemingly irreconcilable forces: business and government, teachers and students, parents and children, grading systems and learning. You can inform the audience about everyday items they do not understand: stock market reports, weather symbols, sales taxes, savings accounts, and automobiles.

One word of warning: always make sure your attention-getter is related to the topic. Jokes told for their own sake are a weak way to begin a speech. Another undesirable way to start is to write some provoking word on the board and then say, "I just wanted to get your attention." All of the examples in the ten methods of gaining attention are from student speeches. They show that students can be creative in order to gain and maintain audience attention.

Relating the Topic to the Audience

A speaker can relate almost any topic to an audience in some way, preferably in the introduction of a speech. This assures the audience that there is a connection between them and the topic. A speaker should find many helpful examples in the previous section on audience attention. A student gave a speech on women's rights, a topic the audience cared little about. However, in her introduction she depicted the plight of married women who have fewer job opportunities and receive less pay than their male co-workers. The speaker asked the audience how they would feel under such circumstances. How would the men like their wives and girl-friends to earn less than men in the same jobs? Most of the men wanted their girlfriends and wives to be able to earn as much money as possible. The audience listened to the speech with more interest because the speaker took pains to relate the topic both to men and women in class.

A common way for a speaker to put an issue into perspective for an audience is to state the issue in their terms. Here is an example from a student speech on the effect of drinking laws:

> How many of you have been to a house party recently? I'm sure everyone enjoyed the good music, the friends, and all the beer going around. If your house is like ours, almost everyone will be drinking, but what if the police were to come in checking I.D.s? I know of six people in our house who are minors, and I'm sure there are more around campus. Next year will be worse. The new drinking age has caught some college students this year and has made college parties more complicated and maybe a thing of the past.

The speaker was relating the topic to her particular audience. Her assumptions that many in the class went to parties, many knew illegal drinkers, and many were confused by the new laws ensured a relationship between audience and topic.

Remember that it is at this point in the speech that the speaker attempts to promote the general nature of the topic. The audience must not feel that the topic is being imposed on them for their own good; instead, they should feel that the speaker is presenting ideas, information, and actions that will be useful to them. If you did a good job of audience analysis (chapter 4), then you will be confident that your topic is meaningful to the audience.

In the last section, we discussed relating the topic to the audience and covered ten strategies for doing so. In this section we will look at three strategies for relating the topic to you as speaker.

You can wear clothing that will signal your credibility on a topic, that shows your relationship to the topic and the occasion. One student aroused the audience's interest in the topic and the speaker by showing up with a hardhat on his head, a sweat rag around his neck, and a flashlight in his hand. He was encouraging his classmates to take up the questionable sport of exploring the university's steam tunnels.

Other ideas for using appropriate clothing to signal your relationship to the topic are to wear a warmup suit for a speech on exercise, or a laboratory coat for a speech on chemistry experiments, or a dress or suit for a speech on how to interview for a job. In all of these cases, the speaker's attire reminds the audience of the topic and makes the speaker look like an authority.

A second strategy for relating yourself as speaker to your topic is a more extreme situation than simply dressing for the topic and the occasion. In **role-playing,** the speaker actually tries to act the part of a person while delivering the speech.

A Presbyterian minister startled his congregation by appearing for his sermon in the garb of a Roman guard at the cross when Jesus Christ was crucified. His "sermon" told the story from the point of view of the Romans, the conquering army who saw Christ as an uncommon criminal causing trouble in an occupied territory. Because the minister was a fine actor, he quickly got the congregation involved in the subject of his speech.

A student giving a speech on life in the Middle Ages, dressed in the attire of the times and played the role of a merchant many centuries ago. He made history come to life for the audience with his detailed knowledge of society at that time. In both cases, the minister and the student made themselves highly credible sources on the topic by what they said and how they appeared in their role.

A third strategy for relating yourself as a speaker to your topic requires no special clothing and no role-playing. Instead, all you have to do is reveal yourself, especially how you have knowledge about the topic.

Sometimes **self-disclosure** is confessional: "I had malaria," "I am an alcoholic," or "I was the victim of a mugger."

This method has considerable impact on the audience mainly because it violates the audience's expectations. A daring disclosure in a public speaking class occurred when a mild-mannered young man revealed that he had been in a Louisiana prison on a drug offense—for six years. He spoke with great feeling about the effects of our penal system on an individual.

Not all self-disclosures have to be so dramatic. Indeed, some of the best pose a common problem, such as this one:

> I am a Catholic girl and I have a Baptist boyfriend. Our different religions have challenged us both but have strengthened, rather than weakened, our relationship because we have to explain our faiths to each other. With that in mind, I'd like to share with you the similarities between two seemingly different religions.

Another student spoke on structural barriers to the handicapped and revealed that she knew about the subject because of a hip operation that forced her to learn how to walk all over again. Both of these students disclosed information that the audience had not known but enhanced their credibility and captured the audience's attention.

Self-disclosure must be used carefully in public speech. Most self-disclosure occurs in interpersonal communication when only two or three people are engaged in conversation. Be sure that you can handle the disclosure. One woman decided to tell a class about her sister's recent death from leukemia, but she found she could do nothing but cry. The speaking situation is one that is already filled with a certain amount of tension, and you do not want to overload yourself with more emotion than you can handle.

Self-disclosure must be considered carefully for a second reason. As we stated, self-disclosure generally occurs when one person provides personal information to one or two others. In general, we do not tell highly personal information to a large number of people. Perhaps the story of a suicide in your family will gain the attention of the audience, but do you want twenty of your peers knowing such information? Do not self-disclose information that is potentially embarrassing to yourself or to people who care about you.

Self-disclosure must be honest information. Don't invent an occurrence or exaggerate an experience beyond recognition. You will not be viewed as a trustworthy speaker if you practice deception and dishonesty in your speeches. One student began his speech by telling a story of how a friend of his had set his body on fire to protest U.S. involvement in conflicts in other parts of the world. He went on to say that the friend had suffered first-, second-, and third-degree burns and that he had to have plastic surgery later. When the students in the class expressed their regrets to him after the speech, he laughed and said he had made up the story and the friend. The classmates felt betrayed. The speaker earned their scorn for his deceit, and he found that they would not believe what he said in his later speeches.

Stating Purpose and Forecasting Organization

The fourth and final function of an introduction is stating the specific purpose and forecasting the organization and development of your speech. This step should be taken late in the introduction because it reveals for the audience the length and direction of your speech.

The *statement of specific purpose,* optional in some persuasive speeches, tells the audience of the informative or persuasive intent of your speech. **Forecasting** tells the audience how you are going to cover the topic. Here is an example that clearly indicates both the specific purpose and the organization:

> This morning I will try to persuade you to start buying your books at the student co-op bookstore because the textbooks are less expensive, the used books receive a higher price, and the profits go for student scholarships.

The type of speech is persuasive. The specific purpose is to have the audience stop their book trade at the commercial bookstore and to start buying and selling books at the student co-op. The speech will have three main points.

Here are some additional examples of statements of purpose and forecasting from student speeches. The statement of purpose is underlined in each for emphasis:

> Follow my advice this evening and <u>you can earn ten dollars an hour</u> painting houses, barns, and warehouses. First, I will show you how to locate this kind of work. Next, I will teach you how to bid on a project. And, last, I will give you some tips on how to paint well enough to get invited back.

My purpose is <u>to help you understand your own checking account</u>. I will help you "read" your check by explaining the numbers and stamps that appear on the face; I will help you manage your checking account by showing you how to avoid overdraw charges; and I will demonstrate how you can prove your check cleared.

Forecasts and statements of specific purpose can take many forms. They do not have to blatantly state that you wish "to inform" or "to persuade," but your intentions should be clear to you and to your audience.

Demonstrating the Functions in a Speech

To see how the four functions operate together in a single introduction, examine the student introduction in figure 9.1. The side notes indicate which function is being fulfilled. Notice that the speaker gains and maintains attention, relates the topic to himself and to the audience, and forecasts the development of the speech. Remember that using a story is just one strategy that can be used in an introduction.

One last suggestion to set your mind at ease about introductions. You might wonder, how can I compose an introduction before I know what is in the body of my speech? Do whatever is easier for you. If you find it easier to develop the body of the speech first and then write an introduction, then do it that way. If you are a person who likes to have a plan before you commit to a project, then write the introduction first and build the speech around your statement of purpose and forecast.

Mid-Speech Sag

At this transition point in the chapter—between information on introductions and information on conclusions—let us pause for a moment and think about what comes between the introduction and the conclusion.

The same day this chapter was being written one of the authors heard the chief justice of the state supreme court give a luncheon address.[5] He started with the story of a young lawyer who was out in the countryside on a call when he ran low on gas and had to stop at a one-pump "station" that looked more like a shack. Outside the shack was an old man sitting on a chair with a large, junkyard dog at his feet. "Does your dog bite?" asked the lawyer cautiously as he slowly opened his car door. "Nope," said the old man. The lawyer jumped from the car and stepped to the pump when the dog snarled and growled so loud that the lawyer leaped into his car and slammed the door. "I thought you told me that your dog doesn't bite," said the lawyer with undisguised anger in his voice. "He don't," said the old man, "but this dog does."

An Example of an Introduction

DEATH RACE

Begins with a narrative, a story to gain attention

Role-plays a veteran checking out his gear to maintain attention

Story is a subtle means of relating himself to the topic: He has had the experience

Arouses curiosity about the topic to maintain attention

Story employs drama, adventure, and conflict

With sweat beading on my forehead and adrenalin gushing through my body, I solemnly survey my mission. Gusting winds cut through my jeans as a cloudy sky casts shadowy figures on the surroundings. I check through my gear one final time, for a failure of any item can spell certain death for me. Let's see. Good tread on tennis shoes. Check. Fluorescent vest turned on. Check. I take time to reflect on my previous missions. Yes, you could say that I am a veteran. I've been there and back many times. Two hundred or so successful assignments without a serious injury. A good record. A couple of close calls, but never anything more than a sprained ankle or a hurt ego. But today is a new day. I must not let my record lull me into carelessness. I'm ready. The time is now, for if I wait one minute longer, I'll be late for class!

The thoroughfare is crowded and I can barely see my destination. Cautiously I look both ways, up and down the street, once, twice, three times before I venture out. An opening breaks and I begin to hurry. Wait! A Mack truck just pulled out and is rushing toward me. Will he see the flashing warning lights? Will he read the big yellow sign proclaiming my right of way? As he rumbles recklessly toward me, I realize that the answer is no. I cover the remaining twenty feet in a couple of leaps and bounds. Exhausted, my mission is complete. I have successfully crossed a campus street.

Does this story sound familiar to you? How many times a day do you have to risk life and limb to cross a campus street? How often have you been angered by the drivers who ignore the pedestrians, the crosswalks, and the warning lights? We have all had the experience.

Begins to announce the topic

Relates topic to audience Announces topic, forecasts development, and states specific purpose

Today I want to discuss with you what can be done to end this terror for the innocent pedestrian on campus. I want to talk about three suggestions that I have for alleviating the problem of crosswalk warfare: closing certain streets, increasing off-campus parking, and installing lights and crosswalks in strategic areas.

Figure 9.1 An example of an introduction.

The speech started off strong and it ended with an upbeat conclusion, but the rest of the speech—like so many—suffered from **mid-speech sag**. That is, all the energy, humor and excitement was built into the beginning and the ending. The middle was like a tape recording of legal cases and decisions that mainly inspired sleep. In the middle of the speech, the body became largely a collection of evidence delivered with a minimum of enthusiasm.

At this midpoint in the chapter, we wanted to remind you that most of the time in a speech is spent in the middle, the body. Keeping the audience interested in that part of the speech is a continuing challenge. You can do it by repeatedly revealing how the speech is related to the audience, because if it isn't related, you shouldn't be saying it. You can do it by using many of the attention-gaining-and-maintaining techniques that are mentioned earlier in this chapter; they are not for exclusive use at the beginning of a speech. Finally, you can keep in mind that it is easier to get an audience's attention than it is to keep it, easier to arouse the audience at the beginning and end than in the body of the speech, and it is simplest to keep the audience's attention throughout a speech if the content speaks to them.

You talk to an audience about what is vital to them—their jobs, their kids, their neighborhood, the threats to their existence, the opportunities that meet their aspirations—and they will listen to you. They will not fall asleep. The content should be the most captivating aspect of a speech. The humor, the gestures and movement, the attention-gaining techniques are simply allies in the speaker's attempt to impart information and influence behavior.

Concluding Your Speech: Four Functions of a Conclusion

We have discussed the introduction of the speech very thoroughly. Let us now consider the ending or conclusion of the speech. Just like the introduction, the conclusion of a speech fulfills certain functions: (1) to forewarn the audience that you are about to stop; (2) to remind the audience of your central idea or the main points in your message; (3) to specify precisely what the audience should think or do in response to your speech; (4) to end the speech in an upbeat or memorable manner that will make the audience members want to think and do what you recommend.

• •

Conclusionary Functions

1. To forewarn the audience that you are about to stop
2. To remind the audience of your central idea or main points
3. To specify what the audience should do in response
4. To end the speech in a striking manner

• •

Let's examine each of these functions of a conclusion in greater detail. The **fore-warning function** warns the audience that you are about to stop. Can you tell when a song is about to end? Do you know when someone in a conversation is about to complete a story? Can you tell in a TV drama that the narrative is drawing to a close? The answer to these questions is usually "yes," because we get verbal and nonverbal signals that songs, stories, and dramas are about to end. But, how do you use the brake light function in a speech?

Forewarning the Audience of the End

The most blatant, though trite, method of signaling the end of a speech is to say, "In conclusion . . ." or "To summarize . . ." or "In review . . ." Another way is to physically move back from the lectern. Also, you can change your tone of voice to have the sound of finality. There are hundreds of ways to say, "I'm coming to the end." For instance, as soon as you say, "Now let us take my four main arguments and bring them together into one strong statement: you should not vote unless you know your candidates," you have indicated an impending conclusion.

The second function of a conclusion—to remind the audience of the central idea in your message—is the **instant-replay function.** You could synthesize a number of major arguments or ideas into a single memorable statement. A student giving a speech on rock music concluded it by distributing to each classmate a sheet of paper that had the names of local rock stations and their locations on the radio dial. You could also simply repeat the main steps or points in the speech. For instance, a student who spoke on the Heimlich Maneuver for saving a choking person concluded his speech by repeating and demonstrating the moves for saving a person's life.

Reminding Your Audience of the Main Points

The third function of a conclusion is to clearly state the response you seek from the audience, the **anticipated response.** If your speech was informative, what do you want the audience to remember? *You* tell them. If your speech was persuasive, how can the audience show their acceptance? A student who delivered a speech on peridontal disease concluded by letting her classmates turn in their candy for a package of sugarless gum. Other students conclude by asking individuals in the audience to answer questions about the content of the speech: "Judy, what is the second greatest cause of lung cancer?" Whether your speech is informative or persuasive, you should be able to decide which audience behavior satisfies your goals.

Specifying What the Audience Should Do

The fourth function of a conclusion—the **striking ending function**—is to end the speech in an upbeat or memorable manner so that the audience will remember it and want to do what you recommend. A student many years ago gave a speech with a clever ending that summarized his arguments and gave it a memorable

Ending the Speech in a Striking Manner

ending. His speech was on car accidents, the wearing of seat belts, and the disproportionately large number of college-aged people who die on the highways. He talked about how concerned we are that an accident not be our fault. His conclusion: "It does not matter who is right in the case of an automobile accident. It is not who is right that counts in an accident; it is who is left." It was a grim conclusion that made the main point memorable.

Avoid endings that are overly dramatic. A student at a large midwestern university was giving a speech on the fourth floor of a large classroom building. His topic was insanity. As he gave the speech, it became increasingly apparent to the class that he might have been speaking from personal experience. The longer he spoke, the more obvious it became: his words became increasingly slurred, his eyes went from restless to slightly wild, and his mouth and eyelids went slack. At the very end of the speech, he walked to an open window and jumped out. The class rushed to the window to see the speaker safely caught in a net held by his fraternity brothers. Had there been a mixup in communication and the fraternity brothers had appeared at the wrong time or window, overdramatization could have led to a permanent conclusion.

This chapter has concentrated on beginnings and endings, the skills necessary for developing the introduction and the conclusion of a public speech.

In the first section, you learned that there are four functions of an introduction: to gain and maintain attention, to relate the topic to the audience, to relate the speaker to the topic, and to forecast the organization and development of the speech. You were given ten strategies for gaining and maintaining attention and three strategies for relating the speaker to the topic.

In the second section, you learned that there are four functions of a conclusion: the forewarning function that warns the audience of the impending conclusion, the instant replay function that reminds the audience of your central idea and reviews your main points, the anticipated response function that tells the audience how you would like them to respond to your message, and the striking ending function which ends the speech in a memorable manner.

Next we will turn to the language of the public speech.

Summary

Application Exercises

1
Gaining and Maintaining Attention

Think of a speech topic. Then take any three of the ten methods of gaining and maintaining attention listed in the text to introduce your topic.

2
Signaling the Conclusion

Watch your professors for a few days. How do they indicate that classes are over? How many of them use ordinary ways to signal the end, such as saying, "For tomorrow read pp. 229–257"? What are some more imaginative ways that your teachers conclude their classes and lectures? Do any of them use methods that you could imitate in a public speech?

3
Concluding a Speech

Between class sessions, develop a conclusion that can be tried on a small group of classmates. See if you can fulfill the four functions given in the text. Try especially to develop skill in summarizing, synthesizing, and stating the main point of your message in language that will be striking and memorable.

Application Assignments

1
Performance

Deliver a two- to four-minute introduction to a speech. Be sure your introduction fulfills the functions explained in this chapter. The criteria for evaluation are the extent to which you

1. Gain and maintain the audience's attention through some means relevant to the topic.
2. State the topic of the speech and its relationship to the immediate audience.
3. Describe your qualifications for delivering a speech on this topic (i.e., the relationship between you and the topic).
4. Arouse interest, generate curiosity, or highlight the need for the audience to hear the body of the speech.
5. Forecast the subject, development, and organization of the body.

Do not go beyond the introduction in this performance; instead, try to make the audience eager to hear more.

2
Written Script

Write a script of your introduction. Include side notes that indicate how it fulfills its functions.

▼▼▼

Vocabulary

anticipated response Revealing to an audience what you want them to think, know, or do as a result of your speech.

forecasting A function of the introduction that reveals to the audience the organization and development of the speech.

forewarning function A function of the conclusion of a speech in which the speaker indicates an impending ending by verbal and nonverbal means.

instant-replay function A function of the conclusion of a speech, in which the speaker summarizes, synthesizes, or repeats the main points of the message.

mid-speech sag A phenomenon that occurs when the speaker places too little emphasis on making the body of the speech as captivating as the introduction and the conclusion.

role-play Acting the part or role of another person or character during your speech.

self-disclosure A speaker's revelation of a characteristic that the audience is unlikely to know already; a device used in public speaking to gain and maintain an audience's attention.

striking-ending function Ending a speech in an upbeat or memorable manner.

▼▼▼

Endnotes

1. "Child Care Fact Sheet," in *Women at Work,* published by the National Commission on Working Women, 2000 P St. N.W., Suite 508, Washington, D.C. 20036, Fall 1985.
2. L. S. Harms, "Listener Judgments of Status Cues in Speech," *Quarterly Journal of Speech* 47 (1961): 168.
3. The student found the Reagan quotation in "Reagan's One Liners," *New York Times,* February 6, 1981, A13.
4. Dr. Johnetta Cole's toast was quoted in Bill Wallisch, "20 Seconds to Profundity: How to Handle the Broadcast Media," *Educational Record: The Magazine of Higher Education,* Spring 1988, 16.
5. This speech was delivered by the Honorable Chief Justice Thomas Moyer of the Ohio Supreme Court to a meeting of Rotary International, Athens, Ohio, December 13, 1988.

Language and Your Speech

10

Question Outline

I.   What are some differences between spoken and written language?

II.   What are eight different ways to share meanings by defining words, phrases, and concepts?

III. What kinds of language behavior should you avoid if you want to be a literate speaker?

IV.   What are four ways to improve your powers of description?

V.   What is information overkill?

Proper words in proper places, make the true definition of a style.

JONATHAN SWIFT

Introduction

Speaker: Well, I don't think you can call it "child abuse" when you are just spanking your kid for doing something wrong!

Audience Member: It is child abuse because you are just using your physical power to overcome the kid instead of using reasoning. When the kid gets bigger and stronger, he will use the same methods on you: might makes right!

Speaker: You're wrong! My parents used the belt on me, and I'm going to use it on my kid. No mamby-pamby soft-heart is going to tell me that spanking is "child abuse." I call it "discipline."

We like to think that other people share our meanings for words. When we say "child abuse," we mean child abuse, and we expect others to share the same meaning of the words that we have in our own mind. If the dispute gets serious, we turn to "the final arbiter," the dictionary.

Unfortunately, our commonly-held beliefs—that others share the same meanings and that the dictionary settles disputes—are both misconceptions. **Language** is an arbitrary symbol system that has developed over time and is full of inconsistencies. Language developed to serve our needs, not to please grammarians.

Language is important for you to study in public speaking because much of the message you communicate to an audience depends on the words you choose to express your intended meaning. You should remember that language is arbitrary, that words vary in their ability to be understood and in their availability for an audience, that words are often ambiguous, and that words are strategic choices you have to make as a speaker.

Arbitrariness

The **arbitrariness** of language refers to the fact that meanings for words have developed over time, and that the relationship between a word and its various meanings is the product of people's inventiveness with the language. To one person a carbonated sweetened drink in a bottle or can is "pop," to another "soda," to still another "a soft drink."

Very likely you have learned a specialized vocabulary from your experience or field of study that is not shared by your audience. You cannot consult the dictionary as the final arbiter of meaning because what really matters to you as a speaker are the audience's interpretations of words and the meanings. Fortunately, as a public speaker, you will be in a position to share meanings with the audience.

A second set of characteristics of language is its ability to be understood and its **availability** to an audience. A word is highly understandable if the speaker and the audience use it frequently in their everyday lives. One measure of a word's ability to be understood is its length: the words that we use most often tend to be abbreviated. "Motion pictures" become "films" or "flicks." "Television" becomes "TV" or "the tube."

Availability refers to the word we most likely will use to state a perception. We use words to describe various courses, such as *ag, home ec, double E,* and *stat,* which are not only highly understandable, but the most available, the most likely ones we select to talk about those courses.

Public speakers who use language effectively are sensitive to both the ability to be understood and the availability of words they select for a speech.

Availability

A third characteristic of language is **ambiguity.** Ambiguity is the difficulty of determining exactly what a word is likely to mean to an audience. In certain circumstances, a person uses words as signals to reduce ambiguity. For example, a sign that says "Stop" is not supposed to be ambiguous, because it means that everyone should come to a complete halt, check for safety, and proceed. On the other hand, a sign that says "Yield" is somewhat more ambiguous because in some cases you should stop completely and wait, while in others you need only slow down to check the flow of traffic.

Much of our everyday language is highly ambiguous. For instance, suppose someone calls you a "fundamentalist." What does that term mean? The word is ambiguous because there is no universally agreed-upon meaning for it. Similarly, if you say that someone is "beautiful," the term is ambiguous because reasonable persons may disagree on what beauty is. As a public speaker you will have to learn ways to lessen ambiguity and to increase the chances that the audience shares your intended meanings.

Ambiguity

Finally, language in public speaking involves **strategic choice.** That is, you as speaker must choose words deliberately, intentionally, and purposefully. You must choose words strategically so they accurately describe what you have in mind and so the audience shares enough of the meaning to understand your message. For example, suppose you were to describe the building you grew up in. Would you call it an apartment, a shack, a mansion, a hovel, a high-rise, a condominium, a townhouse, or a tenement? These words all have a certain similarity, but they do not communicate the same message. The word you choose depends on both

Strategic Choice

Home.

the meaning you intend to communicate and the availability of the word for your audience. You gain nothing by calling the building a condominium or a hovel if your audience is unfamiliar with those words. They may be accurate descriptors, but they may fail to communicate because of low availability.

In this chapter you will find ways to overcome some of the most common problems of using language in a public speech. Language may be arbitrary, high or low in ability to be understood and availability, ambiguous, and strategic, but it is also functional. You can learn ways to use language more effectively in your public speeches.

One approach to the study of language is to discuss it at a theoretical level, as we did in the preceding section. Another approach is to consider what language problems arise when student speakers actually deliver their speeches in class. This is the approach we will take in the rest of this chapter. The examination is not exhaustive; you or your instructor may know of language problems peculiar to your classmates, your college, or your region. Language problems discussed here are among the most common in the public speaking classroom. What are some of the language problems that confront student, instructor, and audience in the public speaking class?

Solutions to Language Problems

One problem arises when *the speaker uses written rather than spoken language* in the speech. Many students are more comfortable if they write out their speeches. When they deliver them in front of the class, they have either partially memorized the speeches, or they are reading them.

Using Spoken Language

Compare, for example, these three excerpts from student speeches. Which seem more like written language? Which, on the other hand, seem more like spoken language?

A. The designer's art is probably the least appreciated and truly understood craft of the modern day. Truly fine design is inherently unobtrusive but crucial to the utility of a given object; only when bad design is present do most people notice design at all. . . .[1]
B. The story of the Salem witch trials is an allegory for modern times. The urge to hunt witches has not vanished. Replace the idea of the wicked witch dressed in black with concepts such as race or nationality. . . .[2]
C. "Hey man, let's get high!" Is this a familiar scene with you? I bet as a student in this college you have at one time or another come into contact with "cannabis." You say, "What's cannabis?" Well, what about "pot" or "grass?" Ah yes, I see they sound familiar. . . .[3]

There is nothing incorrect in any of these student speeches. However, if you guessed that sample C was the most like spoken language, you would be correct. The passage is conversational. It invites audience response by asking questions and is the only passage to directly address the audience. Samples A and B seem to be more literary—more like written than spoken language. Sample A is full of long words. Sample B assumes that the audience knows what an allegory is. Neither sample is conversational nor directly addresses the audience, though sample B does ask us to consider our attitudes toward nationality and race as being similar to earlier attitudes toward witches.

You can make your speeches sound more like spoken than written language if you recognize the distinction between concrete and abstract words. **Concrete language** evokes a more specific image in another person's mind. It is "closer" to its referent (the concept or object for which it stands). All words "stand for" or symbolize something else, but a concrete word "stands for" or symbolizes something in particular. **Abstract language** consists of less specific references to ideas. In this sense, the abstract term is "farther from" its referent: it does not tend to evoke a specific image in the listener's mind.

The word *justice* is an abstract term. If you asked your classmates their meaning for the term, you would receive many answers. However, if you told the class how your car broke down in the parking lot and you received twenty dollars in fines for which there was no appeal, then you would be rendering the concept of justice—or injustice—in concrete terms.

You should consider how to translate some of our earlier examples into more concrete language. Sample A is probably the most abstract of the three selections. Here it is again:

> The designer's art is probably the least appreciated and truly understood craft of the modern day. Truly fine design is inherently unobtrusive but crucial to the utility of a given object; only when bad design is present do most people notice design at all. . . .

Notice the abstractions: *the designer's art, craft, modern day, truly fine design, utility, object, bad design,* and *people.* These terms are all so broad that the images evoked in the audiences' minds are practically uncontrolled.

See what happens in your mind when this passage is "translated" into more specific, concrete language:

> Are you comfortable in the chair you are sitting in? Someone designed that chair for you; yet, you are unlikely to think about the chair you sit in, the table you eat at, or the clothes that you wear unless the chair is too small, the table too narrow, or the collar too tight.

Is it easier for you to see and feel your chair, your table, and your clothes than to envision the "designer's art"? Now look at some of the examples of abstract and concrete language in table 10.1. The concrete examples have much more impact than their abstract counterparts. Similarly, in your own speeches, you will find that the audience responds better when you "translate" abstract ideas and concepts into more concrete terms. No speech will be without some abstractions, but you should learn to recognize the difference between concrete and abstract language so that you can speak more effectively.

The language of public speaking is closer to the language of conversation than to the language of literature. If speakers sound as if they are reading from a book, then they are using written rather than oral style. A speech is likely to consist of specific, concrete words rather than abstract language, and it is more likely to consist of simple rather than complex words. Even changes in subject—signaled by a new paragraph in writing—are likely to be more frequent in speaking than they are in writing. A speech is also likely to employ questions rather than an army of complex sentences; it is likely to use relational or personal pronouns (we,

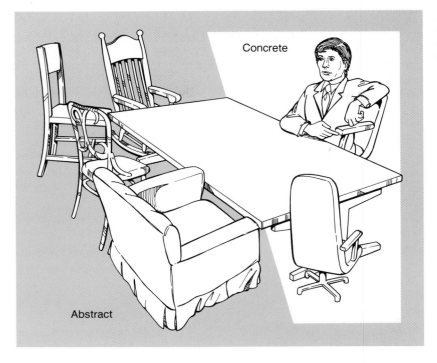

Table 10.1 A comparison of abstract and concrete language

Abstract	Concrete
Dog	Spot
Some people say	*Time* reports
Recent reports	Today's *New York Times* says
Music	Whitney Houston's "Thinking About You"
Fast	Ninety miles per hour
Department store	Sears
Killed	Murdered in cold blood
Runner	Sprinter in 100-yard dash
Far away	Four hundred and ninety miles away

our) rather than impersonal ones (one, they); it is likely to use the everyday language of colloquial expression rather than the formal language of the high court; it is likely to use blatant transitions ("Now that we have covered that point, let's move to the second point"); it is likely to be repetitive; and it is likely to contain language adapted to the particular audience.[4]

Language and Your Speech   **183**

Table 10.2[5]

The Language of Speaking	The Language of Writing
Uses short, simple sentences with action verbs and one idea per sentence	Uses longer, complex, compound, and compound-complex sentences
Uses contractions, sentence fragments, short words, slang	Uses few contractions, no fragments, difficult words
Tends to employ personal stories, experiences	Tends to use an impersonal voice
Employs concrete, specific, picture-producing words	Often uses abstract words, difficult to picture
Uses personal pronouns: I, me, we, us, you, they	Uses "one," "a person," "he or she"
Receives immediate feedback	Receives delayed or no feedback
Tends to say the same thing several ways—repetitive	Tends to be concise with little or no repetition
Words are reinforced with facial expression, voice, gesture	Words reinforced by bold type, pictures, punctuation
Transitions reinforced by gesture and movement	Transitions restricted to words
Vocalized pauses distract	No vocalized pauses
Pauses and silence for dramatic effect or emphasis	Dashes, dots, and empty space indicate pause or silence

Using Shared Meanings

A second trouble spot for speakers comes from using words the audience does not understand. The student who is interested in canoes speaks of "straight strokes," "j-strokes," and "sweep strokes." The student who makes his own butter talks about the "dasher" and the "clabber," "bilky" milk and butter that "gathers." The student who speaks on aerobics uses terms like "arteriosclerosis," "cardio-vascular-pulmonary system," and "cardiorespiratory endurance." Do you know what these students are talking about? The words they are using are all specialized terms, sometimes called *jargon,* that are used by people who know more than the ordinary person does about canoeing, buttermaking, and exercise.

At the outset you should recognize that there is nothing particularly wrong with using terms that the audience does not understand—as long as you explain the terms in language they *can* understand. Another way of stating the principle involved is that you should explain your terms in the audience's language. The student giving a speech on making butter explains that "The dasher consists of a stick similar to a broom handle. A cross made of two slats, four inches long

Language and Your Speech

and two inches wide, is nailed to the end of the handle. The dasher is inserted into the churn, and the churn's opening is covered by a tightly fitting wooden lid with a hole in the middle for the dasher."[6] The student speaker defines a word his audience is unlikely to know by comparing it to a broomstick and revealing how it is constructed.

You can make your speeches more effective by learning various methods of communicating meaning to an audience. The following eight methods are a sampling of ways to evoke the meanings you intend. Each method is labeled, defined, and illustrated.

- -

Types of Definitions

1. Comparisons	5. Etymology
2. Contrasts	6. Differentiation
3. Synonyms	7. Operational definition
4. Antonyms	8. Experiential definition

- -

Comparisons

Something unfamiliar can be defined by showing how it is similar to something the audience is more familiar with. A student who was defining *wassailing* explained that the term meant "going on a spree or a binge," or "painting the town red." As the Bible puts it, "eat, drink, and be merry."[7]

The idea is to compare the unknown (that which the speaker saw) with the known (that with which the audience is familiar), as the student did when he said that two G's are the same as you would feel "on the big hill of the tornado rollercoaster."

The public speaker must be careful to avoid comparisons that have been overused, such as "smooth as silk," "pretty as a picture," or "hard as a rock." These overused similes or comparisons are called clichés. Instead, try to create comparisons that help the audience envision what the speaker describes—such as the speaker who viewed a basketball from a distance of one centimeter looks "like the pebbly bottom of a backwood stream;" or the speaker who described snow as a "soft, rolling white carpet."

Contrasts

Something unfamiliar can be defined by showing how it is different from something else the audience is more familiar with. A speaker who was attempting to communicate the meaning of "assertiveness" explained the concept like this:

> Assertiveness can be contrasted with the more familiar idea of aggressiveness. Aggressiveness is characterized by pushiness and threats, while assertiveness is characterized by clarity. The aggressive person might say "Get over here and help me"; the assertive person might say "I need your help."[8]

Synonyms	To define a term with synonyms is to use words that are close to or similar in meaning and more familiar to the audience. "Being spaced out," said a speaker who was defining the term, "is similar to having the mind go blank, being dumbfounded, or being disoriented."[9]
Antonyms	To define a term with antonyms is to use words that are opposite in meaning and that are more familiar to the audience. Hence, being "spaced out" is "not being alert, keen, or responsive."[10]
Etymology	To define a term by means of its etymology is to give its origins or history. A desk dictionary will reveal the language or languages from which a word is derived. More specialized sources like the *Dictionary of Mythology,* the *Oxford English Dictionary,* and the *Etymological Dictionary of Modern English* will provide more detailed accounts. In a speech of definition, a speaker used the etymology of a word to explain its significance:

> What does *rhinoplasty* mean? Well, without a dictionary, you might feel that you're lost. But if you break up the word into its two parts, *rhino-* and *-plasty,* the meaning becomes clearer. You might not know the meaning of *rhino-* itself, but if you think of an animal whose name bears this prefix, namely the rhinoceros, and of the most distinctive feature of this beast, its rather large snout, you would probably guess correctly that *rhino-* refers to the nose. The meaning of the suffix *-plasty* also seems elusive, but a more common form of it, *plastic,* reveals its meaning of "molding or formation." Put together, these meanings have been modified to create the current medical definition of *rhinoplasty:* "a plastic surgical operation on the nose, either reconstructive, restorative, or cosmetic." Put quite simply, a *rhinoplasty* is a nose job.[11]

Differentiation	To define a term by means of differentiation is to distinguish it from other members of the same class. Notice how a student used differentiation to show the difference between two things that many people would see as very much alike:

> Some people think a jury trial is a jury trial; they don't realize that a jury trial can be quite different, depending on whether the case being tried is a civil or a criminal case. If it is a criminal case, then the jury will have to decide guilt or innocence beyond a reasonable doubt; if the trial is a civil case, then the preponderence of evidence should decide whether the plaintiff or the defendant wins the case. The end result of a jury trial in a criminal case is guilt or innocence, with the former resulting in punishment. The end result of a jury trial in a civil case is damages, either granted or not.[12]

An operational definition reveals the meaning of a term by describing how it is made or what it does. A cake can be operationally defined by the recipe, the operations that must be performed to make it. A job classification, such as secretary, can be operationally defined by the tasks that the person in that job is expected to perform: a secretary is a person who takes dictation, types, and files papers. Here is an operational definition from a student speech:

Operational Definition

> Modern rhinoplasty is done for both cosmetic and health reasons. It consists of several mini-operations. First, if the septum separating the nostrils has become deviated as a result of an injury or some other means, it is straightened with surgical pliers. Then, if the nose is to be remodeled, small incisions are made within each nostril, and working entirely within the nose, the surgeon is able to remove, reshape, or redistribute the bone and cartilage lying underneath the skin. Finally, if the nose is crooked, a chisel is taken to the bones of the upper nose, and they are broken so that they may be straightened and centered.[13]

A term can be explained by revealing a person's experience with it. Often words are ones that are used only by a specific group who have shared experiences. The kids at a local high school call the rural kids "reds." In some circles calling someone a "red" might mean that they are a communist, but in this case the high schoolers mean that the "reds" are "rednecks," a slang expression for country folks. Another example of a term that can only be understood through experiential definition are the "posties" on campus. The "posties" are students who have served as writers and editors of the university's daily newspaper, *The Post*. Perhaps you too can think of terms that are used by a gang, an organization, or an ethnic group that can be explained only by revealing those people's experience with the word.

Experiential Definition

Other methods of defining terms exist, but the eight we've discussed—comparison, contrast, synonyms, antonyms, etymology, differentiation, operational definition, and experiential definition—will help you share meanings with your audience. You communicate more clearly as a speaker when you define your terms.

You also can avoid the embarassment of communicating something that you do not intend. A student gave a speech in which she frequently used the word *cruising*. Every time she used it, the members of the audience looked at each other in amusement. At the time, the word *cruising* was used by students to mean "seeking a sexual partner." However, the speaker was using it as professional foresters do, referring to the marking and measuring of trees. Remember that defining your terms can improve your communication.

Achieving Literacy

Literacy as applied to the written word means a person's ability to read and write at some minimally acceptable level. Literacy may also be applied to the spoken word. Some indications of oral illiteracy and how to overcome it are explored in the following sections.

. . . .

Signs of Oral Illiteracy

1. Mistakes in grammar and pronunciation
2. Vocalized pauses and verbal fillers
3. Using clichés and euphemisms

. . . .

Signs of Oral Illiteracy

One sign of **oral illiteracy** is that speakers make mistakes in grammar and pronunciation. Speakers who say "Him and I went," "If we was staying there," or "People reach a point in their life," are signaling to those who know the rules of grammar that the speakers do not. Similarly, a speaker who cannot pronounce the words in a speech reveals to the audience an ignorance about the subject. Anyone knowledgeable about the topic would know how to pronounce the words.

Less serious, but equally problematic, is the overuse of certain words that may cause the audience to start listening for the next repetition. Some speakers repeat the word *now* every time they begin a new sentence; others repeat the word *so*. Certain words and phrases are often used as "fillers" or vocalized pauses. They change considerably from year to year, but one phrase that has been around for several years is *you know*. Undoubtedly, many of the people in your class have other words and phrases that they use as verbal fillers.

A third indication of oral illiteracy is the use of other people's language to explain your own position. One example is the use of **clichés** such as "You only get out of it what you put into it," "All's fair in love and war," and "Beauty is only skin deep." Another example is the use of **euphemisms** or socially acceptable expressions such as the words *bathroom, powder room,* or *ladies' lounge* for the word *toilet*. A third example is more difficult to illustrate, but it consists of mouthing the words of others every time you have to state your position on an issue. You might, for instance, explain your position on busing by using your father's argument and his words. You might cling to some other authority such as Lauro F. Cavazos on education. Perhaps you simply take your husband's, wife's, friend's, or roommate's position on issues when you are asked to articulate your own. In any case, oral illiteracy includes your being unable to explain your own position without merely adopting someone else's language, arguments, and words.

Speechmakers who speak frequently have a tendency to use the same words repeatedly until their entire speech becomes memorized and impervious to further thought. The politician has his stock speech, the athletic banquet speaker has hers, and the evangelist has his. Such frequent expression of one's own thinking can become little different from thoughtlessly mouthing the words of others. This is especially true when the words have been spoken so often that the speaker is unwilling to revise them even in the face of changing circumstances. Are the words you use in your speeches simply repetitions of expressions you have given time after time? Is there any new knowledge that should be taken into account since you began taking a particular position?

Oral literacy is easiest to describe as the absence of certain characteristics such as

Why You Should Strive for Oral Literacy

—mistakes in grammar and pronunciation
—overusing verbal fillers or vocalized pauses
—using clichés and euphemisms

Why should you strive to become orally literate? Why should you avoid grammatical errors, clichés, and all of the other mistakes that you have been warned against?

Avoid grammatical and pronunciation errors because audiences may discount much of what you have to say simply on the basis of such errors. This does not mean that your language must sound stilted or affected. You can be relaxed and informal without making errors in grammar and pronunciation.

What can you do if you have a problem with grammar or pronunciation? Observe how other people pronounce words and use language. You can turn to your instructor for help. You can turn to the dictionary or a grammar handbook. The student who habitually makes numerous grammatical errors is unlikely to find a quick cure, but poor language can be corrected by students who recognize the social and economic benefits of being able to express themselves correctly and effectively.

Why should you avoid clichés and euphemisms? Clichés are a substitute for thought. There are so many clichés that entire conversations and speeches can be strung together with them. Unfortunately, most clichés are only partial truths. "You only get out of it what you put into it." Is that always true? Have you ever met people, including fellow students, who put a great deal into their college education and get practically nothing out of it? Have you seen others who put nothing into their education and yet reap many more benefits than they seem to deserve? If beauty is only skin deep, is ugliness clear through? The partial truths that we mumble in answer to difficult problems mask the complexity and invite simple answers that discourage the creative thought that might solve a problem or settle an issue.

What is wrong with using the language and words of others? Again, the problem centers on using other people's thinking as a substitute for your own. Your position on an issue may be like someone else's, but did you arrive at that position you call your own by inheriting it from your parents or borrowing it from your friends? You can be considerably more convincing as a speaker if you try to articulate your own ideas instead of simply imitating those you have heard or

Reprinted by permission of NEA, Inc.

FRANK AND ERNEST   by Bob Thaves

read. Likewise, occasionally take a close look at the opinions you have held for a long time. Has a situation changed so much that your position on it is still viable? George Wallace, Alabama politician and two-time presidential contender, repeated segregationist ideas for years without recognizing the changes in circumstances (including the civil rights movement) that so drastically altered the country. He became politically, philosophically, and morally out of step with the times. The same circumstance could be true for us if we did not make the effort to reexamine our own ideas. Literacy in public speaking is more than avoiding grammatical errors—it means you must synchronize your own ideas and language and effectively communicate them.

Improving Descriptive Powers

How can you improve your use of language in public speech? Public speakers need to have a large vocabulary and good **descriptive powers** in order to accurately and vividly convey their thoughts. The person who only knows the primary colors—blue, red, and yellow—is unable to describe a landscape as accurately as the person who knows how to differentiate mauve, chartreuse, indigo, violet, and purple. A person's descriptions typically relate size, shape, color, texture, or even feelings evoked by objects and people.

Let us look first at some examples of descriptions from student speeches. Is a basketball just a round thing usually orange in color? This student looked at a basketball from various perspectives:

> Defining the surface texture is much more crucial to understanding the object than is naming the exterior material. Texture is not only a quality of coarseness, but of topography. At a viewpoint range of, say, one centimeter, a basketball is an undulating surface infiltrated by scores of bulging protuberances, like the pebbly bottom of a backwoods stream. At a range of one hundred meters, it becomes indistinguishable from an orange ball bearing.[14]

A second student described an early snowfall:

> The harshness of the frozen earth had been transformed into a soft, rolling white carpet. The bare trees which had previously been stripped of their majestic, colored leaves now stood proudly flocked.
>
> The sun was beginning to push the night back—revealing a chilling blue sky. The early morning light glistened off the newfallen snow, dancing from one ice particle to another, creating thousands of diamonds everywhere.[15]

Finally, a third student described an accelerated maneuver stall in an airplane:

> The stall is initiated by tipping the plane into a 45° angle turn, pushing the throttle to full power, and pulling back on the stick. The once serene earth has tipped onto its side and is spinning dizzily around me. The spinning fields slowly sink out of sight as I continue to pull back on the stick until all I see is blue sky in the windshield. The force of gravity on my body is steadily increasing. When the maneuver began there were two G's on my body, the same as on the big hill of the tornado rollercoaster. Just before the stall there will be four G's pulling me in my seat. My blood rushes to my feet instead of staying in my brain where I need it. My stomach constricts so I won't throw up. The noise of the engine makes a lugging sound as the plane labors into a steeper and steeper climb. When the airspeed comes within five knots of stalling, an irritating horn blares out its warning.
>
> Suddenly the plane begins to buffet. The stall is imminent. The nose drops violently, and the earth pops up in front of the plane. The four positive G's turn to four negative G's. The force pushes my stomach into my throat. The blood rushes to my brain. I have to act fast, or the stall will turn into a spin. Against instinct, I push the stick forward, level the wings, and apply right rudder. . . .[16]

These speakers could have said, "A basketball is a round plastic thing," "The ground was covered with snow," and "The plane went up fast, stalled, and fell." But such brief, abstract descriptions would give the audience very little opportunity to develop the pictures in their own minds. The specific details in the students' accounts help the audience to visualize and feel what the speakers experienced. The speeches also suggest some methods of description you can use in your own speeches.

Reprinted by permission of
NEA, Inc.

FRANK AND ERNEST by Bob Thaves

*Use Precise,
Accurate
Language*

One method of describing something is to use precise, accurate language. In the description of the basketball, the speaker views the ball from distances of one centimeter and one hundred meters—not from close and far away. The language is very precise. The plane tips to a 45° angle; it does not simply turn on its side. The language is very specific.

*Build Your
Vocabulary*

A second method of describing something is to use a variety of words and expressions. The basketball's surface texture is described as "coarseness," "typography," and "an undulating surface infiltrated by scores of bulging protuberances." The snow is "soft," "rolling," and "white." The "serene earth" in the stalling maneuver becomes "spinning fields" as the engine makes a "lugging sound" and "labors into a steeper and steeper climb." The vocabulary in each case is impressive in its variety and appropriateness.

*Employ
Denotative and
Connotative
Meanings*

A third method of describing something is to use the connotative dimension of words. **Denotative meaning** is the dictionary meaning, the objective meaning without an emotional component. **Connotative meaning** is what the word suggests, its emotional content. For instance, if you refer to a woman as a "broad," the denotative definition may mean a female, but the connotative definition probably means a sex object. The same thing holds for a man referred to as a "hunk."

A look at our student speeches shows how one uses connotative meaning to enliven a description. To refer to the "typography" of a basketball suggests a map with a raised surface to indicate mountains, hills, and valleys. To say that a tree was "stripped" suggests forceful removal, and "proudly flocked" might suggest the spray "snow" used to decorate Christmas trees.

*State the Familiar
in an Unfamiliar
Way*

A fourth method of describing something is to state the familiar in an unfamiliar way to make it more striking and memorable. "The bird carried the sky on its wings" is more exciting imagery than "the bird flew across the sky." Similarly, in the student descriptions, the imagery is more striking when a basketball at one hundred meters is "an orange ball bearing" and in the snow scene when "the sun was beginning to push the night back."

To make your speeches more effective, use precise, accurate language; employ a wide vocabulary; use both the denotative and connotative meaning of words; make comparisons; and state the familiar in an unfamiliar way. Learn new words by reading self-help books, stories, and poems; by listening carefully to how literate people use the language. Use resources like the dictionary, the thesaurus, and handbooks on grammar and usage. Learning how to express yourself through language is not an easy task, though people who do it well make it look easy. A public speaking class gives you the opportunity to start working on your vocabulary, the accuracy and precision of your language, and your descriptive powers.

We have discussed difficulties that speakers have with language and some methods of overcoming those problems. We turn now to one final area of concern, **information overkill.** The primary point of this section is that it is relatively easy for a knowledgeable speaker to provide more information and ideas than a diverse audience, without expertise in a particular area, can easily absorb. Usually this is exactly the type of audience you face in a public speaking class. The warning to avoid information overkill is not aimed at speakers addressing a homogeneous audience whose members, like the speaker, are well acquainted with the ideas and specialized language necessary to express them.

Overkilling with Information

An example of the problem of information overkill comes from a student who was delivering a speech in class on the topic of photovoltaics. His first three sentences were appropriate enough as an attention-getter, but observe what happened next:

> With America's energy independence growing weaker every day because of dwindling oil reserves, it is paradoxical that energy is available in the United States at over five hundred times the United States' present rate of consumption. Where does this energy come from? The sun, of course. When the sun is high in the sky, energy radiates on the earth's surface at a little more than one kilowatt per meter squared. The equivalent of one gallon of gas, 36 kilowatt-hours, falls on the area of a tennis court every ten minutes. In the least sunny part of the United States, the northeast according to chart 1, one football field could provide all the energy used by 66 average American families of 4.7 people during a year's time. . . .[17]

Probably, for most members of the audience, the references to tennis courts and football fields did relate the unfamiliar to the familiar, but how many people in a classroom audience know the meaning of "one kilowatt per meter squared," "36 kilowatt-hours," or the significance of "66 average American families of 4.7

Information overkill can confuse an audience.

people during a year's time"? The information flow was too rapid for the introduction of a speech to a diverse, unspecialized audience. The language was too unfamiliar, undefined, and unpalatable. The problem of information overkill was caused by a density of ideas and language complexity.

The speaker did not improve his communication. By the middle of the speech, he was saying this:

> I will use this silicon cell as my example. Electricity is generated in the silicon cell when electrons are freed from the valence on the outermost shell of the silicon atom by light. When the electron is freed, it creates a hole, which is a positively charged carrier, whereas the electron is a negatively charged carrier. If the photovoltaic cell was of uniform consistency, no current would be generated, since holes and freed electrons would be in the same proportion; hence, they would all recombine. . . .

The speaker was clearly talking above the audience's capacity to understand. He used the language of electrical engineering and physics without considering that most audience members were unfamiliar with atoms, valences, positive and negative charges, currents, electrons, and photovoltaic cells. Even if the speaker had defined all of these terms, the speech would have been inappropriate for a generalized audience. The speech does, however, illustrate the meaning of information overkill through language.

In this chapter you learned that language is an arbitrary system of communication in which words evoke meanings in other people's minds. You found that public speakers face certain problems with language. One problem is that beginning speakers, and even some experienced ones, tend to use written rather than spoken language in their speeches. A solution to this problem is to understand the difference between abstract and concrete language and to follow the suggestions in chapter 11 on delivery. Another problem is how to establish shared meanings. This can be solved by means of comparisons, contrasts, synonyms, antonyms, etymologies, differentiation, and operational and experiential definitions. A third problem area is achieving oral literacy. This can be accomplished by avoiding (1) grammatical and pronunciation errors, (2) the overuse of certain words as verbal fillers or vocalized pauses, and (3) the use of clichés and euphemisms. A fourth problem is how to improve your descriptive powers. This can be done by (1) using precise, accurate language, (2) building vocabulary, (3) using both denotative and connotative meanings, and (4) stating the familiar in an unfamiliar fresh way. Finally, you learned to avoid difficult language and information overkill in public speeches.

Summary

▼▼

1
Translating Terms

Application Exercises

"Translate" the abstract terms in the column on the left into more specific, concrete terms in the blanks on the right.

1. A recent article _____
2. An ethnic neighborhood _____
3. A good professor _____
4. A big profit _____
5. A distant land _____
6. A tough course _____
7. A tall building _____
8. He departed rapidly _____
9. She dresses poorly _____
10. They are religious _____

2
Defining Your Terms

Examine the words in the column at the left. Consider which method of definition you would use to help your classmates understand your meaning by placing the name of the method in the middle column. Then in the column at the right show how you would use that method.

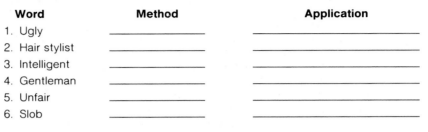

Word	Method	Application
1. Ugly	_____	_____
2. Hair stylist	_____	_____
3. Intelligent	_____	_____
4. Gentleman	_____	_____
5. Unfair	_____	_____
6. Slob	_____	_____

▼▼

Application Assignments

1
The Speech of Definition

Deliver a two- to three-minute speech in which you define a term unknown to a majority of your audience by using at least two of the methods of defining discussed in this chapter. You are encouraged to use sources of information like the dictionary or a thesaurus to help you determine various ways of defining your terms.

Optional: Provide a manuscript of your speech with side notes indicating where you used the two different methods of defining. *Note:* An example of a speech of definition can be found in chapter 13. This speech can serve as a model for this assignment.

2
The Speech of Description

Deliver a three- or four-minute speech in which you describe a person, place, object, or experience by indicating size, weight, color, smell, texture, and/or feelings. The speech does not require outside sources, but you may wish to use a thesaurus or dictionary to help you produce a description without using clichés.

Optional: Provide a script of your speech with side notes indicating which methods of description you used.

Note: An example of a speech of description can be found in chapter 13. This speech can serve as a model for this assignment.

▼▼

Vocabulary

abstract language   The use of words that tend to be broad and unspecific, and refer to ideas likely to evoke a variety of meanings; the opposite of concrete language.

ambiguity   A characteristic of language that relates to the multiple meanings evoked by words.

arbitrariness   A characteristic of language referring to the relationship between a word and the various meanings people assign to it over a period of time.

availability   A characteristic of language referring to the likelihood of a word's being selected to describe a particular perception; words most likely to be selected as descriptors are high in availability.

cliché   A statement that has lost its impact because it has been overused.

concrete language   The use of words that are relatively close to their referent; words that tend to be precise and specific and evoke particular meanings; the opposite of abstract language.

connotative meaning   What a word suggests to the listener or reader; subjective meaning resulting from emotional involvement.

denotative meaning   The objective meaning of a word, standardized by such sources as a dictionary.

descriptive powers   The ability to vividly convey one's thoughts; usually related to sensory matters (size, shape, weight, texture, smell, and feelings experienced) and relayed to others by means of precise, accurate language, a wide vocabulary, connotative and denotative meanings, comparisons, and fresh imagery.

euphemism   An agreeable expression substituted for one that may offend or sound unpleasant.

information overkill   The use of excessive jargon or specialized language and an oversupply of factual data for a particular audience.

language   An arbitrary symbol system developed over time to communicate meaning.

oral illiteracy   Speaking with errors in grammar or pronunciation, unintended vocalized pauses, verbal fillers, an overdependence on others' language or ideas, or an overreliance on your own language and ideas.

strategic choice   Words are chosen for the purpose of communicating with an audience.

▼▼

Endnotes

1. From a speech delivered by Matthew Eash in Fundamentals of Public Speaking, Iowa State University.
2. From a speech delivered by Jana Milford in Fundamentals of Public Speaking, Iowa State University.
3. From a speech delivered by David Kastner in Fundamentals of Public Speaking, Iowa State University.
4. Based on Harold P. Zelco and Frank E. X. Dance, "Oral Style Characteristics," *Business and Professional Speech Communication,* 2d ed. (New York: Holt, Rinehart, and Winston, 1978), 152–54.
5. Based on figure 8.1 in Albert J. Vasile and Harold K. Mintz, *Speak with Confidence,* 5th ed. (Glenview, Ill.: Scott, Foresman and Company, 1989), 152. The original list was enriched by contributions from Robert O. Skovgard, ed., *Openings* (Dayton, Oh.: The Executive Speaker Co., 1984), 2, cited in Roger Ailes, *You Are The Message: Secrets of the Master Communicators* (Homewood, Ill.: Dow Jones-Irwin, 1988), 41.
6. From a speech delivered by Warren Varley in Fundamentals of Public Speaking, Iowa State University.
7. From a speech delivered by Roberta Mau in Fundamentals of Public Speaking, Iowa State University.

8. From a speech delivered by Jergen Nelson in Fundamentals of Public Speaking, Iowa State University.
9. From a speech delivered by John Rector in Fundamentals of Public Speaking, Iowa State University.
10. From a speech delivered by Sandra Eckerman in Fundamentals of Public Speaking, Iowa State University.
11. From a speech delivered by Mark DuPont in Fundamentals of Public Speaking, Iowa State University.
12. From a speech delivered by Barbara Tarter in the Communication and Persuasion Course, Ohio University.
13. Dupont.
14. From a speech delivered by Matthew Eash in Fundamentals of Public Speaking, Iowa State University.
15. From a speech delivered by Susan Schiltz in Fundamentals of Public Speaking, Iowa State University.
16. From a speech delivered by Warren Varley in Fundamentals of Public Speaking, Iowa State University.
17. The speaker of this negative example will remain anonymous for obvious reasons.

Delivery

11

Besides, as is usually the case, we are much more affected by the words which we hear, for though what you read in books may be more pointed, yet there is something in the look, the carriage, and even the gesture of the speaker, that makes a deeper impression upon the mind.

PLINY THE YOUNGER

199

Introduction

Demosthenes, the famous classical orator, was asked "What are the three most important aspects of public speaking?" His answer: "Delivery, delivery, delivery."

Roger Ailes, a graduate of Ohio University and one of the consultants credited with George Bush's 1988 election victory, says

> ". . . *You are the message.* What does that mean exactly? It means when you communicate with someone, it's not just the words you choose to send to the other person that make up the message. You're also sending signals of what kind of person you are—by your eyes, your facial expression, your body movement, your vocal pitch, tone, volume, and intensity, your commitment to your message, your sense of humor, and many other factors. . . . *You are the message* comes down to the fact that unless you identify yourself as a walking, talking message, you miss that critical point."[1]

Ancient orator and modern media consultant alike regard delivery as exceedingly important in public speaking. If you begin learning delivery with less than your usual esteem, you might bolster your confidence with these words of American author Ralph Waldo Emerson: "All the great speakers were bad speakers first."[2]

Four Modes of Delivery

The four modes of delivering a speech are (1) extemporaneous, (2) manuscript, (3) impromptu, and (4) memorized. These four modes are appropriate for different topics, audiences, speakers, and situations. When you complete this section, you should be able to decide which mode to use in each situation.

Extemporaneous Mode

The **extemporaneous mode** of delivery is the one most commonly taught in the public speaking classroom. It is the speech teachers' favorite because it is the most versatile mode, demands attention to all aspects of public speaking preparation, and is the mode a speaker is likely to use most often.

What exactly is extemporaneous speaking? Extemporaneous speaking sounds conversational, looks spontaneous, and seems effortless. But extemporaneous speaking is the result of much effort. The speaker selects a topic appropriate for the audience, completes research on the topic, organizes the main points and supporting materials, practices the speech with a working outline or key words, and then delivers the speech with maximum eye contact, gestures, and movement. The speaker may occasionally glance at notes, but the emphasis is on communicating the message to the live audience.

Extemporaneous speaking is something that you may have done many times without realizing it. Have you ever prepared for a class by reading the assignment, caught the drift of the professor's questions, jotted a few words on your notes, and given an answer in class? Your answer was a brief, extemporaneous speech. Have you ever sat in a meeting about an issue you knew something about, written a few phrases to remind you of your line of argument, and then addressed

the group with your point of view? Your "speech" was extemporaneous because it included your background preparation, organization of your idea, brief reminders, and a conversational delivery.

The extemporaneous speech is not practiced to the point of memorization. In fact, it is not delivered with exactly the same words even in practice. The idea is to keep the content flexible enough to adapt to the audience. If the audience appears puzzled by something you said, then you can include a definition, description, or example to clarify your position. Audience members like to be "talked to," not "lectured at." The extemporaneous mode results in high quality talk, freedom from notes, generous eye contact, and immediate adaptation to the audience.

Let us now consider the second mode of delivery, the manuscript mode. The speaker writes out and reads *verbatim* a manuscript speech. The **manuscript mode** of delivery is most appropriate when a speaker has to be precise. A president who delivers a foreign policy speech in which the slip of a word could start a war, a minister who carefully documents his sermon with biblical quotations, and a politician who releases information to the press are examples of speakers who might adopt this mode.

An example of the use of this mode occurred one week on campus when the school invited several speakers to present their points of view on religion. Every lecture drew a huge audience. The speakers, all professors, were a humanist, a Protestant, and an atheist. The humanist presented his point of view in a speech

Manuscript Mode

virtually without notes. His speech was almost paternal, full of human virtue, and devoid of conflicting opinions. The Protestant, a Lutheran, delivered his speech a few days later. Many students in the audience were also Protestants, mainly Lutherans, and the speaker had considerable support from his audience. He, too, delivered his speech with few notes. A few days later, the atheist presented his speech. Instead of standing on the well-lighted stage as the others had done, he delivered his speech seated in the middle of the auditorium with a single spotlight shining on him in the darkness. He read every word from a carefully argued manuscript. Though he argued well, he had few followers in the audience. The response was polite but restrained.

The following weekend all three speakers faced each other and the audience in a discussion of their positions. Because the atheist's position was unpopular with both his fellow speakers and the audience, he was asked most of the questions. He received the audience's reluctant admiration because, in verbal combat, his previous mode of delivery enabled him to have a solid position on almost every question. The humanist and the Protestant had difficulty remembering exactly what they had said, while the atheist answered nearly every inquiry *verbatim* from memory. It was difficult for anyone in the audience or on the stage to distort the atheist's position. It was clearly a case in which a manuscript delivery was the most appropriate mode for the speaker, audience, and situation.

The advantages of a manuscript speech are obvious: the manuscript prevents slips of the tongue, miswording, and distortion. Of course, there are also disadvantages. It is difficult to be spontaneous or to respond to audience feedback with a manuscript, and it is quite difficult to make any significant changes during delivery. Many of the bodily aspects of delivery are limited by the script. If you have to read every word accurately, you cannot be watching your audience at the same time, or move about and gesture uninhibitedly, as you can when giving an extemporaneous speech.

Impromptu Mode

The word *impromptu* means "in readiness." The **impromptu mode** of delivery actually *is* "on the spur of the moment." Unlike the extemporaneous mode, the impromptu mode really involves no planning, preparation, or practice. You may be ready for an impromptu speech because of your reading, experience, and background, but you do not have any other aids to help you know what to say.

You undoubtedly have already delivered impromptu speeches. When your teacher calls on you to answer a question, your answer—if you have one—is impromptu. You were ready because you read the assignment or prepared for class, but you probably did not write out an answer or certain key words. When someone asks you to introduce yourself, explain something at a meeting, reveal what you know about some subject, or give directions, you are delivering your answer in an impromptu fashion.

One of the advantages of an impromptu speech is that it reveals what you are like in unplanned circumstances. In a job interview you might be asked to explain why you are interested in the company, want a particular job, or expect such a high salary. Your impromptu answers may tell a potential employer more about you than if you were given the questions ahead of time and had prepared your answers. Similarly, the student who can give an accurate, complete answer to a difficult question in class shows a mastery of the subject matter that is, in some ways, more impressive than it might be in an exam or other situation in which he or she may give partially planned answers. One advantage of the impromptu mode is that you learn how to think on your feet. A major disadvantage of impromptu delivery is that it is so spontaneous that it discourages audience analysis, planned research, and detailed preparation.

The **memorized mode** of delivery is one in which the speaker has committed the speech to memory. It entails more than just knowing all of the words; it usually involves the speaker's rehearsal of gestures, eye contact, and movement. The speaker achieves this mastery of words and movement by practicing or delivering a speech over and over in much the same way that an actor or actress masters a dramatic script.

Memorized Mode

The memorized mode is common in oratory contests, on the lecture circuit, and at banquets. It is appropriate for ceremonial occasions where a minimum of spontaneous empathy with the audience occurs. Campus lecturers often earn $5,000 or more a night for merely filling in the name of a different college in their standard speech. Politicians usually have a stock speech that they have delivered so many times they have memorized it. Some speakers have delivered the same speech so many times that they even know when and how long the audience is going to applaud. The main advantage of the memorized mode is that it permits maximum use of delivery skills: every variation in the voice can be mastered, every oral paragraph stated in correct cadence, every word correctly pronounced at the right volume. With a memorized speech, you have continuous eye contact and you eliminate a search for words.

On the other hand, a memorized speech permits little or no adaptation during delivery. If the audience appears to have missed a point, it is difficult for a speaker to explain the point in greater detail. A second disadvantage is that recovery is more difficult if you make a mistake: if you forget a line you have to search for the exact place where you dropped your line. A third disadvantage, especially for beginning speakers, is that a speech sometimes *sounds* memorized: the wording is too glib, the cadences are too contrived, and the speech is too much of a performance instead of a communicative experience. Nevertheless, there is still a place for the memorized speech in your public speaking repertoire. In some formal situations there may be little need for adaptation.

Your mode of delivery must be appropriate for you, your topic, audience, and situation. Memorizing five pages of print may not be your style. A manuscript speech is out of place in a dormitory meeting, a rap session, or any informal gathering. Ultimately, the mode of delivery is not the crucial feature of your speech. In a study to determine whether the extemporaneous or manuscript mode was more effective, two researchers concluded that the mode of delivery simply did not determine effectiveness. The speaker's ability was more important. Some speakers were more effective with extemporaneous speeches than with manuscript speeches, but others used both modes with equal effectiveness.[3]

Vocal Aspects of Delivery

In the last chapter, we considered the various modes of delivery in the public speech. We turn now to a discussion of specific vocal aspects of delivery. Keep in mind the central goal of public speaking is to communicate a message to an audience as effectively as possible. Your knowledge of the content of your speech looms larger in importance than what you do with your hands or your eyes. Indeed, some authors suggest that the best way to improve your delivery is not to emphasize it directly.[4] Instead, let your effective delivery flow naturally. As you grow in confidence in front of an audience, your delivery is likely to improve because you do not have to think about it. In an extemporaneous speech, for instance, the "best" delivery may be one in which you appear to be conversing with the audience. All of your delivery skills can be aimed at using your voice in ways that reflect a conversational quality in your speech.

In this chapter you will examine a relatively large number of variables that occur in delivering a speech. You should first learn to understand these aspects of delivery so that you can practice them in your continuing effort to grow in confidence as a public speaker. Studying the vocal aspects of speech delivery is like studying "verbal punctuation." When you want to underline what you are saying, slow down. When you want to draw attention to your words as you would with italics, then speak slowly and make the word stand out in contrast by saying it softer or louder than the words around it. If you want a comma in your speech, then pause. If you want to indicate a period, pause longer.

You will learn more by examining the six vocal aspects of delivery: pitch, rate, pauses, volume, enunciation, and fluency.

. . . .

Vocal Aspects of Delivery in Public Speaking

1. Pitch
2. Rate
3. Pauses
4. Volume
5. Enunciation
6. Fluency

. . . .

Pitch is the highness or lowness of the speaker's voice, its upward and downward   Pitch
inflection, the melody produced by the voice. Pitch is what makes the difference between the "Ohhh" that you utter when you earn a poor grade on an exam and the "Ohhh" that you say when you see someone really attractive. The "Ohhh" looks the same in print, but when the notes become music, the difference in the two expressions is vast. The pitch of your voice can make you sound animated, lively, and vivacious, or it can make you sound dull, listless, and monotonous. As a speaker you can learn to avoid the two extremes: you can avoid the lack of pitch changes that result in a monotone, and the repetitious pitch changes that result in a singsong delivery. The best public speakers use the full range of their normal pitch. They know when to purr and when to roar, and when to vary their pitch between.

Pitch control does more than make a speech aesthetically pleasing. Certainly one of the more important features of pitch control is that it can be employed to alter the way an audience responds to words. Many subtle changes in meaning are accomplished by pitch changes. Your pitch tells an audience whether the words are a statement or question, sarcastic or ironic, and whether you are expressing doubt, determination, or surprise.

You learn pitch control by constant practice. An actor who is learning to say a line has to practice it many times, in many ways, before he can be assured that most people in the audience will understand the words as he intends them. The public speaker rehearses a speech in front of a sympathetic audience to receive feedback on whether the words are being understood as she intends them. Perhaps you sound angry or brusque when you do not intend to. Maybe you sound cynical when you intend to sound doubtful. Possibly you sound frightened when you are only surprised. You may not be the best judge of how you sound to others. Therefore, place some trust in other people's evaluations of how you sound. Practicing pitch is a way of achieving control over this important aspect of delivery.

Rate

Rate, the second characteristic of vocal delivery, is the speed of delivery. Normally, American speakers say between 125 and 190 words per minute, but audiences can comprehend spoken language much faster. Four psychologists in an article entitled "Speed of Speech and Persuasion" noted that speech rate functions to improve the speaker's credibility and that rapid speech improved persuasion.[5] Another study, however, showed that when students shortened their pauses and increased their speaking rates from 126 to 172 words per minute, neither the audience's comprehension nor their evaluations of the speaker's delivery was affected.[6] Thus, you should not necessarily conclude that faster speaking is better speaking.

Instructors often caution beginning speakers to "slow down." The reason is that beginning speakers frequently vent their anxiety by speaking very rapidly. A nervous speaker makes the audience nervous as well. On the other hand, fluency comes from confidence. A speaker who is accustomed to audiences and knows the subject matter well may speak at a brisk rate without appearing to be nervous. An effective speaker sounds natural, conversational, and flexible. He or she can speak rapidly or slowly, depending on the circumstances.

The essential point, not revealed by the studies, is that speaking rate needs to be adapted to the speaker, audience, situation, and content of the speech. First, become comfortable with your rate of speaking. If you normally speak rather slowly, you might feel awkward talking like a competitive debater. If you normally speak at a rapid pace, you might feel uncomfortable speaking more slowly. As you learn to speak publicly, you will probably find a rate that is appropriate for you.

Second, adapt your rate to the audience and situation. A grade-school teacher does not rip through a fairy tale; the audience is just learning how to comprehend words. The public speaker addressing a large audience without a microphone might speak like a contest orator to make sure the audience comprehends his words.

Martin Luther King, Jr., in his famous "I Have a Dream" speech began his address at a slow rate under 100 words per minute, but as he became more passionately involved in his topic and as his audience responded he finished at almost 150 words per minute.

Audience, situation, and content help to determine your speaking rate.

The content of your speech may determine your rate of delivery. A story to illustrate a point can be understood at a faster rate than can a string of statistics or a complicated argument. The rate should depend on the effect you seek. Telling

a story of suspense and intrigue would be difficult at a high rate of speed. Rarely does speaking "too fast" refer to words per minute; instead, "too fast" usually means the rate at which new information is presented without being understood. Effective public speakers adjust their rate according to their own comfort, the audience, situation, and the content of their speeches.

A third vocal characteristic is the **pause.** Speeches are often stereotyped as a steady stream of verbiage. Yet the public speaker can use pauses and silences for dramatic effect and to interest the audience in content. You might begin a speech with rhetorical questions: "Have you had a cigarette today? Have you had two or three? Ten or eleven? Do you know what your habit is costing you a year? A decade? A lifetime?" After each rhetorical question a pause allows each member of the audience to answer the question in his or her own mind.

Another kind of pause—the **vocalized pause**—is really not silent at all. Instead, it is a way of delaying with sound. The vocalized pause is a nonfluency that can adversely affect an audience's perception of the speaker's competence and dynamism. The "ahhhs," "nows," and "you knows" of the novice speaker are annoying and distracting to most audiences. Unfortunately, even some highly experienced speakers have the habit of filling silences with vocalized pauses. One organization teaches public speaking by having members of the audience drop a marble into a can every time the speaker uses a vocalized pause. The resulting punishment, the clanging of the cans during the speech, is supposed to break the habit. A more humane method might be to rehearse your speech for a friend who

Pauses

Delivery   **207**

can signal you more gently every time you vocalize a pause. One speech teacher helps her students eliminate vocalized pauses by rigging a small red light on the lectern. Every time the student speaker uses a vocalized pause, the instructor hits the light for a moment. Do not be afraid of silence; most audiences would prefer a little silence to a vocalized pause.

One way to learn how to use pauses effectively in public speaking is to listen to how professional speakers use them. Paul Harvey, the Chicago radio commentator, practically orchestrates his pauses. A long pause before the "Page Two" section of his news broadcast is one technique that has made him an attractive radio personality. Oral Roberts, Billy Graham, and TV anchorpersons similarly use pauses effectively.

Volume

A fourth vocal characteristic of delivery is **volume,** the relative loudness of your voice. In conversation you are accustomed to speaking at an arm's length. When you stand in front of an audience, some of them may be quite close to you, but others may be some distance away. Beginning speakers are often told to "project," to increase their volume so that all may hear the speech.

Volume is more than just projection, however. Variations in volume can convey emotion, importance, suspense, and subtle nuances of meaning. You whisper a secret in conversation, and you stage whisper in front of an audience to signal conspiratorial intent. You speak loudly and strongly on important points and let your voice carry your conviction. An orchestra never plays so quietly that the patrons cannot hear it, but the musicians vary their volume. Similarly, a public speaker who considers the voice an instrument learns how to speak softly, loudly, and at every volume in between to convey his or her intended meaning.

Enunciation

Enunciation, the fifth vocal aspect of delivery, is the pronunciation and articulation of words. Because your reading vocabulary is likely to be larger than your speaking vocabulary, you may use words in your speeches that you have never heard before. It is risky to deliver unfamiliar words. One student in a speech class gave a speech on the human reproductive system. During the speech he made reference to a woman's "vir-gin-yah" and her "you-teár-us." The suppressed laughter did not help the speaker's credibility as a competent commentator. Rather than erring in public, practice your speech in front of friends, roommates, or family who can tell you when you make a mistake in pronunciation or articulation, or check pronunciation in a dictionary. Every dictionary has a pronunciation key. For instance, the entry for the word *deification* in *Webster's New World Dictionary of the American Language* is:

de–i–fi–ca–tion (dē′ə–fi–kā′ shən), n.[ME.; OFr.],
1. a deifying. 2. deified person or embodiment.[7]

The entry indicates that the word has five syllables into which it can be divided in writing and which carry distinct sounds. The pronunciation key says that the *e* should be pronounced like the *e* in ēven, the ə like the *a* in ago, and the *a* like the *a* in ape. The accent mark (′) indicates which syllable should receive heavier

Pitcher	Picture
Collage	College
Massage	Message
Áddress	Address´

Words that sound the same or similar may evoke quite different meanings, as illustrated here.

emphasis. You should learn how to use the pronunciation key in a dictionary, but if you still have some misgivings about how to pronounce a word, ask your speech teacher for assistance.

Another way to improve your enunciation is to learn how to prolong syllables. Such prolonging makes your pronunciation easier to understand, especially if you are addressing a large audience assembled outside or in an auditorium with no microphone. The drawing out of syllables can be overdone, however. Some radio and TV newspeople hang onto the final syllable in a sentence so long that the device is disconcertingly noticeable.

Pronunciation and articulation are the important components of enunciation. Poor **articulation,** poor production of sounds, is so prevalent that there are popular jokes about it. Some children have heard the Lord's Prayer mumbled so many times that they think that one of the lines is "hollow be thy name."

The problem of articulation is less humorous when it happens in your own speech. It occurs in part because so many English words that sound nearly alike are spelled differently and mean entirely different things. In consequence, words are conveyed inaccurately. A class experiment will illustrate this problem. One student whispered a phrase from a presidential address, and a line of students whispered the message from person to person. The phrase was "We must seek fresh answers, unhindered by the stale prescriptions of the past." By the time the message left the third person, it was "When we seek stale answers to the prescription." The eighth person heard the message "When the snakes now answer the question." Similar problems can occur in a public speech if a speaker does not take care to articulate words properly.

Fluency

The sixth vocal characteristic of delivery is **fluency**—the smoothness of delivery, the flow of the words, and the absence of vocalized pauses. Fluency is difficult because it cannot be achieved by looking up words in a dictionary or by any other simple solution. Fluency is not even very noticeable. Listeners are more likely to notice errors than the seemingly effortless flow of words and intentional pauses in a well-delivered speech. You can, however, be too fluent. A speaker who seems too fluent is perceived as "a fast talker," "slicker than oil." The importance of fluency is emphasized in a study that showed audiences tend to perceive a speaker's fluency, the smoothness of presentation, as a main ingredient of effectiveness.[8]

To achieve fluency, you must be confident of the content of your speech. If you know what you are going to say, and if you have practiced it, then disruptive repetition and vocalized pauses are less likely to occur. If you master what you are going to say and concentrate on the overall rhythm of the speech, your fluency will improve. Pace, build, and time various parts of your speech so that in delivery and in content they unite into a coherent whole.

Reprinted by permission of UFS, Inc.

We have considered the vocal aspects of delivery. Let us now examine the bodily aspects. Gestures, facial expression, eye contact, and movement are four bodily aspects of speech delivery—nonverbal indicators of meaning—that are important to the public speaker. In any communication, you indicate how you relate to the material and to other people by your gestures, facial expression, and bodily movements. When you observe two people busily engaged in conversation, you can judge their interest in the conversation without hearing their words. Similarly, in public speaking, the nonverbal aspects of delivery reinforce what the speaker is saying. Researchers have found that audiences who can see the speaker, and his or her visible behavior, comprehend more of the speech than audiences who cannot.[9]

Nonverbal Aspects of Delivery

. . . .

Nonverbal Aspects of Delivery in Public Speaking

1. Gestures
2. Facial expression
3. Eye contact
4. Movement

. . . .

Some persons are more sensitive to nonverbal cues than are others. Five researchers who developed a "Profile of Nonverbal Sensitivity" found that females as early as the third grade were more sensitive to nonverbal communication than males. However, men in artistic or expressive jobs scored as well as the women. The researchers' finding suggests that such sensitivity is learned. A second finding on nonverbal communication was that, until college age, young people are not as sensitive to nonverbal communication as older persons are.[10] This, too, supports the notion that we can and do learn sensitivity to nonverbal cues like gestures, facial expressions, eye contact, and movement.

Gestures

Gestures "mean any visible bodily action by which meaning is given voluntary expression."[11] Although you probably are quite unaware of your arms and hands when you converse with someone, you may find that they become bothersome appendages when you stand in front of an audience. You may feel awkward because standing in front of an audience is not, for most of us, a very natural situation. You have to work to make public speaking look easy, just as a skillful golfer, a graceful dancer, and a talented painter all make their performances look effortless. Novices are the people who make golfing, dancing, painting, and public speaking look difficult. Paradoxically, people have to work diligently to make physical or artistic feats look easy.

What can you do to help yourself gesture naturally when you are delivering your speech? The answer lies in your involvement with the issues and with practice. Angry farmers and irate miners appear on television to protest low prices and poor working conditions. Untutored in public speaking, these passionate people deliver their speeches with gusto and determined gestures. The gestures look very natural. These speakers have a natural delivery because they are much more concerned about their message than about when they should raise their clenched fists. They are upset, and they show it in their words and actions. You can deliver a speech more naturally if your attention is focused on getting your message across. Self-conscious attention to your own gestures may be self-defeating: the gestures look studied, rehearsed, or slightly out of synchronization with your message. Selecting a topic that you really care about can result in the side effect of improving your delivery, especially if you concentrate on your audience and message.

Gestures differ depending on the size of the audience and the formality of the occasion. With a small audience in an informal setting, gestures are more like those you would use in ordinary conversation. With large audiences and more formal speaking situations, gestures are larger and more dramatic. In the classroom the situation is often fairly formal and the audience relatively small so gestures are ordinarily bigger than they would be in casual conversation, but not as exaggerated as they would be in a large auditorium.

Another way to learn appropriate gestures is to practice a speech in front of friends who are willing to make constructive comments. Constructive criticism is one of the benefits your speech teacher and fellow students can give you. Actresses spend hours rehearsing lines and gestures so that they will look spontaneous and unrehearsed on stage. You may have to appear before many audiences before you learn to speak and move naturally. After much practice, you will learn which arm, head, and hand movements seem to help and which hinder your message. You can learn, through practice, to gesture naturally in a way that reinforces your message instead of detracting from it.

Another nonverbal aspect of delivery is **facial expression.** Socrates, one of humanity's greatest thinkers said: "Nobility and dignity, self-abasement and servility, prudence and understanding, insolence and vulgarity, are reflected in the face and in the attitudes of the body whether still or in motion."[12] Some experts believe that the brain connects emotions and facial expressions and that culture determines what activates an emotion and the rules for displaying an emotion.[13]

Ekman and Friesen believe that our facial expression shows how we feel and our body orientation (e.g., leaning, withdrawing, turning) expresses the intensity of our emotion.[14] Pearson, in her book on *Gender and Communication,* cites studies showing differences between male and female facial expressions. For instance, women use more facial expressions and are more expressive than men; women smile more than men; women are more apt to return smiles; and women are more attracted to others who smile.[15]

Facial Expression

Because facial expressions communicate, public speakers need to be aware of what they are communicating. A good example is that smiling can indicate both goodwill—and submissiveness. Animals, like chimpanzees, smile when they want to avoid a clash with a higher status chimpanzee. First year students smile more than upper class students.[16] Constant smiling may communicate submissiveness instead of friendliness, especially if the smiling seems unrelated to the content of the speech.

As a public speaker you may or may not know how your face looks when you speak. Observers can best check out this aspect of delivery. The goal is to have facial expressions consistent with your intent and your message.

Eye Contact

A second nonverbal aspect of delivery that is important to the public speaker is **eye contact.** This term refers to the way a speaker observes the audience while speaking. Studies and experience indicate that audiences prefer maintenance of good eye contact,[17] which improves source credibility.[18] Eye contact is one way you indicate to others how you feel about them. You may be wary of a person who will not look at you in conversation. Similarly, in public speaking, eye contact conveys our relationship with the audience. If you rarely or never look at your audience, they may be resentful of your seeming disinterest. If you look over the heads of your audience or scan them so quickly that you do not really look at anyone, you may appear to be afraid. The proper relationship between you and your audience should be one of purposeful communication. You signal that sense of purpose by treating the audience as individuals with whom you wish to communicate a message and by looking at them for responses to your message.

Eye contact, the frequency of looking and the duration of looking, varies by culture, personality, and gender.[19] White people tend to use more eye gaze than black people, and blacks tend to gaze less while listening than do whites. A white speaker could wrongly interpret a black audience member's averted eyes as disinterest. Latin Americans, Southern Europeans, and Arabs tend to gaze directly on the other person's face, while Asians, Northern Europeans, and Indian-Pakistanis turn their bodies toward others but avoid focusing on the other person's face.

Personality too affects eye contact. People who are extroverted, authoritative, or dominant look more frequently at people to whom they are speaking. So do people who have a high need to be included, liked, and wanted. Gender also affects eye contact with women—more so than men—looking at others both while listening and speaking.

How can you learn to maintain eye contact with your audience? One way is to know your speech so well and to feel so strongly about it that you have to make few references to your notes. The speaker who does not know her speech well tends to be manuscript-bound. You can encourage yourself to keep an eye on the audience by delivering an extemporaneous speech from an outline or key words. One of the purposes of extemporaneous delivery is to help you adapt to your audience. Adaptation is not possible unless you are continually monitoring the

audience's reactions to see if they understand your message. Other ways of learning eye contact include scanning or continually looking over your entire audience, addressing various sections of the audience as you progress through your speech, and concentrating on the head nodders. In almost every audience there are some individuals who overtly indicate whether your message is coming across. These individuals usually nod "yes" or "no" with their heads, thus the name *nodders*. You may find that you can enhance your delivery by finding the friendly faces and positive nodders who signal when the message is getting through to them.

Movement

A third physical aspect of delivery is **movement,** or what you do with your entire body during a speech presentation. Do you lean forward as you speak, demonstrating to the audience how serious you are about communicating your message? Do you move out from behind the lectern to show that you want to get closer to the audience? Do you move during transitions in your speech to signal physically to the audience that you are moving to a new location in your speech? These are examples of purposeful movement in a public speech. Movement without purpose is discouraged. You should not move just to work off your own anxiety like a caged lion.

Always try to face the audience even when you are moving. For instance, even when you have need to write information on the board, you can avoid turning your back by putting your notes on the board before class or putting your visual material on posters. You can learn a lot about movement by watching your classmates and professors when they speak. You can learn what works for others and for you through observation and practice.

Think of physical movement as another way for you to signal a change in emphasis or direction in your speech. In the same way that a new paragraph signals a directional change in writing, moving from one side of the podium to the other can signal a change in your speech. All of the movements mentioned so far have been movements with a purpose. On the other hand, purposeless movement—movement unrelated to the content—is discouraged. Examples of purposeless movement are rocking back and forth or side to side or the "caged lion" movement where the speaker circles the front of the room like the lion in a zoo.

The presence of a podium or lectern affects the formality of the speech. When a podium is present, the speaker is expected to use it, and the result is a higher level of formality than would otherwise be the case. The podium or lectern suggests a speaker-superior relationship with the audience, while the absence of a podium suggests more of an equal relationship with the audience. Your professor may have an opinion about the use of the podium, so you should inquire about its use.

The distance between the speaker and the audience is also significant. A great distance suggests speaker superiority. That is why pulpits in most churches loom high and away from the congregation. A speaker often has a choice about how closely to move to or away from the audience. In the classroom the speaker who clings to the far wall may appear to be exhibiting fear. Drawing close suggests intimacy or power. You need to decide what distances make you and your listeners most comfortable.

Effective delivery has many advantages. Research indicates that effective delivery, the appropriate use of voice and body in public speaking, contributes to the credibility of the speaker.[20] Indeed, student audiences characterize the poorest speakers by their voices and the physical aspects of delivery.[21] Poor speakers are judged to be fidgety, nervous, and monotonous. They also maintain little eye contact and show little animation or facial expression.[22] Good delivery tends to increase the audience's capacity to handle complex information.[23] Thus, your credibility, the audience's evaluations of your being a good or a poor speaker, and your ability to convey complex information may all be affected by the vocal and physical aspects of delivery.

To put this section on the physical aspects of speech delivery in perspective, remember that eye contact, facial expression, gestures, and movement are important, but content may be even more important. The very same researcher who found that poor speakers are identified by their voices and the physical aspects of their delivery also found that the best speakers were identified by the content of their speeches.[24] Two other researchers found that more of an audience's evaluation of a speaker is based on the content of the speech than on vocal characteristics such as intonation, pitch, and rate.[25] Still another pair of researchers found that a well-composed speech can mask poor delivery.[26] Finally, one researcher reviewed studies on informative speaking and reported that, while some research indicates audiences who have listened to good speakers have significantly greater immediate recall, other findings show that the differences are slight. His conclusion was that the influence of delivery on comprehension is overrated.[27]

Practice your speech in the room where you will deliver it.

What are you to do in the face of these reports, that good delivery influences audience comprehension positively but also that the influence of delivery on comprehension is overrated? What are you to do when one study reports that poor vocal characteristics reveal a poor speaker and another states that good content can mask poor delivery? Until more evidence is available, the safest position for you as a public speaking student is to regard both delivery and content as important. What you say and how you say it are both important—and probably in that order.

A student confessed to one of the authors that he had disobeyed instructions. Told to write a brief outline from which to deliver the speech, the student instead was afraid to speak in front of the class without every word written out. He practiced the speech by reading the whole manuscript word for word. After rehearsing the speech many times, he wrote the entire speech in microprint on note cards so it would appear to be delivered from a brief outline on the cards. However, as he began his speech he found that he couldn't read the tiny print on his cards, so he delivered the entire speech without using the cards at all. All the practice had helped him; the micro-manuscript had not.

To help you perfect your own delivery, you might want to follow these steps that many students find useful.

Perfecting Your Delivery

1. Start with a detailed working outline that includes the introduction, the body, and the conclusion. Remember to include all main points and supporting materials.

2. Distill the working outline into a speaking outline that simply includes reminders of what you intend to include in your speech.
3. Practice your speech alone first, preferably in front of a mirror so you will notice how much or how little you use your notes. Ideally, eighty to ninety percent or more of your speech should be delivered without looking at notes.
4. Next practice your speech in front of your roommate, your spouse, your kids, or anyone else who will listen. Try again to maintain eye contact as much as possible. After the speech ask your observer if he or she understood your message—and seek his or her advice for improving the speech.
5. Practice your speech with minimal notes in an empty classroom or some similar place that gets you accustomed to the size and situation. Focus on some of the more sophisticated aspects of delivery like facial expression, vocal variety, gestures, and movement.
6. If possible, watch a video tape of your own performance for feedback. If practice does not make perfect, at least it will make you confident. You will become so familiar with the content of your speech that you will focus more on communicating it to your audience.

A common error among beginning speakers is that they finish composing their speech late the night before delivery, leaving no time for practice. The most beautifully written speech can be a delivery disaster, so protect yourself by leaving time for three to five practice sessions. Then you will be self-assured, and your delivery will show that confidence.

Summary

This chapter on delivery began with four modes of delivery: extemporaneous, manuscript, impromptu, and memorized mode. The mode of delivery that most speech professors prefer for classroom instruction is the extemporaneous mode, which allows for minimal use of notes but invites spontaneity and maximum focus on message and audience.

Next we reviewed the vocal aspects of delivery: pitch, rate, pauses, volume, enunciation, and fluency. These characteristics of the voice need to be orchestrated by the speaker into a symphony of sound and movement that sounds attractive to the audience. Monotony and unintentional vocal blunders like the dreaded vocalized pause are the enemies of good delivery.

Nonverbal aspects of delivery was the third section in this chapter. It examined gestures, facial expression—including smiling, eye contact, and movement. The key to this art is naturalness, sincerity, and sensitive responsiveness to the audience. You learn to look and move in ways that you find comfortable and that the audience finds inviting.

Finally, we concluded with some ideas about perfecting your delivery. Starting with a script of your speech or preferably a sentence outline, you move with practice toward fewer and fewer notes and more and more attention to your audience. The key word is practice. Too much practice can turn your extemporaneous speech into a memorized one, but too little can turn your well-composed speech into a comedy of errors. Allowing time to practice your speech is about as tough as finding a topic in a reasonable amount of time, but those who practice usually receive the best evaluations.

▼▼

1
Selecting a Mode of Delivery

Examine each of the topics, audiences, and situations here and indicate which mode of delivery would be best by placing the appropriate letter in the blank on the left.

A = Manuscript mode, B = Extemporaneous mode,
C = Impromptu mode, D = Memorized mode.

_____ 1. You have to answer questions from the class at the conclusion of your speech.

_____ 2. You have to describe the student government's new statement of policy on student rights to a group of high-level administrators.

_____ 3. You have to deliver the same speech about student life at your college three times per week to incoming students.

_____ 4. You have to give parents a "walking tour" of the campus, including information about the buildings, the history of the college, and the background of significant places on campus.

_____ 5. You have to go door-to-door demonstrating and explaining a vacuum cleaner and its attachments that you are selling.

2
Bodily Aspects of Delivery

Observe a talented public speaker—a visiting lecturer, a political speaker, a sales manager—and study his or her gestures, facial expressions, eye contact, and movement. Then answer the following questions.

1. Do the speaker's gestures reinforce the important points in the speech?
2. Does the speaker's facial expression reflect the message and show concern for the audience and the topic?
3. Does the speaker maintain eye contact with the audience, respond to the audience's reactions, and keep himself or herself from becoming immersed in the manuscript, outline, or notes?

4. Does the speaker's movement reflect the organization of the speech and the important points in it?

5. Are the speaker's gestures, facial expressions, and movements consistent with the occasion, the personality of the speaker, and the message being communicated?

3
Evaluating Your Delivery

For your next speech, have a classmate, friend, or relative observe and evaluate your speech for delivery skills. Have your critic use this scale to fill in the blanks on the left.

1 = Excellent, 2 = Good, 3 = Average, 4 = Fair, 5 = Weak

Vocal Aspects of Delivery

_____ Pitch: highness and lowness of voice; upward and downward inflections

_____ Rate: words per minute; appropriate variation of rate for the difficulty of content

_____ Pause: intentional silence designed to aid understanding at appropriate places

_____ Volume: loud enough to hear; variation with the content

_____ Enunciation: correct pronunciation and articulation

_____ Fluency: smoothness of delivery; lack of vocalized pauses; good pacing, rhythm, and cadence without being so smooth as to sound artificial, contrived, or overly glib

Nonverbal Aspects of Delivery

_____ Gestures: natural movement of the head, hands, arms, and torso consistent with the speaker, topic, and situation

_____ Facial expression and smiling behavior: consistent with message; used to relate to the audience; appropriate for audience and situation

_____ Eye contact: natural, steady without staring, includes entire audience, and is responsive to audience feedback

_____ Movement: purposeful, used to indicate organization, natural, without anxiety, use at podium and distance from audience

▼▼▼

Application Assignment

Practicing Delivery Through Oral Interpretation

Select a poem, play, short story, or speech that will provide you with three to five minutes of content so you can focus on the delivery of your selection. As with your other speeches, this one should be practiced until you can deliver it without heavy dependence on your notes. Introduce your selection and deliver it. Have the teacher and audience say what aspects of delivery were best performed in your speech.

articulation A vocal aspect of delivery, indicating the effective production of sound. See *enunciation*.

enunciation A vocal aspect of delivery that involves the pronunciation and articulation of words; pronouncing correctly and producing the sounds clearly so that the language is understandable.

extemporaneous mode Delivery in which the speaker proceeds through careful preparation and practice to deliver a speech that appears spontaneous and conversational. This mode is characterized by maximum eye contact and minimal use of notes.

eye contact A bodily aspect of delivery that involves the speaker's looking directly at the audience in order to monitor their responses to the message. In public speaking, eye contact is an asset because it permits the speaker to adapt to audience responses and to assess the effects of the message.

facial expression A bodily aspect of delivery that involves the use of eyes, eyebrows, and mouth to express feelings about the message, the audience, and the occasion. Smiles, frowns, grimaces, and winces can help a speaker communicate feelings.

fluency A vocal aspect of delivery that involves the smooth flow of words and the absence of vocalized pauses.

gestures A bodily aspect of delivery that involves movement of head, hands, and arms, to indicate emphasis, commitment, and other feelings about the topic, the audience, and the occasion.

impromptu mode Delivery in which the speaker talks spontaneously without special preparation. Question-and-answer sessions after a speech follow this mode of delivery because the speaker has to address answers to questions that may not have been anticipated.

manuscript mode Delivery in which the speaker writes out every word of the speech and reads the speech to the audience with as much eye contact as possible; appropriate in situations where exact wording is very important.

memorized mode Delivery in which the speaker commits the entire manuscript of the speech to memory, either by rote or repetition; appropriate in situations where the same speech is given over and over to different audiences.

movement A bodily aspect of delivery that refers to a speaker's locomotion in front of an audience; can be used to signal the development and organization of the message.

pause An intentional silence used to draw attention to the words before or after the interlude; a break in the flow of words for effect.

pitch A vocal aspect of delivery that refers to the highness or lowness, upward and downward inflections of the voice.

rate A vocal aspect of delivery that refers to the speed of delivery, the number of words spoken per minute; normal rates range from 125 to 190 words per minute.

vocalized pause A nonfluency in delivery characterized by sounds like ''Uhhh,'' ''Ahhh,'' or ''Mmmm'' or the repetitious use of expressions like ''O.K.,'' ''Like,'' or ''For sure'' to fill silence with sound; often used by speakers who are nervous or inarticulate.

volume A vocal characteristic of delivery that refers to the loudness or softness of the voice. Public speakers often project or speak louder than normal so that distant listeners can hear the message. Beginning speakers frequently forget to project enough volume.

Endnotes

1. Roger Ailes, *You are the Message: Secrets of the Master Communicators* (Homewood, Ill.: Dow Jones-Irwin, 1988), 20.
2. Ralph Waldo Emerson, "Power" in *The Conduct of Life, Nature, and Other Essays* (Dutton, 1860).
3. Herbert W. Hildebrandt and Walter Stevens, "Manuscript and Extemporaneous Delivery in Communicating Information," *Speech Monographs* 30 (1963):369–72.
4. Otis M. Walter and Robert L. Scott, *Thinking and Speaking* (New York: Macmillan, 1969), 124–33.
5. Norman Miller et al., "Speed of Speech and Persuasion," *Journal of Personality and Social Psychology* 34 (1976):615–24.
6. Charles F. Diehl, Richard C. White, and Kenneth W. Burk, "Rate and Communication," *Speech Monographs* 26 (1959):229–32.
7. *Webster's New World Dictionary of the American Language—College Edition* (New York: The World Publishing Company, 1957), 386–87.
8. Donald Hayworth, "A Search for Facts on the Teaching of Public Speaking," *Quarterly Journal of Speech* 28 (1942):247–54.
9. Edward J. J. Kramer and Thomas R. Lewis, "Comparison of Visual and Nonvisual Listening," *Journal of Communication* 1 (1951):16–20.
10. Robert Rosenthal et al., "Body Talk and Tone of Voice: The Language Without Words," *Psychology Today* 8 (1974):64–68.
11. *Nonverbal Interaction,* Adam Kendon, "Gesture and Speech: How They Interact," John M. Wiemann and Randall P. Harrison, eds., vol. II of *Sage Annual Reviews of Communication Research* (Beverly Hills, Calif.: Sage Publications, 1983), 13.
12. Socrates, Xenophon, *Memorabilia III* in *Nonverbal Communication: Readings with Commentary,* Shirley Weitz, ed. (New York: Oxford University Press, 1974), vii.
13. Paul Ekman, "Pan-cultural Elements in Facial Displays of Emotion," *Science* 164 (1969):86–88.

14. Paul Ekman and Wallace V. Friesen, "Head and Body Cues in the Judgment of Emotion: A Reformulation," *Perceptual and Motor Skills,* 24 (1967):711–24.
15. Judy Cornelia Pearson, *Gender and Communication* (Dubuque, Ia.: Wm. C. Brown Publishers, 1985), 250.
16. Pearson, p. 249.
17. Martin Cobin, "Response to Eye-Contact," *Quarterly Journal of Speech* 48 (1962):415–18.
18. Steven A. Beebe, "Eye Contact: A Nonverbal Determinant of Speaker Credibility," *Speech Teacher* 23 (1974):21–25.
19. Virginia P. Richmond, James C. McCroskey, and Stephen K. Payne, *Nonverbal Behavior in Interpersonal Relations* (Englewood Cliffs, N.J.: Prentice-Hall, Inc., 1987), 82–83.
20. Erwin Bettinghaus, "The Operation of Congruity in an Oral Communication Situation," *Speech Monographs* 28 (1961):131–42.
21. Ernest H. Henrikson, "An Analysis of the Characteristics of Some 'Good' and 'Poor' Speakers," *Speech Monographs* 11 (1944):120–24.
22. Howard Gilkinson and Franklin H. Knower, "Individual Differences Among Students of Speech as Revealed by Psychological Tests—I," *Journal of Educational Psychology* 32 (1941):161–75.
23. John L. Vohs, "An Empirical Approach to the Concept of Attention," *Speech Monographs* 31 (1964):355–60.
24. Henrikson, pp. 120–24.
25. Ronald J. Hard and Bruce L. Brown, "Interpersonal Information Conveyed by the Content and Vocal Aspects of Speech," *Speech Monographs* 41 (1974):371–80.
26. D. F. Gundersen and Robert Hopper, "Relationships between Speech Delivery and Speech Effectiveness," *Speech Monographs* 43 (1976):158–65.
27. Charles R. Petrie, Jr., "Informative Speaking: A Summary and Bibliography of Related Research," *Speech Monographs* 30 (1963):81.

Presentational Aids

12

Question Outline

I. Why should you use presentational aids?

II. When should you use presentational aids?

III. What should you avoid in using presentational aids?

IV. How can you relate your visual aids to your topic, situation, and audience?

V. What is the relationship between your presentational aids and your message?

Light hath no tongue,

but is all eye.

JOHN DONNE

Introduction

"A picture is worth a thousand words." This old saying is true for the public speaker who finds that presentational aids can save words and clarify messages.

We live in a highly visual world. In the late 1980s people watched television six hours and more per day. Computers can produce bar graphs, pie charts, and pictures faster than people can absorb them. In this visual world, the role of presentational aids in public speeches has developed into a fine art.

You will not be able to speak with confidence until you learn how to use presentational aids to communicate your message to an audience. This chapter will present the fundamentals of the art.

Why Use Presentational Aids?

Presentational aids are an economical way to supplement and clarify your message. They should not be seen as a replacement for your speech but as an important helper in communicating a message to an audience. Also, presentational aids arouse your audience's interest in your speech and make it memorable.

The speaker began the body of her speech with an enlarged photograph she had obtained from a local insurance company. The presence of flashlights and car lights indicated that the picture had been taken at night. The picture showed shoes. The shoes were spread across the road and in the ditch as if boxes of them had fallen off a truck. They were the shoes of teenagers. Thirteen high school seniors had died in a head-on, two-car crash near the city limits. The impact of the two speeding cars had knocked the shoes off most of the victims and had blasted them across the road and into the ditch.

The speaker was discussing the unusually high number of car accidents among our youth. Her photo showed no mangled wreckage, no blood, and no bodies. The shoes told the story.

Presentational aids are not only economical, they are often clearer than words alone. The public speaker trying to show how our financial situation has changed over a five-year period could use hundreds of words and many minutes explaining the effects of inflation, but a bar graph could show it more clearly in a couple of minutes.

Pictures, graphs, charts, and maps are often more interesting to an audience than words. The newspaper *USA Today* was the subject of jokes when it was first published. Cynics called it "McNews" and said that it would win a Pulitzer prize for the most outstanding paragraph. But *USA Today* revolutionized the newspaper business by illustrating the importance of graphics—pictures, drawings, maps, and color. The editors who thought the paper was superficial and simple found themselves scrambling to improve their own graphics. People found the highly visual newspaper more interesting than columns of print. Live audiences, too, find graphics interesting.

Finally, audiences find visualization memorable. We learn much of what we know through sight. According to Elena P. Zayas-Baya in the *International Journal of Instructional Media*,[1] we learn

1% through taste	11% through hearing, and
1.5% through touch	83% through sight
3.5% through smell	

The effect of our senses on memory is equally dramatic. You are likely to remember

10% of what you read	50% of what you see and hear
20% of what you hear	80% of what you say, and
30% of what you see	90% of what you say and do

This chart illustrates how much you are likely to retain.

	3 hours later	3 days later
Telling alone	70%	10%
Showing alone	72%	20%
Showing and telling	85%	65%

Seeing is an important component of learning and retaining information. That is exactly what you are trying to do with presentational aids—helping the audience to see what you are talking about, economically, clearly, interestingly, and memorably.

Some experimental studies support the use of presentational aids. In one study university students were exposed to a series of words and/or pictures and were tested on their ability to recall what they had seen. When the students were exposed to two stimuli at a time (i.e., sound plus pictures or printed word plus line drawings), they remembered better than they did with just one stimulus.[2] Another study demonstrated that two-dimensional objects, simple figures against a background, were better remembered when they moved than when they stood still.[3]

A third study used male and female subjects from junior high to college age and tested them for audio and visual cues. The experimenters determined that these audiences were more influenced by what they saw than by what they heard.[4] For the public speaker, the message is clear: presentational aids reinforce your message and will probably be the part of your speech that the audience remembers.

Six questions to ask yourself before using presentational aids are:

1. What is the composition of my audience?
2. What is the occasion?
3. What is the setting?
4. What is the message?
5. What is the cost?
6. What are the rules?

Your answers to these questions will help you decide if, what kind, and how many presentational aids are appropriate for your speech.

Audience

What is the composition of my audience? This question considers the age, education, status, and reason for attending your speech. In other words, the question considers audience analysis as examined in chapter 4.

The younger your audience, the more necessary presentational aids become. Preschool and elementary children are captivated by visual aids. That is why elementary teachers have to learn how to use them daily.

People who have had little formal education may be more dependent on graphic illustrations, while highly educated people are more accustomed to interpreting what they hear. Regardless of educational level, some materials like statistics, mathematical formulas, and weather maps are very difficult to comprehend without accompanying visuals.

High-status people have to be treated carefully lest they feel that the speaker is "talking down" to them with a visual presentation, but boards of directors, developers, and fund raisers find that architects, lawyers, and investors often use visual displays to influence their decisions.

If the audience must learn something from the speaker, then presentational aids usually come into play. So informative speeches to most groups invite the use of visuals for clarification and understanding. If the audience is expecting to be entertained, then the need for aids may be less imperative.

Occasion

What is the occasion? Ceremonial occasions often call for decoration—political bunting, ribbons, flags, etc.—but not often for presentational aids. Similarly, rituals like funerals, baptisms, or bar mitzvahs call more for decoration than for presentational aids. Even evangelists and most visiting lecturers depend more on words than on visuals. But some occasions cry for presentational aids.

Instruction is an occasion that practically demands presentational aids, whether it is elementary school, high school, college, or a place of business. Where the purpose is pedagogical and the idea is to impart knowledge to a group, the need for presentational aids is high.

Persuasive situations, too, invite presentational aids. When the military tries to make a case for more funding, Congress is treated to graphs, charts, pictures, and even the very objects of defense. When a speaker is trying to convince an audience to stop drinking, start exercising, and continue eating appropriately, that speaker usually tries to persuade the audience with facts and figures presented visually. In short, the very kinds of speeches that predominate in the classroom—informative and persuasive speeches—are the very ones that need visual reinforcement if the audience is to understand and remember the message.

What is the setting? The place where the speech is to occur helps determine if Setting and what kind of presentational aids should be used. The size and shape of the room can forbid their use or make them appropriate. Huge rooms demand specialized gear: large screens, projectors, amplifiers, and light. Small rooms—like classrooms—are appropriate for a wide variety of presentational aids.

A classroom, lecture hall, or conference room is usually designed for visual display; they usually come equipped with a viewing screen, chalkboard, and places to put posters. A church sanctuary, a lounge, or a private office may be ill equipped for visual presentation. You have to decide what is possible to do in the particular setting in which your speech is to occur.

The setting should not be seen as an absolute limitation. One speech communication professor tells of the student who said his visual aid was too large for the classroom. The student had designed a mini-car with award-winning mileage. Larger than a midget racer, the mini-car required a site out-of-doors. The teacher made an exception by permitting the speech to be delivered outside on the building patio, with the audience attending. After an inspiring speech about the mini-car, the speaker jumped into his self-designed auto and drove off. Speakers can—with permission—alter the setting for their presentational aid.

What is the message? Some messages are so simple or so compelling that pre- Message sentational aids are superfluous, but most messages have parts that are tough to comprehend without some visual assistance. The complexity of the material is the main variable that determines the appropriateness of presentational aids: the more complex or difficult to understand verbally, the more necessary the presentational aids.

Most quotations, narrations, and case studies do not demand visual reinforcement; most messages about economic changes over time, statistical trends, series of dates, financial reports, sales records, and weather predictions do demand visual reinforcement. You have to exercise the interpersonal skill of empathy: what parts of your speech will be better understood by the audience if they are presented visually or with an audio tape?

What is the cost? Poster board is cheap, film is more expensive, and video tape Cost or quadraphonic sound in the classroom could be prohibitively expensive. Expense has to do with both time and money: few students have the time to make and develop slides, film, or video. Fortunately, the chalkboard, flip-charts, posters, physical objects, and handouts—the most common presentational aids of all—are neither very expensive nor very time-consuming. You have to consider how much time and money you can afford to spend on your public speech.

Rules

What are the rules? When you are pondering the use of presentational aids, you should consider their safety and legality. Students often ask teachers about using drugs, drug paraphernalia, alcohol, guns, and fire in the classroom. Teachers tell of students pulling out a gun when talking about banning handguns or about a student who brought a flaming wastebasket into the room to talk about the effectiveness of various fire extinguishers.

You should use your imagination and creativity when you plan your speech, but you need to consider also the safety and legality of your speech. If you have any doubt about the safety or legality of something you plan for your speech, check first with your teacher.

Now that you know some of the broad questions to ask about your presentational aids, or PAs as the students call them, you are ready to consider some of the types of PAs available for your use in a public speech.

Types of Presentational Aids

There are many kinds of presentational aids, but you will be able to use them easier if you think of them in categories.[5] We begin with the kinds of visual aids used the most—graphics—and move through display boards and equipment to persons and things—which are used less often in public speeches.

Graphics

Graphics include photographs; pie, line, and bar graphs; drawings; charts; and maps. All of these are in the public speaker's repertoire.

Photographs

Photographs are useful in a public speech if they are large enough for the audience to see. A student from the Philippines gave a speech about her native land accompanied by large travel posters borrowed from a travel agency. The large pictures of the beaches, the city of Manila, and the countryside reinforced what she told the audience about her country.

Avoid passing snapshots or small pictures because the audience will not be listening to your speech. Instead, use large pictures, as the student did who showed a large satellite photograph of the region, with circles drawn to indicate how far various AM, FM, and TV signals would carry. Any picture that needs to be passed is too small for use in a public speech.

Graphs

Graphs are of three types—pie, line, and bar. The pie graph looks like a pie cut in slices. The entire pie equals 100% and each slice equals some smaller percentage. Although some people have difficulty determining percentages by looking at a pie graph, your pie graph will serve you well if everyone can see it, if it is divided into fewer than six slices, and if the parts are clearly labeled.

The pie graph in figure 12.1 indicates the percentage by age group of the nearly ten thousand shoplifters who were caught in one year.

The second type of graph is the line graph. The advantage of a line graph is that it can be quite exact. The disadvantage is that audiences often have difficulty reading and interpreting the vertical and horizontal information. They can see

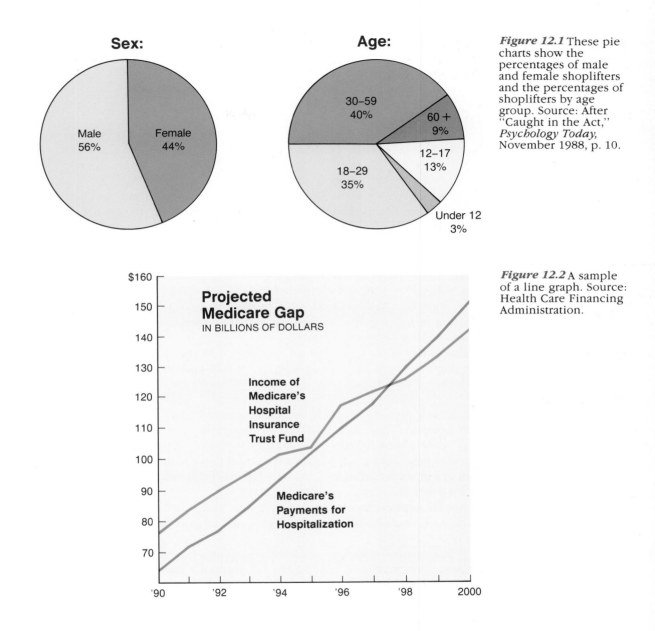

Sex:

Male 56%
Female 44%

Age:

30–59 40%
60 + 9%
12–17 13%
18–29 35%
Under 12 3%

Figure 12.1 These pie charts show the percentages of male and female shoplifters and the percentages of shoplifters by age group. Source: After "Caught in the Act," *Psychology Today,* November 1988, p. 10.

Projected Medicare Gap
IN BILLIONS OF DOLLARS

Income of Medicare's Hospital Insurance Trust Fund

Medicare's Payments for Hospitalization

$160
150
140
130
120
110
100
90
80
70

'90   '92   '94   '96   '98   2000

Figure 12.2 A sample of a line graph. Source: Health Care Financing Administration.

the lines but they do not have the slightest notion of what they mean. The speaker usually has to help an audience interpret a line graph.

Even on the line graph in figure 12.2, the message may not be clear from the data, that in the 1990s Medicare's payments will exceed the trust fund designed to pay them.

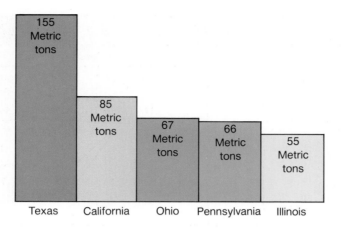

Figure 12.3 This bar graph shows the states with the highest carbon emission rates measured in metric tons. Source: After "USA Snapshots: A Look at Statistics that Shape the Nation," *USA Today,* December 20, 1988, p. 1A.

The third type of graph is the bar graph. The advantage of the bar graph is that it is easy to read and comprehend; the disadvantage is that it is not a very exact measure. Audiences do seem to have an easy time understanding the meaning of a bar graph, so their use in public speeches is encouraged. For a traditional bar graph see figure 12.3.

Regardless of the type of graph you employ in your speech, the pie, line, or bar graph needs to be large enough for the audience to see everything on the visual aid, including any print that explains the pie, the lines, or the bars.

Charts and Tables

A chart is a presentational aid that summarizes information, lists steps, or otherwise displays information difficult to convey orally. For example, you might want your audience to know the emergency numbers to call in your area for police, fire, rape crisis, abuse, etc. A chart is an easier way to display that information than to announce it. Similarly a chart showing the names and prices of personal computers is easier to comprehend in print.

A table usually consists of columns of numbers. A table of numbers is particularly useful because columns of numbers are nearly impossible to communicate orally.

When composing a chart or table, be careful not to overload the chart with too much information. Table 12.1 is an example of a chart that overwhelms the audience with information. Table 12.2 is a simplified version of some of the same information, written in a more digestible form.

Reprinted with permission by the American Council on Education.

Table 12.1 University presidents' prior positions by type of institution

| | Prior Position | | | | | | | | | | | | | | | |
| | President | | V.P.[1] | | Dean/ Director[2] | | Faculty/ Chair | | K–12 | | Outside Academe | | Other | | No Response | |
	No.	%	No.	%	No.	%	No.	%	No.	%	No.	%	No.	%	No.	%
All Presidents (n = 2,105)	361	17.2	880	41.8	390	18.5	169	8.0	48	2.3	136	6.5	110	5.2	11	.5
Doctorate-granting (n = 164)	51	31.1	60	36.6	26	15.9	7	4.3	—	—	8	4.9	11	6.7	1	.6
Comprehensive (n = 359)	67	18.7	166	46.2	51	14.2	23	6.4	7	2.0	22	6.1	21	5.9	2	.6
Baccalaureate (n = 553)	77	13.9	233	42.1	99	17.9	60	10.8	8	1.5	41	7.4	34	6.1	1	.2
Specialized (n = 228)	30	13.2	56	24.5	55	24.1	38	16.7	—	—	37	16.2	9	3.9	3	1.3
Two-year (n = 801)	136	17.0	365	45.6	159	19.9	41	5.1	33	4.1	28	3.4	35	4.4	4	.5

[1]Includes Senior or Executive Vice President, Vice President for Academic Affairs, other Vice President, Assistant or Associate Vice President
[2]Includes Dean, Director, Assistant/Associate Dean, Director of Student Services

Table 12.2 Table of numbers simplified from 12.1 for easier audience understanding.

What job did university presidents have before?

Type of School	Were Presidents Before	Were Vice Pres. Before	Were Deans Before
All Presidents	17%	42%	19%
4-Year College	14%	42%	11%
2-Year College	17%	46%	20%

Instead of explaining every number to an audience, you should help them interpret the data. For example, with table 12.2 you could point out that most college presidents were vice presidents or were already presidents of other colleges when they assumed the presidency. Actually, the most interesting information is not on the chart: ninety percent of male presidents are married; only slightly more than one-third of all women presidents are married. Said the author: ". . . the overwhelming majority of college presidents are white, male, married, and in their early fifties."[6]

Figure 12.4 This drawing made this speaker's poster more attractive to the audience.

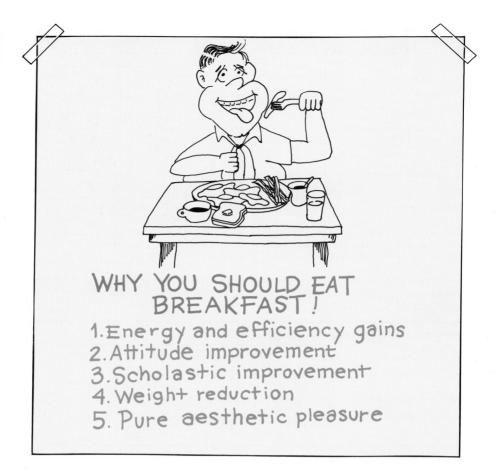

Drawings

Public speakers can use illustrations prepared by themselves or others. One woman who was a talented artist presented her speech on the various species of ducks. Each specie was illustrated by a large colored drawing. She did not say that she had drawn them herself until the question-and-answer session. Nonetheless, her classmates were suitably impressed with her speech and her artistry.

The main things to remember about drawings and illustrations are: they must be relevant to the message; they must add something to the speech that cannot be provided by language alone; and they must be large enough for all to see.

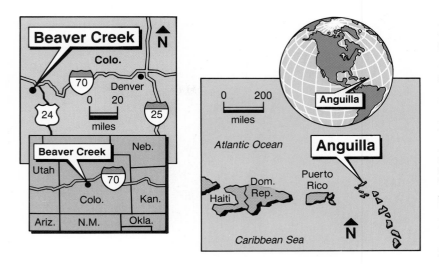

Maps

Some informative speeches tell an audience about locations that are difficult to specify without a map. Some informative speeches encourage students to write to legislators, but the audience does not know who their legislator is without the name and a legislative map. As long as your map is large and the lines are clear, it can be useful in your public speech.

You have now seen the appropriate use of photographs; pie, line, and bar graphs; charts and tables; drawings; and maps. In order to review all that you have learned about kinds of presentational aids and types of graphics, you are invited to use the checklist at the end of this chapter.

Display Boards

Three kinds of display boards are commonly used by public speakers: chalk or slickboards, posters, and flip-charts. Let us examine them systematically and consider the possibilities of each.

Chalkboards or Slickboards

In most classrooms, the chalkboard is the most available presentational aid. It is good for stating your name and the title of your speech, for keeping the audience's attention on the main points of your speech, for spelling out difficult words, and for showing simple drawings. The advantage is that you can use a blackboard or slickboard spontaneously if you wish; the disadvantage is that, to use them effectively it is necessary to turn your back on your audience.

The main difficulty faced by speakers who try to write on the board is that their writing cannot be read. If you expect your audience to be able to read what you write, you have to write legibly:

1. Use print instead of cursive writing.
2. Use bold, block letters.
3. Use chalk that shows well on the board (white or yellow on green or black boards).
4. Use lettering that is 2" high and ¼" wide for every 25 feet of viewing distance.

Another useful suggestion is to use a pointer when talking about items on the board so you do not have to turn your back on the audience.

A slickboard is uncommon in the classroom, but relatively common in conference rooms. It is like a blackboard except that it has a slick white or light-colored surface that accepts water markers of many colors.

Both slickboards and chalkboards are good for diagrams, definitions, outlines, brief reviews, a line or two of poetry, and mathematical problems or formulas. Both can make your speech seem too pedagogical, too much like a classroom lecture instead of an extemporaneous speech.

Avoid writing on the board during your speech by writing your message before class. If you do not want your classmates to see your written message until you speak, then cover it with a sheet of newspaper. If you have any doubts about your teacher's attitude concerning the use of the board, check with the teacher.

Figure 12.7 A poster showing calories burned in different activities.

The handwritten poster reads:

ITEM	CAL/HR.
Skiing downhill	530
Skiing x/country	625
Tennis - singles	380
Tennis - doubles	270
Ice skating	390
Mountain climbing	650
Racquetball	600
Bicycle riding	500
Walking	260
Jogging	450
Horse riding	360
Dancing (continuous)	225
Sitting	75

Posters

Posters overcome many of the disadvantages of the presentational aids listed so far. Because they must be prepared ahead of time, they can be designed for easy viewing. Because they are made of heavy, high-grade paper, a black magic marker can produce a highly visible message. And because they are prewritten, the speaker need not turn his or her back on the audience when the poster is being discussed.

A student giving a speech on child abuse used posters to highlight his message. He had five main points and five posters, each displaying a true or false question. He placed all five posters on the chalk tray and introduced the speech by asking his audience to answer the questions.

Most abused children come from poor families. True   False

Most children are abused by their own mothers. True   False

Most people now in prison were abused as children. True   False

And so on. The audience was uncertain of the correct answers, but their curiosity was aroused. The speaker used each of the questions as a main point in the speech. The posters eliminated the speaker's need for notes—they were on the posters.

Some suggestions for using posters might help you use them effectively:

1. Keep your message simple. The audience should be able to quickly grasp what you are illustrating.
2. Make sure the poster and the print are large enough for everyone to see (remember, the teacher usually sits in the back of the room).
3. Use clips or masking tape to keep the poster up while you are referring to it. Avoid the embarrassment of having to pick up your poster off the floor, or having it curl off the wall.

Look at the posters in figures 12.7 and 12.8 for some ideas.

Figure 12.8 A poster showing the main points of a speech on rappeling.

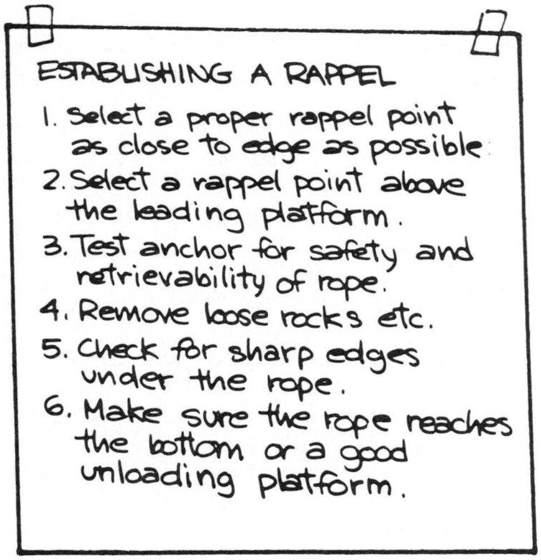

Whether you choose to use chalk- or slickboards, posters, or flip-charts, remember that their purpose is to reinforce your message, not to be used for their own sake.

Flip-Charts

A flip-chart is a large pad of paper, usually on a stand, that allows the speaker to flip the sheets over or tear them off as they are used. Colored pens may be used on this medium as long as they do not soak through to the next sheet.

Flip-charts are frequently used in business presentations to give structure, define, explain, or gather ideas. In a brainstorming situation, for example, the ideas can be listed on the page, torn off, and stuck to the wall or board with masking tape for later review or evaluation.

A flip-chart can have some material already printed on the page, but the advantage to the flip-chart is that it allows spontaneity. The flip-chart shares some of the disadvantages of the chalk- or slickboard in that the speaker usually has to turn his or her back to the audience in order to write, and the speaker must write legibly in block print large enough for all in the room to see. Lettering must usually be at least 3″ high and the width of the broad edge of a magic marker.

Another advantage of the flip-chart is that it is portable and relatively inexpensive. Like a board, it can be used for definitions, difficult words, and simple drawings to illustrate or reinforce your message.

Next we will look at some presentational aids that demand specialized equipment.

Computer-Generated Graphics

With the personal computer and its sophisticated software has come the opportunity to make handouts, illustrations, transparencies, and slides from materials created on the video screen. Perhaps you have heard of "desktop publishing;" well, the capability you are examining here is called "desktop presentations."

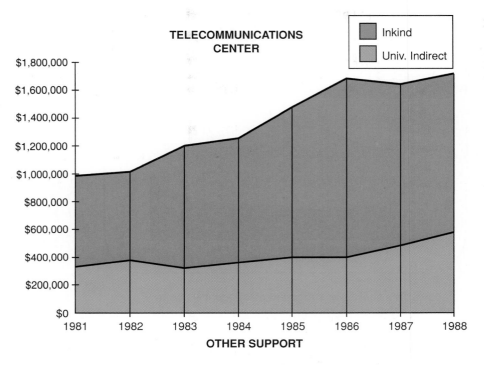

TELECOMMUNICATIONS CENTER

Legend:
- Inkind
- Univ. Indirect

Y-axis: $0, $200,000, $400,000, $600,000, $800,000, $1,000,000, $1,200,000, $1,400,000, $1,600,000, $1,800,000

X-axis: 1981, 1982, 1983, 1984, 1985, 1986, 1987, 1988

OTHER SUPPORT

Figure 12.9 This graph was created on a computer as a handout for a speech about public radio and TV revenue in the 1980s.[14]

An example is Microsoft.Powerpoint®, a software program used on a MacIntosh® Plus computer and a laser printer. This program created the graph in figure 12.9, an illustration used in a speech about where a public radio and television station received its revenue in the 1980s. The graphic was used as a handout in the speech. Meanwhile, the speaker used the graph and the four-part explanation in figure 12.10. The audience did not see the material in figure 12.10, but the computer program printed a reduced version of the graphic and a boldfaced printed list of explanations for the speaker.

For a very important presentation, you can convert computer-generated graphics into acetate transparencies for an overhead projector, slides for a slide presentation, or even 35-millimeter color strips for use with a projector. The MacIntosh Plus with PowerPoint can even be used by itself as a "slide show" operated either on a timed sequence or manually. The computer can show your visual creations just as a slide projector does except the audience sees the graphics on the video screen.[7]

Figure 12.10 This graph with explanations was used by the speaker to help him remember the handout and to remind him of the explanations. The entire page was computer-generated and laser-printed.

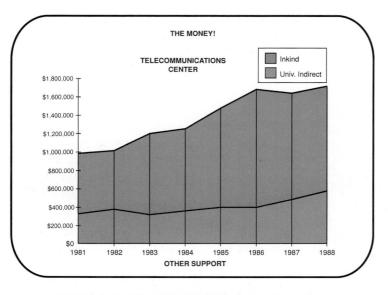

1. **This shows the support of other agencies both within the University and without.**

2. **The indirect support from the University includes things like physical plant activities, administrative support, etc. It's total value in 1988 was $584,558 - up 21% from 1987.**

3. **The inkind support of Center activities by other agencies includes services from OEB, ETS, the State Department of Education, etc. That support had a value of $1,113,961 in 1988 - down 2% from the prior year.**

4. **Together these support items added $1,698,519 to the strength of the Center.**

This section on display equipment begins with a warning. Do not use display equipment unless you know what you are doing. The types of equipment we are referring to are movies and slides, video tapes, audio amplification and recording equipment, and opaque and overhead projectors. Let us look at each in turn for their possibilities in your public speaking.

Great for demonstrating, illustrating, and clarifying, movies and slides have equally disastrous disadvantages: they tend to become the speech instead of serving as reinforcement, emphasis, or supplement. They reduce the spontaneity of an extemporaneous speech because they must be premade. Also, they require the use of a projector, an item that few people own and that must, therefore, be checked out of a media center or rented. In short, movies and slides are expensive.

Another problem with movies and slides is that they usually require a darkened room. A dark room hides the speaker and all the nonverbal cues that make public speaking effective. We tell about movies and slides here not because we think that every student should learn how to use them, but because we have seen them used effectively on rare occasions.

One student used a film very persuasively in a fifteen-minute speech on violence in football. The speaker was a varsity football player who showed only three minutes of punt returns in his speech, but used his own voice to explain what was happening. He showed how football players can disable a player who does not call for a safe catch. He told how the coaches taught them to hurt the opposing player with fists, face masks, and helmets. Notice that most of the speech consisted of violence in football, and that the brief bits of film were used simply to illustrate the truth of what he said.

Another student who used slides very effectively was a rough-and-tumble fellow who always wore a black leather jacket, jack boots, and lots of chrome studs. He was a biker. Imagine the audience's surprise when he gave a speech encouraging the use of safety helmets when riding a motorcycle. He dimmed the lights, but did not blacken the room, and showed five slides during his speech. Each slide had a badly battered helmet in vivid color. His speech on using helmets built a story around each battered helmet, because each person whose helmet was shown had lived through a serious accident only because of the helmet. It turned out that this tough-looking fellow taught motorcycle safety to teenagers on his own time.

Movies and slides as a presentational aid require skill in using the equipment. The speaker needs to practice on the same equipment that will be used in class and needs to be prepared to complete the speech without it if the projector bulb burns out, the film continues to slip, or the slides come out upside down.

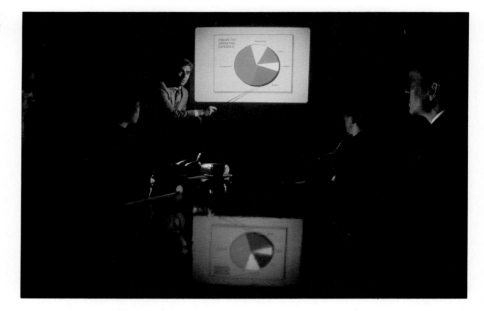

Some suggestions for the effective use of slides:

1. Limit yourself to one basic idea per slide and keep the message or picture short and simple.
2. Arrange your information with more width than height. A slide is one third wider than it is high.
3. Check for visibility of the screen and slides or movie in the room where the audience will do the viewing.
4. Check your slides and film to see if they work in the projector—before you use it in class.
5. If possible, use a remote slide changer, or with film, a helper, so you do not have to stay by the machine.
6. Practice with your visual aids in the same place where your speech will be delivered. You can avoid the problem faced by the student who practiced at home only to find out that the only electrical outlet in the classroom was out of order.

Slides and film can add dramatic impact and involvement to your speech, but think twice before using them if you are inexperienced. Also, whenever you use mechanical devices in your presentation, you should have a backup plan in case your devices should fail. The best public speakers are ready for anything—including a fast change of plans.

A student delivering a speech on TV advertising, more specifically on its use of women to sell products, used a videocassette and a video player to show the class some thirty-second examples to illustrate her point.

Video

VCRs, videocassette recorders, are becoming as common as radios and televisions in American homes. They can be used effectively in a speech, if they are used sparingly to illustrate, reinforce, or emphasize main points. They should be used when seeing something on video would get the point across better than trying to picture it with words.

Although it is possible to produce your own materials on videotape, the most common use of video in public speeches is using brief excerpts from television to illustrate your point. Nearly all material that appears on network and pay TV, as well as all rental videos, are protected by copyright. You are unlikely to be sued by a major network for showing thirty seconds of a copyrighted program because the courts have been relatively lenient about using materials for educational purposes. Nonetheless, you might want to check with your teacher to see about the use of video in your public speech.

The equipment necessary is a videotape and a VCR with a large monitor. The mechanics of effective use include:

1. Showing your video in below normal light, but not in complete darkness.
2. Adjusting the volume, contrast, and position before the presentation.
3. Centering the monitor in the front of the room for optimal viewing (maximum viewing distance is twelve times the diagonal width of the monitor, or 19 feet for a 19-inch diagonally measured screen).
4. Practicing with your equipment before your presentation.

Try to make your videotaped presentation as natural as possible by treating it as an integral part of your speech. Avoid a big buildup on the one hand or making excuses for your video on the other. And be prepared to substitute your own material in case of mechanical failure. When machines fail, you will still be expected to succeed.

Audio

Audio refers to what you hear. It can include both the projection of the natural voice with a microphone or the use of audiotape to play voice or music.

The microphone is rarely used in classroom speeches, but it is often used in speeches where the audience is larger than twenty-five, when the speech is delivered outside, or where the room is too large for unaided speaking.

Microphones are of two basic types. One type is attached to the lectern or podium. Another type can be carried with or without a cord so the speaker has freedom of movement. Both require that the speaker stay relatively close to the microphone itself to be heard.

If you have never used a microphone before, practice with one before you give your speech. One reason for rehearsal is that you are likely to be startled by the sound of your own voice. Just as your voice does not sound the same to you when you hear it recorded on tape, it will not sound like your own when it is amplified either. Being startled by the sound of your own voice can be distracting when you are trying to concentrate on your speech.

Another reason to practice before delivering a speech is to learn the appropriate distance to stay from the microphone. Broadcasters call it "popping the mike" when a speaker stands so close that plosive sounds like words beginning with k, p, and t blow too much air into the instrument. If you stay a distance of 12 inches away you are unlikely to "pop" the microphone. On the other hand, you do have to speak toward it because averting your head will cause your voice to fade or disappear.

Audio recorders are another form of audio equipment that is a useful presentational aid. In a speech about types of music, a few short excerpts can best illustrate what you mean in your informative speech differentiating among AOR (album-oriented radio), CHR (contemporary hits radio), and easy listening radio formats.

One of the effective uses of audio occurred when a student secured the tape of a sheriff questioning a suspected drug pusher. The part of the tape used began at the point where the young pusher's story fell apart, and he started to implicate himself and others. The minute and a half of tape was a dramatic illustration of what happens to drug pushers when they are caught. The confession was enough to make the audience glad they were not suspects.

The mechanical aspects of using tape recorders in a public speech include:

1. Setting the volume before the presentation so that all can hear.
2. Placing your tape so it will start exactly where you wish.
3. Having the machine turned on and warmed up before you speak.
4. Practicing several times with the tape to ensure that you can use it smoothly.

You might want to have someone else take care of turning the machine off and on, but if you exercise this option, practice the speech and the use of the recorder with that person until you establish complete trust in each other.

Some practical suggestions concerning the recorder's use during your speech include:

1. Avoid saying anything while the tape is playing: a "voice-over" is inappropriate in this case.
2. Integrate the taped portion into your speech so that it becomes a natural extension of your talk.
3. Avoid any big buildup or excuses.

If you observe these mechanical and delivery suggestions, you can make an audio recording an important supplement to your speech.

Have someone you trust help you with your equipment.

Overhead and Opaque Projectors

An overhead projector is a machine that shines through an acetate (clear plastic) sheet. Any images or letters drawn on the acetate with magic marker or grease pencil will be projected and enlarged on a white wall or movie screen.

The advantage of this device is that you can face the audience while you speak. The lights immediately over the screen should be dim, but otherwise the room can be bathed in normal light so the audience can see the speaker. The lettering or images can be prepared ahead of time (excellent idea) or drawn spontaneously during the speech (less desirable).

Some suggestions for using the overhead projector include:

1. Express one idea on each transparency. Otherwise the screen becomes too crowded with verbiage and too complex for easy understanding.
2. Compose lettering one inch high for every twenty-five feet of viewing because one inch letters will be considerably larger when projected on the screen.
3. Place most of your message toward the top of the transparency, and avoid using the bottom, since it tends to run off the screen.
4. Place your transparencies in hard paper frames and number them for ease of handling, or the sheets *may not* separate for you during your speech.
5. Practice using the overhead projector while you practice your speech until use of the transparencies becomes natural.

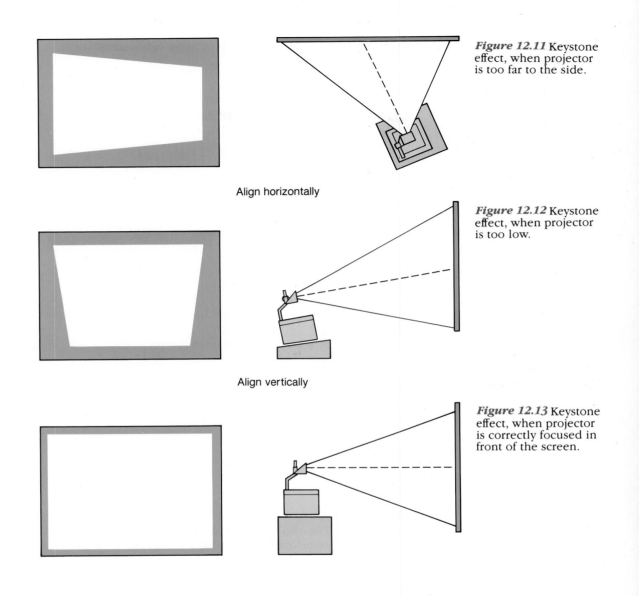

Align horizontally

Figure 12.11 Keystone effect, when projector is too far to the side.

Align vertically

Figure 12.12 Keystone effect, when projector is too low.

Figure 12.13 Keystone effect, when projector is correctly focused in front of the screen.

At first you may find that your projected light on the screen looks like the images in figures 12.11 and 12.12. In figure 12.11, the projector needs to be aligned horizontally until the keystone image becomes a rectangle; in figure 12.12, the projector needs to be aligned vertically. To completely avoid any keystone effect, the projector needs to be centered perpendicular to the screen like the arrangement in figure 12.13.

Some helpful hints about delivery when using an overhead projector include:

1. Talking a bit louder to compensate for the sound of the machine's fan.
2. Pointing with a pencil instead of your finger to eliminate any unwanted shadows.
3. Making sure that you have your transparencies numbered on your working outline and on the transparency frames to ensure that they are used in correct order during the speech.

Finally, you would be well advised to bring an extra bulb and more than one marker. Follow these suggestions and your use of the overhead projector can be an asset to your speech.

Two creative ways to use transparencies are the "reveal" method and the "overlay" method. The "reveal" method blocks out parts of the information on the transparency, and is then revealed as the speaker proceeds (fig. 12.14).

The "overlay" method allows you to use one transparency to make one point and a second transparency placed over the first to make another point. In figure 12.15, the speaker first shows a line graph in one color and then places the second over the first to illustrate how the situation changed during the same period of time the following year.

The opaque projector is an instrument that can project the image of small objects or the top surface of thick items like a magazine. Many of the suggestions for use of the overhead projector apply to the opaque projector as well: both have noisy fans requiring voice projection, both use screens and lights that can result in the keystone effect, and both require a practice session or two to ensure smooth and uninterrupted use.

Display Persons and Things

Another type of presentational aid used in public speaking is displays, using living models, objects, handouts, and even yourself.

Living Models

W. C. Fields once warned about performing on the same stage with a small child or an animal: they tend to steal the show away from the performer. Speakers should be aware of the same danger when they consider using persons or things as presentational aids: human "helpers" can catch the smell of grease paint and steal the show from you.

Charles Roberts, the chair of a communication department at McNeese State University in Louisiana, tells of a gentleman who gave a demonstration speech on body painting. When he completed his speech, few could remember his main points, but they certainly remembered the woman in the demonstration who stood there for ten minutes in her string bikini.

A living model is a person or persons used in your speech to illustrate an important point. A woman explaining the fine points of ballet found it impossible to deliver the speech and illustrate the moves herself. So she asked another ballet artist to show the audience what she was talking about as she described the moves.

Figure 12.14 The "reveal" method of using a transparency.

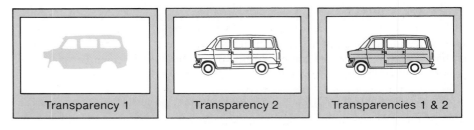

Figure 12.15 The "overlay" method used multiple transparencies to show layers or levels.

A person speaking about pumping iron, playing an instrument, or practicing first aid or lifesaving might similarly find a living model useful in a public speech.

Some suggestions for the use of living models include:

1. Selecting a person whom you know to assist you in the speech usually works better than selecting a volunteer from an unsuspecting audience.
2. Except when the living model is demonstrating something, he or she should sit down or otherwise move out of the audience's line of vision so the focus shifts to the speaker instead of dwelling on the living model.
3. The model who performs should be introduced, since their credibility will affect your own in the speech that you share.
4. Living models should be dressed appropriately for the topic, the audience, and the situation.

One of the author's vivid memories of a student speech included the thirty-second display of a living model. The speaker was a Big Eight varsity football player. The class thought he was a pretty large specimen at 6'2" and 220 pounds. The speech discussed how football was changing and that giants were being recruited into the game. At that point, in walked a first-year football player who was 6'11" and over 300 pounds. He stood there for thirty seconds while he was introduced and then lumbered back into the hall. The speaker had made his point with a living model.

Physical Objects

Another presentational aid is the use of physical objects in a public speech. The architecture student who is talking about house design might use miniature models large enough for the audience to see. The art student might show a few pieces of wood sculpture to show how wood can be hewn into marvelous shapes. And the physics student might demonstrate some laws of gravity and momentum by showing an audience how a pendulum swings.

Some suggestions about the use of physical objects include:

1. Selecting an object that can be seen by everyone.
2. Avoiding passing an object since that is a distraction from yourself and your speech.
3. Making the object an integral and natural part of your speech through your own practiced familiarity with it.
4. Addressing the audience instead of talking at or to the object being discussed.

When you consider using an object in your speech, be aware that the most common problems with physical objects is that they could be too small, too complicated, or too dangerous for classroom use.

The student who tried to give a speech on contact lenses found, to his dismay, that no one past the second row could see what he was showing. The student who tried to show all of the parts of a small engine became hopelessly confusing to her audience as she came to her fiftieth small part. And the students who come

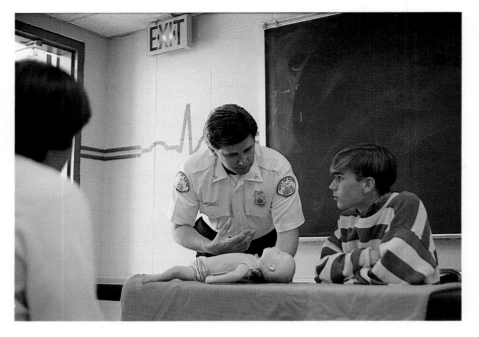

to class with fireworks, handguns, or even a bottle of liquor will find that they are either breaking a community or college ordinance or are so disturbing the audience that the speech is ineffective.

Before using any handouts, inquire about your professor's attitude toward them. Some speech communication teachers have a very negative attitude about handouts because they see them as a constant distraction, not only during the speaker's presentation but also for the speakers who follow.

Handouts

Handouts, if allowed, can be a useful supplement and can reinforce or show what the speaker means. Perhaps a person speaking about the danger signs of cancer could depend on the audience to take notes, but a more certain way to ensure that the audience has a record of the danger signs is to distribute them on a handout at the end of the speech. Maybe an audience could remember all of the radio stations, their call letters, and their position on the FM band, but a more definite way is to distribute a chart for future reference.

The distribution of handouts creates problems that you can cleverly avoid. What you want to avoid is wasting your speaking time by passing out papers;

having long rows of people passing, dropping, and rattling papers; having audience members fighting over too few copies; and producing the equivalent of "The Wave" as the papers ripple across the room. Some of the ways to avoid these problems include: (1) counting out the handouts by row ahead of time, (2) enlisting in advance the help of others so handouts can be distributed quickly, (3) having the audience pick up the handout after class, and (4) making sure that everyone has a handout.

Some suggestions for the effective use of handouts include:

1. Make your handouts simple so they do not have to be studied for understanding.
2. Type or print your handouts so they are readable.
3. Try to keep your handout to a single page so it is easy and quick to distribute.
4. Be certain that having your information in print is the most effective way to communicate that information to your audience.

By following these suggestions you can make sure that a handout is an effective means of communication.

Yourself

Whether you realize it or not, you are a presentational aid. The way you look, the way you dress, and the way you behave in front of the audience are part of your presentation. You are an important part of your message.

You do not have to dress up for every presentation unless that is an expectation in your class. Instead, dress in a manner appropriate to the topic and the audience. The person delivering a speech on how to interview for a job can reinforce the point by dressing the way a person should dress for an interview. The speaker demonstrating how to dissect a fetal pig ought to wear lab clothes. And the speaker talking about fashion should look like an authority on that subject.

The slovenly speaker is telling the audience how he feels about himself and about the audience. People who give public speeches often dress in a way that shows respect for the audience. Consider carefully how you fare as a presentational aid in your own public speech.

Summary: A Checklist for Presentational Aids

As a final step in critically evaluating your own use of visual aids and their use by others, ask yourself the following questions:

1. Have I used presentational aids to supplement and reinforce important points in my speech? Presentational aids should not be used for their own sake; instead, they should always be used for clarity, illustration, or explanation.
2. Have I been careful not to let my presentational aids dominate my speech so much so that they have become the speech? Do not become so infatuated with your living model, your charts and graphs, and your objects that they become your speech.

3. Have I prepared my presentational aids as much as possible in advance of the speech so I do not have to be absorbed in their use when I give my speech? Most presentational aids, especially the printed, taped, and projected ones should be ready before you give the speech.
4. Have I made my presentational aids big, loud, and central enough for everyone to see or hear? A presentational aid can detract from your speech if it becomes a deterrent to effective communication.
5. Have I explained my presentational aid so the audience knows its message and its purpose? Presentational aids rarely explain themselves, so the speaker is expected to reveal their role in the speech.
6. Have I avoided passing my presentational aid? Passing handouts may be permissible, but objects and pictures will detract from your speech if passed during the presentation.
7. Have I practiced with my equipment, my living model, and my other presentational aids so that they are smoothly integrated into my speech?
8. Have I spent a reasonable amount of time preparing my presentational aids? Too little preparation can result in chaos; too much can keep you from other important aspects of your public speech.

Armed with the information in this chapter, you are ready to use presentational aids in an intelligent and effective manner. You will find, as others have, that practice in using presentational aids will help you speak with confidence.

▼▼

Application Exercises

1
Proper Topics for Presentational Aids

Either individually or in a small group compose a list of ten topics that require audio or visual presentational aids. For example, a speech on the topic of "Comparative Shopping for Certificates of Deposit" demands interest rate figures, time periods, and figures from various banking or lending institutions.

2
Proper Presentational Aids for Topics

After completing Application Exercise 1 you will have a list of ten topics. Now examine the topics carefully and list for each the presentational aids that would be most appropriate for that topic. For example, on the topic of comparing certificates of deposit, you could list: a chart showing local rates from five banks; a slide showing how the yields change depending on how often interest is compounded, etc.

**Application
Assignment**

The Presentational Aids Speech

In a five-minute speech demonstrate how to do something by using presentational aids. Choose a topic (perhaps from the list you generated in Application Exercise 1) that invites the use of presentational aids.

▼▼

Endnotes

1. Elena P. Zayas-Baya, "Instructional Media in the Total Language Picture," *International Journal of Instructional Media, 5 (1977–78):*145–50.
2. Bernadette M. Gadzella and Deborah A. Whitehead, "Effects of Auditory and Visual Modalities in Recall of Words," *Perceptual and Motor Skills* 40 (February, 1975):255–60.
3. Delores A. Bogard, "Visual Perception of Static and Dynamic Two-Dimensional Objects," *Perceptual and Motor Skills* 38 (April, 1974):395–98.
4. Bella M. De Paulo et al., "Decoding Discrepant Nonverbal Cues," *Journal of Personality and Social Psychology* 36 (March 1978):313–23.
5. Some of the material and illustrations in this chapter on visual aids come from an uncopyrighted classroom handout by K. Kealey and entitled "Presentational Aids."
6. Madeline F. Green, "A Profile of the American College President," *Educational Record,* Spring 1988, 47.
7. The authors thank N. Joseph Welling, Director of the Telecommunications Center at Ohio University, for the two graphic creations in figures 12.9 and 12.10 and for a quick course in computer-generated graphics.

Informative Speaking

13

Question Outline

I. What are four purposes of informative speaking?

II. What are two rhetorical principles of informative speaking?

III. What are some principles of learning that can be applied to the informative speech?

IV. How can you organize your informative speech?

V. What are four types of informative speeches?

The improvement of the understanding is for two ends: first, for our own increase of knowledge; secondly, to enable us to deliver and make out that knowledge to others.

JOHN LOCKE

Introduction

Angelique Valdez is a single mother of three young children. A sophomore, she is older than many of the other students, and her day at school can best be described as hectic.

On this particular morning she has an 8:00 class which means she must be up at 6:00 A.M. to bathe, dress, and prepare breakfast for the kids. At 7:30 she is at the day care center where she has to tell the teacher that her youngest daughter will be picked up at 1:30 so she can keep an appointment with the doctor.

She gets to class just five minutes before the bell. She is lucky because she has to ask the professor how long the term paper is supposed to be and whether or not it is supposed to be double-spaced.

On her way to the next class she sees her friend Diane, another busy student-mother, and arranges to meet her for lunch at the Oasis, a gathering place for non-traditional students.

At noon Diane asks her what she should do about her two-year-old who cried much of the night. If it is an ear infection, she asks, does she have to go to the doctor or will an over-the-counter drug do the trick? Angelique recommends the free clinic and in turn asks Diane about where she can get information for her speech which is due next week.

We will not continue to follow Angelique throughout her day because the point is already well made: Angelique, like the rest of us, asks for and gives information many times each day. The only difference between our everyday conversations and the informative speech, which we learn about in this chapter, is that the speech is longer, better researched, and given to more people. The similarities between the preceding conversations and the informative speech are more numerous: you tell people about things they want to know, need to know, or can use; you adapt your knowledge to increase their understanding; and you define, explain, and give examples that help them apply your knowledge to their situation.

How do you know what you know? How do you know how to play football, make a dress, drive a car, read a book, or write an essay? For many years, parents, teachers, coaches, employers, and friends have helped you increase your knowledge. In many cases, the vehicle for learning probably has been the informative speech. A physical education instructor may have taught you how to bowl, dance, and participate in team sports. Other teachers undoubtedly taught you how to read, write, and take examinations. Employers may have taught you how to serve a customer, type a letter, or give a sales pitch.

After completing your formal education, you may find yourself conveying what you know to your children, employees, or fellow workers. The purpose of this chapter is to examine the primary means of communicating information to other people: the informative speech. You will discover the purposes of informative speaking, the rhetorical principles for communicating information, and principles of learning that are especially important for communicating information to an audience. At the end of this chapter you will find a checklist for the informative speech and assignments that apply what you learn in this chapter. Once completed, you will know enough about informative speaking to increase your confidence as a public speaker.

Informative Speaking

An informative speech can be defined as one that increases an audience's knowledge about some subject, one that helps the audience learn more about an issue or idea. The four purposes of informative speaking are to create a desire for information, and to help the audience to understand, remember, and apply that information.

. . . .

Four Purposes of Informative Speaking

1. Creates a desire for information
2. Helps the audience to understand
3. Helps the audience to remember
4. Invites the audience to apply information

. . . .

The first purpose of informative speaking is to generate a desire for information. Audiences, like students, are not always receptive to new information. You have observed teachers who were skilled at inspiring your interest in poetry, advanced algebra, chemistry, or physical education. You will have an opportunity to demonstrate whether you are skilled at communicating information to an audience of classmates. If you read this chapter carefully, you should become an effective informative speaker. The first step is to arouse the audience's interest in your topic.

To create a **desire for information** in your audience you must arouse their need for, or interest in, the information. Can you show how your information will improve their everyday lives? Can you demonstrate to the audience that they can gain the respect and admiration of their peers by knowing what you have to tell? Can you raise questions in the speech for which the audience will seek answers? One way you can learn to generate this hunger for information is to become a systematic observer of your own instructors. How do they arouse your interest? How do they get you to learn information, even in courses that you are required to take? You can adopt others' methods to improve your own ability to generate a desire for information.

How does a person create a desire for information in a speech? One student began like this:

My speech today is on the subject of hydroponics. [The class looked slightly mystified.] How many of you know what hydroponics is? [Two students out of twenty-two raised their hands.] I see that only a few of you know what hydroponics is. Our technology is ahead of our ability to absorb it. Educated people should know what it is. Today you will find out.

After this introduction, the audience was convinced that most of them did not know the topic of the speech, and, as educated people, they began to feel they *ought* to know. The speaker had successfully aroused their interest for information.

Another student created a desire for information by posing questions to which the members of the audience would seek answers in the speech. She began: "Do you know what your chances are of getting skin cancer? Do you know when you are likely to get it? Do you know if anything can be done to cure it?" The questions aroused the audience's curiosity about the answers, which were given later in the speech. Other student speakers have asked: "Do you know how to save money on food?" "Can you repair your own stereo?" "Can you tell a poor used car from a good one?"

The student who has carefully analyzed an audience can find ways to instill a desire for information that will make the audience want to hear the informative speech.

Reprinted by permission of
UFS, Inc.

The second general purpose of informative speaking is to increase the ways in which the audience can respond to the world. The more we know, the greater our repertoire of responses. The poet can look at a boulevard full of trees and write about it in a way that conveys its beauty to others. The botanist can determine the species of the trees, whether their leaves are pinnate or palmate, and whether they are healthy, rare, or unusual. The chemist can note that the sulphur dioxide in the air is affecting the trees and know how long they can withstand the ravages of pollution. A knowledgeable person may be able to respond to the trees in all of these ways. Acquiring more information provides us with a wider variety of ways to respond to the world around us.

Helps the Audience to Understand

The informative speaker's goal is to increase the audience's understanding of the topic. Whether the audience is interested in the topic before you speak about it is less important than the interest you arouse during your speech.[1] The effective informative speaker analyzes an audience to find out how much it already knows about a subject, so that he or she does not bore the informed or overwhelm the uninformed. The effective speaker narrows the topic so that he or she can discuss an appropriate amount of material in the allotted time. Finally, the effective speaker applies his or her own knowledge to the task to simplify and clarify the topic.

How can you encourage the audience to understand your topic? You can apply the following ideas to your own informative speeches:

1. Remember that audiences understand main ideas and generalizations better than specific facts and details.[2] Make certain that you state explicitly, or even repeat, the main ideas and generalizations in your own informative speech. Limit your speech to two to five main points.
2. Remember that audiences are more likely to understand simple words and concrete ideas than complex words and abstract ideas.[3] Review the content of your informative speech to determine if there are simpler, more concrete ways of stating the same ideas.

3. Remember that early remarks about how the speech will meet the audience's needs can create anticipation and increase the chances that the audience will listen and understand.[4] In your introduction be very explicit about how the topic is related to the audience. Unless your speech is related to their needs, they may choose not to listen.
4. Remember that the audience's overt participation increases their understanding. You can learn by listening, and you can learn by doing, but you learn the most—and so will your audience—by both listening *and* doing.[5] Determine how to encourage your audience's involvement in your speech by having them raise hands, stand up, answer a question, comment in a critique, or state an opinion.

If you will remember and apply these four suggestions in your informative speech, you will probably increase the audience's understanding of your topic.

Helps the Audience to Remember

The third general purpose of informative speaking is to help the audience remember important points in your speech. How can you get them to retain important information? One method is to reveal to the audience specifically what you want them to learn from your speech. A speaker can tell you about World War I and let you guess what is important until you flounder and eventually forget everything you heard. However, the audience will retain information better if the speaker announces at the outset, "I want you to remember the main causes of World War I, the terms of the armistice, and the immediate results of those terms." Similarly, a student speaker may say, "After this speech I will ask several of you to tell me two of the many causes for blindness that I will discuss in my speech." Audiences tend to remember more about an informative speech if the speaker tells them specifically at the outset what they should remember from the speech.

. . . .

Methods of Encouraging Retention

1. Tell audience what you want them to remember
2. Indicate to audience which ideas are most important
3. Repeat main ideas
4. Pause to indicate important points
5. Gesture to indicate important points

. . . .

A second method of encouraging an audience to remember (and one also closely tied to arousing audience interest) is to indicate clearly in the informative speech which ideas are main ones and which are **subordinate,** which statements are generalizations to be remembered and which are details to support the generalizations. Careful examination of students' textbooks and notebooks shows that in preparing for examinations students highlight important points with a highlighter pen. You can use the same method in preparing your informative speech.

Highlight the important parts and convey their importance by telling the audience, "You will want to remember this point . . .", "My second main point is . . .", or "The critical thing to remember in doing this is. . . ."

Other methods that encourage an audience to retain important information include repeating an idea two or three times during the speech and pausing or using some physical gesture to indicate the importance of the information.[6] At least one experiment showed that speaking in a loud voice, repeating important matters infrequently, and repeating important matters too often (four repetitions) did *not* enhance the audience's ability to answer questions based on the information in the speech.[7] When you listen to your instructors' and classmates' informative speeches, try to determine what the speakers do to inspire you to remember the information. Then see if you can apply those same techniques in your own informative speech.

The fourth general purpose of informative speaking is to encourage the audience to use or apply the information during the speech or as soon afterward as possible. An effective speaker determines methods of encouraging the audience to use information quickly. Sometimes the speaker can even think of ways that the audience can use the information during the speech. One student, who was delivering an informative speech on the Japanese art of origami, for example, had everyone in class fold paper in the form of a bird with moveable wings. Another student speaker had each classmate taste synthetic foods made with chemicals. Still another student invited everyone to try one dance step to music. These speakers were encouraging the audience to apply the information from their speeches to ensure that they retained the information.

Why should the informative speaker encourage the audience to use the information as quickly as possible? One reason is that information applied immediately is remembered longer. Another reason is that something tried once under supervision is more likely to be tried again. An important purpose of informative speaking is to evoke behavioral change in the audience. It is easy to think of informative speeches as simply putting an idea into people's heads, of increasing the amount they know about some topic. However, there is no concrete indication that increased information has been imparted except by observing the audience's behavior. Therefore, the informative speaker seeks **behavioral response** in the audience.

What behavioral response should the informative speaker seek? Many kinds are possible. You can provoke behavioral response by inviting the audience to talk to others about the topic, or to actually apply the information (e.g., trying a dance step) or to answer questions orally or in writing. If the audience cannot answer a question on the topic before your speech but can do so afterward, you have effected a behavioral response in your audience.

The four general purposes of informative speaking, then, are to create a desire for information in the audience, to increase audience understanding of the topic, to encourage the audience to remember the information, and to apply the information as quickly as possible.

Invites the Audience to Apply Information

Next we will examine two rhetorical principles and five learning principles that relate to informative speaking.

Rhetorical Principles of Informative Speaking

Relates the Speaker to the Topic

Two **rhetorical principles** are related to any public speech, but they need special emphasis in informative speaking because they are so often overlooked. These two principles focus on the relationship between the speaker and the topic, and the audience and the topic.

The first rhetorical principle states that you, the informative speaker, must show the audience the relationship between yourself and the topic. What are your qualifications for speaking on it? How did you happen to choose this topic? Why should the audience pay particular attention to you on this subject? As we pointed out in the chapter on source credibility, audiences tend to respond favorably to high-credibility sources because of their dynamism, expertise, trustworthiness, and common ground. This credibility is unrelated to understanding: an audience apparently learns as much from a low-credibility source as from a high-credibility source. However, the audience is more likely to apply what they do comprehend if they respect the speaker as a source.

Consider this hypothetical example. Suppose a husky male athlete gives an informative speech to your class on macramé, an activity that helps him relax. Would the men in the class comprehend the information as well if a female art major delivered the same information? Research says that the comprehension would be the same: they would learn about macramé equally well from a high- or low-credibility source.[8] But, would the men in the class be more likely to actually try macramé themselves if the male athlete suggested it? We believe that the athlete and art major would be equally successful at teaching macramé, but the athlete would be more likely to secure a behavioral response from the men in the audience. Here is an example of how one student related the topic to himself:

> You heard the teacher call my name: Gary Klineschmidt. That is a German name. My grandparents came from Germany and the small community in which I live is still predominantly German with a full allotment of Klopsteins, Kindermanns, Koenigs, and Klineschmidts. Many German customs are still practiced today in my home and in my hometown. Today I want to tell you about one German custom that has been adopted by many Americans and two German customs that are practiced primarily by people of German descent.

The speaker established a relationship between himself and his topic by stating explicitly the origins of his authority to speak on German customs.

The point is that you must relate the topic to yourself, so that the audience will respect and apply the information you communicate. Giving a speech on street gangs? Let the audience know if you belonged to one. Giving a speech on skydiving? Tell the audience how many times you have dropped. Giving a speech on hospital costs? Tell the audience the cost of your last hospital stay.

A second rhetorical principle of informative speaking is to relate the topic to the audience early in the speech. We have already indicated that this tactic is a wise one for ensuring audience interest and understanding. Again, you must be explicit. It may not be enough to assume that the audience understands the connection between themselves and the topic. Instead, it is best to be direct: specifically tell the audience how the topic relates to them. Remember, too, that many topics may be very difficult to justify to an audience. An informative speech on taxes is lost on an audience that pays none. An informative speech on raising thoroughbred horses is lost on an audience that has very little money. Therefore, the informative speaker is encouraged to scrutinize audience-analysis information to discover indications of audience interest in a topic.

This example demonstrates the rhetorical principle of relating the topic to the audience:

> Over half of you indicated on the audience analysis form that you participate in team sports. We have two football players, two varsity tennis players, one gymnast, three hockey players, and four persons in men's and women's basketball. Because you already possess the necessary dexterity and coordination for this sport, you are going to find out today about curling.

This speaker carefully detailed the many ways in which the topic was appropriate for the particular audience. When you deliver your informative speech, remember to relate the topic to yourself and your audience.

Relates the Topic to the Audience

Informative speaking is a type of teaching. Listening to informative speeches is a type of learning. If you expect an audience to understand your informative speech and apply the knowledge learned, you must treat the speech as a phenomenon in which teaching and learning occur. Because you, as an informative speaker, are inviting the audience to learn, you can apply these five **principles of learning** to your speech.

Principles of Learning

. . . .

Principles of Learning

1. Build on the known
2. Use humor and wit
3. Use presentational aids
4. Organize your information
5. Reward your listeners

. . . .

Builds on the Known

One principle of learning is that people tend to build on what they already know, and they accept ideas that are consistent with what they already know. An informative speech, by definition, is an attempt to "add to" what the audience already knows. If the audience is to accept the new information, it must be related to information and ideas that they already hold.

Suppose you are going to inform your audience about how to kill cockroaches. If many people in your audience live in old apartments, homes, or dormitories, they may have a need for this information. You have to consider what the audience already knows. They probably know that they can turn on the lights quickly and step on the roaches as they flee for the cracks. But they probably do not know the very best chemical ingredients to wipe out roaches. So, you tell them about chlorpyrifos. You do not have to tell them that chlorpyrifos is actually the simple name for "O, O-diethyl O-3,5,6-trichloro-2-pyridyl phosphorothioate." Tell them what they do not know: that chlorpyrifos is an excellent cockroach killer that remains effective for weeks and is available in only three insecticides—Real-Kill Extra Strength in aerosol spray, Rid-A-Bug, and Real-Kill Liquid Extra in liquid spray.[9] In short, you can build on the audience's probable previous knowledge— manual means of killing insects and the general use of aerosols, sprays, liquids, powders, baits, and fumigant cakes—by adding to their knowledge the specific ingredient that they should look for and by giving them the names of the only three insecticides that contain the ingredient. You could elaborate by pointing out that Propoxur is also a good roach killer, but it has an offensive smell and stains. Build on what the audience knows.

. . . .

Building on the Known Helps an Audience Learn

Gasohol is unleaded gasoline with 10% alcohol added.

Modern daycare institutionalizes the old practice of having aunts, uncles, and grandparents care for a child while the mother is at work.

Working with electrical wiring is like working with water pipes: you can shut off the supply of juice; you should always have something to contain it; and it is very destructive if it gets loose.

. . . .

A speaker can use humor to communicate a message.

A second principle of learning to observe in informative speaking is to use humor and wit. Any of us can find topics about which we know more than our classmates. They may be our religion, hobbies, travels, political position, eating habits, or major in college. However, the aim in informative speaking is to make the information palatable to the audience and to present it in such a way that the audience finds the information attractive. Notice that the principle does not dictate that you must be funny. The principle says "use humor and wit." Wisdom is the information that you know about the topic. Wit and humor are the clever ways you make the information attractive to the audience.

One premed student, for example, decided to give a speech on chiropractors, even though he was clearly prejudiced against them. He decided to handle his prejudice with wit rather than anger or bitterness. He entitled his speech "Chiropractors: About Quacks and Backs." Another student used wit in her speech about parenting. She was unmarried and well-known by her classmates. The audience could hardly hide its shock when she stated in the introduction to her speech, "I did not think anything of parenting until I had my son." Her "son" turned out to be an uncooked hen's egg. She was taking a course on the family, in which she was required to care for her "son," the egg, for one week. When she went out on a date, she had to find a "babysitter" to care for the egg. She had to protect it from breaking as she went from class to class, take it to meals, and tuck it in at night. The introduction of her "son," the egg, added wit to the wisdom of her informative speech on parenting.

Uses Humor and Wit

Often language choices help add vigor to your presentation. A student who was delivering a potentially boring speech on "TV and Your Child" enlivened his speech with witty language. He began this way:

> Within six years almost everybody in this room will be married with a young one in the crib and another on the way. Do you want your youngster to start babbling with the words SEX, VIOLENCE, and CRIME or do you want him to say MOMMY, DADDY, and PEPPERONI like most normal kids?

The speaker hit the audience with the unexpected. It was witty, and it made his speech more interesting to the audience.

Uses Presentational Aids

A third principle of learning is to communicate your message in more than one way. Some people learn best by listening. Other people learn best by reading. Some people learn best when they do what the speaker is explaining. Still others learn best by seeing. Effective informative speakers recognize that different people learn best through different channels. Therefore, such speakers try to communicate their messages in a number of different ways.

A student giving an informative speech about life insurance used a chart to explain to his audience the main differences among whole life, universal life, and term insurance. Because much of his explanation depended on the use of statistics to indicate costs, savings, and loan value, he and the audience found the chart necessary for the informative speech.

You, too, can find a variety of methods of communicating your message to an audience that learns in diverse ways. Some material in an informative speech is simply too detailed and complex to present orally. You might be able to get more of the message across by presenting these complex materials to the audience at the conclusion of your speech. Other complex data may be easier to understand through a graph, a picture, an object, a model, or a person. Consider using every means necessary to get your informative message to the audience.

Organizes Your Information

A fourth principle of learning is to organize your information for easier understanding. Organization of a speech is more than outlining. Outlining is simply the skeleton of a speech. In an informative speech consider other organizational possibilities. How often should you repeat your main point? Where is the best place to repeat it? Where do you try to create a proper setting for learning to take place? Where in the speech should you reveal what you expect the audience to remember? Do you place your most important information early or late in the speech?

Although there probably are no solid answers to these questions, research does hint at some answers.[10]

1. How often should you repeat main points?
   The evidence indicates that two repetitions have little impact and that positive effects fade with four or more, so the best answer seems to be that repeating main ideas three times works best.
2. Where do you create a setting for learning?
   The earlier you create an atmosphere for learning, the better. Make clear to your audience early in the speech exactly what you want them to learn from your presentation.
3. Where should important information be placed?
   The evidence indicates that audiences remember information placed early and late in the speech, so avoid placing your most important material in the middle of your presentation.

A final point about relating your information to your organization: learn how to indicate orally which parts of your speech are main points and which are subordinate or supporting. In writing, subordination is easy to indicate by levels of headings, but people listening to a speech cannot necessarily visualize the structure of your speech, which is why the effective informative speaker indicates early in the speech what is going to be covered. This forecast sets up the audience's expectations; they will know what you are going to talk about and for approximately how long. Similarly, as you proceed through your speech, you may wish to signal your progress by indicating where you are in your organization through transitions. Among organizational indicators are the following:

"My second point is . . ."
"Now that I have carefully explained the problem, I will turn to my solution."
"This story about what happened to me in the service will illustrate my point about obeying orders."

In each case the speaker is signaling whether the next item is a main or subordinate point in the informative speech.

A fifth principle of learning is that audiences are more likely to respond to information if it is **rewarding** for them. One of the audience's concerns about an informative speech is "What's in it for me?" The effective informative speaker answers this question not only in the introduction, where the need for the information is formally explained, but also throughout the speech. By the time a

Rewards Your Listeners

speaker is in the middle of the presentation, the audience may have forgotten much of the earlier motivating information presented; so the speaker continually needs to remind the audience how the information meets its needs.

A student speaker, talking to his audience about major first-aid methods, made this statement in his informative speech:

> Imagine being home from school for the weekend, having a nice, relaxing visit with your family. Suddenly your father clutches his chest and crumples to the floor. What would you do to help him?

The student reminded the audience throughout the speech how each first-aid technique could be applied to victims with heart attacks, serious bleeding, and poisoning. The benefit for the audience was in knowing what to do in each case. Another student began her speech by saying:

> Did you realize that at this very moment, each and every one of you could be, and probably is suffering from America's most widespread ailment? It is not V.D., cancer, or heart disease, but a problem that is commonly ignored by most Americans—the problem of being overweight.

As the speaker proceeded through her information on low-calorie and low-carbohydrate diets, she kept reassuring the audience that they could overcome the problem in part by knowing which foods to eat and which to avoid. The audience benefited by learning the names of foods that could help or hinder their health.

Rewards come in many forms. In the preceding examples, the reinforcement was in the form of readily usable information that the audience could apply. A speaker can use other, more psychological forms of reward. "Do you want to be among the ignorant who do not know what a 'value added tax' is?" The speaker who confidentially tells you about it is doing you a service because you will no longer be ignorant. A student from Chicago found that most of her classmates thought first of muggings when someone mentioned Chicago in conversation. She devoted her informative speech to the positive aspects of living in that city. The result was that the students in the audience had many more positive associations about Chicago, including the fact that one of their fellow students, who looked not at all like a mugger, was from Chicago, and *she* thought it was a good place to live.

| **Structure of the Speech to Inform** | We have considered the purposes of informative speaking, the rhetorical principles of informative speaking, and principles of learning. We are now prepared to examine the structure of an informative speech. We will look at a sample introduction, body, and conclusion. |

An Example of an Introduction to an Informative Speech

Figure 13.1 An example of an introduction to an informative speech.

OUR PRISON SYSTEM

Speaker gains audience attention with questions

Did you know that only 2% of the people in prison today will stay there? Did you know that prisoners who are sentenced to life plus 100 years still get out on parole? And did you know that one of the main reasons that prisoners are released is that our prison system simply is not large enough to hold all of the people who are convicted of crimes? Leonard Larsen of the Scripps Howard News service addressed all of these questions in *The Athens Messenger* on the opinion page this week.

Speaker relates topic to audience

You should have an interest in our prison system because as taxpayers you pay for it, you walk the streets with people on parole, and you vote for the legislators who make our prison policies. Learning about the prisons will make you an informed citizen whose knowledge can help you make wise decisions.

Speaker relates self to topic

I may not appear to be an appropriate person to talk about prisons, but I am a sociology major with a special interest in criminology and our penal system. The course work on the subject has provided me with facts and figures, but my visit to our state penitentiary and the talks with the prisoners, the warden, and one of our state legislators has provided the passion on the subject that inspired me to tell you about it.

Speaker reveals purpose, organization, and development

I am going to inform you today about our state's prison system, its strengths and its weaknesses. Especially I am going to focus on our state's policy on parole, rehabilitation, and early release. On another day, in my persuasive speech, I will be taking a position on how I believe this state can solve some of the weaknesses in the system, but today you will learn the facts.

The introduction for a speech to inform is particularly important because you must (1) establish your credibility by relating yourself to the topic, (2) establish relevance by relating the topic to the audience, (3) gain the audience's attention and interest in the topic by stating it in such a way that you arouse audience curiosity, (4) forecast the content of your speech, and (5) state specifically what you want the audience to learn from your speech. An overall objective in the introduction is to create an atmosphere for learning, in which the audience will be stimulated to comprehend and remember the important parts of your speech. Figure 13.1 shows a student introduction to an informative speech.[11] The side notes indicate the functions being fulfilled.

Figure 13.2 An example of an informative speech outline.

Example of an Outline for an Informative Speech

Title   MAKING THE EXIT INTERVIEW WORK FOR YOU

Introduction   I. The exit interview is a way to find out why an employee is leaving a job.
    A. You need to know about exit interviews as a management tool which can improve your business.
    B. I know about exit interviews because I conduct them for the fast food business for which I work.
    C. I will inform you about the four steps in conducting a patterned exit interview.

Body   II. The four steps in a patterned exit interview are selecting the interviewer, developing a systematic routine, creating a climate, and conducting the interview.
    A. The interviewer should be a person who has worked in the business long enough to ask good questions and to understand the answers.
        1. Some questions should be asked of each person who is interviewed.
        2. All answers should be written or recorded.
    B. The business should routinely move an employee from resignation to exit interview.
    C. The interviewer should create a positive and trustworthy climate in order to learn as much as possible.
    D. The interviewer should conduct the interview thoroughly but without haste.

Conclusion   III. The patterned exit interview can reveal weaknesses in management, improve working conditions, develop better compensation and benefit packages, and reduce turnover.
    A. Employees who have already quit are willing to reveal problems that are otherwise hidden.
    B. One large corporation in the Southwest reduced turnover by 90%, primarily by implementing information learned in patterned exit interviews.

The body of an informative speech should consist of two to five main points supported by illustrations and examples. In the speech outline shown in figure 13.2, the speaker included only two main points in his outline, but each included a great deal of information.[12] The outline presented suggests that the speech was somewhat dry and uninteresting. When the speaker delivered the speech, he added humorous stories and anecdotal material from an internship in which he was involved and in which he conducted patterned exit interviews for a company. He related himself to the topic because of his experience and related the topic to the

Figure 13.3 An example of a conclusion for an informative speech.

Example of a Conclusion for an Informative Speech

Words signal end Restatement	After seeing the graphs and charts on investments, you know as much about investments as I do. You know that when the economy goes wild with inflation, the dollar loses its value and precious medals gain in value. You know that when the stock market goes up and up, the value of bonds tends to go down. And, finally, you know that all investments are a gamble because they change with the economic winds.
Words signal end Application Incentive for remembering	My last advice to you now that you know something about investments is that you protect them by purchasing a variety of investments to balance the gains and losses of economic times. Finally, I would encouarge you to add to your knowledge of investments by taking courses, participating in seminars, and learning by investing. You listened well today, and you learned some information that you did not know before you heard my talk. I think you will find—as I have—that knowledge is a necessary prerequisite for the wise investor.

audience by asking them questions about their own past employment. His speech could have been improved by generating more information hunger in the audience.

The conclusion of an informative speech should restate the main points of the speech, give the audience some incentive for understanding and remembering the content of the speech, and, if possible, reveal how the audience can apply or extend the newly-learned information. The following example demonstrates how all three—restatement, incentive, and application—can be included in the conclusion of an informative speech. In addition, you should determine some way through words or action to signal that you are approaching the end of your speech.

The informative speech typically includes an introduction, a body, and a conclusion. The introduction establishes your credibility, relates the topic to the audience, gains an audience's attention and interest, forecasts the content of the speech, and states specifically what the audience should learn from the speech. The body of the informative speech communicates from two to five main points, with supporting materials like illustrations, examples, and presentational aids. The conclusion restates the main points, provides some incentive for retention, and suggests ways to extend or improve the base of knowledge even further.

Next, we turn to some specific types of informative speeches.

Types of Informative Speeches

The category of informative speeches includes a wide variety of different kinds of speeches. In chapter 10 the speech of definition and the speech of description were briefly discussed. They are two types of informative speeches. In this section we will further explain the speech of definition and the speech of description, and we will introduce the speech of explanation and the speech of demonstration. As you will observe, these speeches all fall under the general heading of informative speeches, but each has unique characteristics.

Speech of Definition

The speech of definition sounds fairly simple and straightforward. You may even be wondering how an entire speech can be based upon definition. After all, defining a word is simply the process of supplying a few other words that explain what the word means. However, if you have read chapter 10, or if you have reflected on the number of "communication breakdowns" you have had because of differences in definition, you know that defining words and concepts is far more complex than it might originally appear to be. Supplying definitions for terms may in fact be the basis of all other types of informative speeches, and it could even be suggested that definition is the most important of the lines of argument used by speakers.

A number of methods of defining were offered in chapter 10. Among the methods discussed were comparison, contrast, use of synonyms, use of antonyms, etymology, differentiation, use of operational definitions, and use of experiential definitions. If you have forgotten any of these types of definitions, you may wish to review that chapter.

A number of speech topics lend themselves to the speech of definition. Listed here are some titles of successful speeches of definition.

1. What Is "Wife Abuse"?
2. What the Russians Mean by *Glasnost*.
3. What Are Chemical Weapons?
4. Understanding the "Greenhouse Effect."
5. What Is an Anti-Lock Brake System?
6. Defining Inflation.
7. P205/75R15: What Are the Numbers on Tires?
8. What Is an *Oxymoron*?
9. What Is Bouillabaisse?
10. Defining "Illegal Drugs."
11. Cholesterol and Your Diet.
12. Defining "Cognitive Therapy."
13. What Is "Touring Suspension"?
14. Dial-a-Porn: The Limits of Privacy.
15. What Is *Perestroika*?

These titles should help you think of other topics appropriate for the speech of definition. Here is a speech of definition without a formal introduction or conclusion. The student was instructed to deliver the body of a speech of definition using at least three means of defining.

George[13]
Jana Milford

George in its adjective form is a word which is unlikely to be found in any dictionary. It is a term which is known only to a limited group of people, but because the term signifies something to those individuals, it can be called a word.

George belongs to a group of adjectives which deal in colloquial use with social acceptability, or, more specifically, with what is fashionable. These adjectives fall into two categories: positive adjectives such as *chic*—meaning cleverly stylish or currently in fashion—and *cool,* and negative adjectives such as *gauche*—defined as lacking social experience or grace. A generalization which extends to words in both categories is that they are often misused. Most of the time one must rely on the situation and the tone of the speaker's voice to determine the intended meaning. *George,* correctly used, belongs to the latter set of adjectives, those suggesting negative characteristics.

Something which is "george" is not only currently out of style, but is also regarded as tasteless to the extent that it never should have been in style, that anyone espousing it would have been crazy. Most persons using the term *george* are aware that differences in taste are results of varied backgrounds and therefore they use *george* as an emphatic declaration of their opinion, not an objective evaluation.

An illustration would probably define the word best. I was shopping with my aunt one fine summer day when a woman in a lime green outfit strolled past. The woman was lime green from head to toe with a silky scarf, a polyester double-knit pantsuit, and vinyl pumps, all of different shades of that vivacious color. Admittedly, lime green might have been an acceptable color in the Paris of the sixties, and I have seen it used in frog costumes recently, but somehow it seemed out of place in the conservative Midwest during the subdued eighties. My aunt, without a trace of sarcasm in her voice said: "That is george."

Margin annotations:
- Denotations
- Synonyms
- Antonym
- Connotation
- Differentiation
- Connotation
- Experiential Definition

Speech of Description

The speech of description is an informative speech in which you describe a person, place, object, or experience by telling about its size, weight, color, texture, smell, and/or your feelings about it. This speech was introduced in chapter 10. The speech of description relies on your abilities to use precise, accurate, specific, and concrete language; to demonstrate a diverse vocabulary; to use words that have appropriate connotative and denotative meanings; and to offer necessary definitions. You may wish to review some of these ideas in chapter 10.

A variety of topics lend themselves to the speech of description. Listed here are some titles of speeches that seemed to work particularly well for this type of informative speech.

1. Portrait of a Los Angeles Bag Lady.
2. How Hormones Affect Human Behavior.

3. Exploring Cuba's Cayo Coco Resort.
4. The World's Fastest Cars.
5. Cincinnati: The City's Past.
6. Life in a Street Gang.
7. Airport Security: What's Next?
8. Trials of the Single Parent.
9. Working in a Crisis Center.
10. Understanding Sculpture.
11. The Smell of Perfume.
12. What to Look for in a Computer..
13. A Case of Child Abuse.
14. Evaluating a Diamond.
15. Training for the Big Fight.

This list of topics should be suggestive, but it is certainly not exhaustive of all of the possible kinds of topics that are appropriate for the speech of description.

This speaker describes a person, place, object, or experience using specific, concrete language, a diverse vocabulary, connotative and denotative meanings, comparisons, and a familiar item described in an unfamiliar way. The student who delivered the speech told about his hometown of Phoenix, Arizona, describing the transition from daytime desert heat to nighttime desert chill. This application assignment is a brief demonstration of the student's powers of description and, therefore, has no formal introduction or conclusion. The marginal notes indicate the means he used in his description.

Transition[14]
Mark Dupont

The heat cannot be escaped. As the sun beats mercilessly on the endless lines of automobiles, waves of shimmering heat drift from the blistering, black pavement, creating an *atmosphere of an oven* and making the minutes drag into eternity. The wide avenues only increase the sense of oppression and crowding as lane after lane clogs with rumbling cars and trucks. Drivers who have escaped the heat of the sun in their air-conditioned cars fall prey to the heat of frustration as they *do battle* with stoplights and autos which have *expired* in the August sun. Valiant pedestrians *wade through the heat,* pausing only to wipe from their foreheads the sweat that stings their eyes and blurs their vision. It is the afternoon rush hour at its peak, Phoenix, Arizona, at its fiercest. The crawl of automobiles seems without end as thousands of people seek out their homes in the sweltering desert city.

Gradually, almost imperceptibly, the *river of traffic* begins its descent past the 100-degree mark; the streets become quieter and more spacious. The mountains enveloping the city begin to glow as their

(marginal notes:)

Comparison with Oven

Comparison with War
Comparison with Death
Unfamiliar Description

Comparison with River

grays and browns awaken into brilliant reds and oranges. The haze which has blanketed the valley throughout the day begins to clear. The lines of buildings become sharper, their colors newer and brighter. The shadows of peaceful palm trees lengthen, inviting the city to rest. The fiery reds and oranges of the mountains give way to serene blues and purples. The water of hundreds of backyard swimming pools, which have been turbulent with the afternoon frolicking of overheated children and adults alike, calms and mirrors the pink and lavender dusk sky. The fading sunlight yields to the lights of homes and streets as the Valley of the Sun becomes a lake of twinkling lanterns reflecting the *sea of stars* above. The *inferno* is gone, forgotten. The rising swell of crickets and cicadas lulls the desert inhabitants into relaxation and contentment. The desert floor gives up its heat, cooling the feet of those who walk on it. The heat of anger and hatred for the valley dissipates, and in the hearts of the people who have braved another summer day in Arizona, there is only the warmth of love for their desert home.

Comparison with Sky and Sea and Hell

The speech of explanation is an informative speech in which you tell how something works, why something occurred, or how something should be evaluated. You may explain a social, political, or economic issue; you may describe an historical event; you may discuss a variety of theories, principles, or laws; or you may offer a critical appraisal of art, literature, music, drama, film, or speeches. A wide collection of topics may be included in this category. Some possible speech titles for the speech of explanation follow.

Speech of Explanation

1. How to Buy a Good Used Car.
2. Understanding Electrical Repair.
3. How to Earn Money by Sewing.
4. Why Drugs Are Dangerous.
5. Why Lend Money to Third World Nations?
6. Understanding the National Debt.
7. How to Write Poetry.
8. Figuring the Interest on your Certificate of Deposit.
9. Why Advertising Works.
10. Yasser Arafat and the PLO.
11. Background on the Battle in Northern Ireland.
12. Hispanics and the Public Schools.
13. Why the Pentagon Needs Less.
14. Who is Donald Trump?
15. Why the World Fears Chemical Warfare.

In the speech of explanation, "A Sweet Killing," the student speaker explains diabetes, reveals what it is, how it affects a person, and what one can do about it.

A Sweet Killing[15]
Laura Kaval

Laura Kaval

Topic Introduced

Everyone with a brother or sister is an expert on sibling warfare. My little blonde brother and I are no different. We have our share of fights. One of us always ended up crying—usually him. My mother prayed that we would both outgrow it, but my brother and I are still fighting. Only now what we are fighting is my brother's disease—juvenile diabetes.

Facts and Figures

According to the American Diabetic Association, another diabetic is diagnosed every sixty seconds.[1] Diabetes with all of its complications is regarded as the third leading cause of death in the United States. It claims over 300,000 lives annually. Diabetes can strike at any age: my brother is sixteen. Although incurable, diabetes can be controlled with early diagnosis.[2] Diabetes is a major health problem, but you can protect yourself with some precautionary measures such as regular visits to your physician.

Definition

Vocabulary

Diabetes is an inability of the body to turn food into glucose, a simple sugar solution, which is responsible for producing energy. The hormone insulin is what makes this process possible. Insulin is produced in the pancreas. When the pancreas fails to produce the proper amount of insulin, the body is unable to process the food. The unprocessed sugar-energy is then released from the body through urination, for it can't be used.[3] Donnell Elizweter of the University of Minnesota and president of the American Diabetic Association states,

Testimonial Evidence

"Early diagnosis and proper control under the supervision of a qualified medical team generally mean a diabetic will be able to live an active and productive life. The trouble is that two out of five diabetics either don't know they have it or choose to ignore it and don't receive proper medical attention."[4]

One Type Defined

Symptoms Listed

There are two different types of diabetes. If a person has juvenile diabetes, as my brother has, where the body creates no insulin supply, there are seven warning signs or symptoms. They include: (1) constant urination; (2) abnormal thirst; (3) unusual hunger; (4) rapid weight loss; (5) weakness/fatigue; (6) nausea/vomiting; and (7) craving for sweets. Juvenile diabetes is treated with direct insulin shots, a planned diet, proper exercise, and regular medical examinations.[5]

Second Type Defined

The second type of diabetes is maturity-onset diabetes. This is where the pancreas produces insulin, but (a) doesn't create enough insulin or (b) the body doesn't use what is made properly. The warning signals are: (1) slow to heal skin; (2) cramps in the legs and feet; (3) blurred vision; (4) genital rash; (5) men's impotence; (6) drowsiness; and (7) excessive weight. Maturity-onset is treated by proper diet, exercise, and occasionally, by oral medication. Many diabetics never have any warning signs or symptoms and are diagnosed during an annual medical examination.[6]

There are several different kinds of tests that you can perform in your own home to help you monitor yours and your family's blood sugar. The first is a urine test. This test is performed by placing two drops of urine in ten drops of water and one Clentest tablet into a container and then shake. By matching the color of the solution to the colors on the side of the package, the amount of blood sugar can be determined. The normal reading is 120. There are also other test tapes, which just need to be dipped in a urine sample and then read.

The second test is a blood test, which is taken by placing a small drop of blood on the end of a test tape. The reading can be taken after the tape dries.[7] These tests are easy and safe and only take a minimal amount of time. These tests are rather inexpensive and are available at most drug stores. It is a small price when it comes to your family's well-being.

These steps to monitor diabetes should be taken by every family to protect their loved ones. If these early detection measures aren't taken, someone you love could become another statistic before you know it. Half of juvenile diabetics face the possibility of death due to kidney failure. Diabetics are two to three times more likely to develop hardening of the arteries, stroke, and heart attack than are non-diabetics; and diabetics are fifty times as likely to develop blood vessel problems.[8]

Actress Mary Tyler Moore, comedian Dan Rowen, baseball player Jackie Robinson, and inventor Thomas Edison were diagnosed as diabetic[9]—and so was my little brother. But because we watch his diet, regulate his insulin, make sure he gets enough exercise and sees his doctor regularly, we are winning our fight. I encourage and strongly urge you to become aware of the warning signs of diabetes and to purchase and use the urine or blood tests regularly to monitor your family's blood sugar. It is also important that your family see a doctor regularly because some symptoms of diabetes can only be detected through a medical examination.

Diabetes causes too many deaths a year and robs too many people of the sight and the touch of their loved ones for you not to take these simple early detection measures. If more people took these precautions, we might not only win the fight but the battle too.

Margin annotations:

- Symptoms Listed
- Fact
- First Test Explained
- Second Test Explained
- Facts and Figures
- Names of Famous Diabetics
- Precautions Cited
- Conclusion

Speech of Demonstration

The next kind of informative speech, the speech of demonstration, is an informative speech in which you show the audience an object, person, or place; in which you show the audience how something works; in which you show the audience how to do something; or in which you show the audience why something occurs. In other words, the speech of demonstration may be similar to the speech of explanation or the speech of description, but the focus in the speech of demonstration is on the visualization of your topic. For instance, one of the suggested topics for the speech of description provided here is a speech about Washington, D.C. If you provided overheads with maps of the city, posters with depictions of major attractions, and photographs of points of interest, the speech would be one of demonstration. Similarly, a speech on horror movies, as suggested above, may be a speech of explanation. If, however, you add short excerpts from various movies illustrating the four reasons that people pay to be frightened, the speech becomes one of demonstration. The key to a speech of demonstration is that you are actually showing the audience something of your topic.

As you consider topics that are appropriate for the speech of demonstration, do not simply recall a speech of explanation or description and add a few pictures, a poster, or an overhead to it and believe that you have an appropriate speech of demonstration. As you attempt to decide on a topic, you should consider those ideas, concepts, or processes that are too complex to be understood through words alone. Similarly, consider the wide variety of items and materials that can be used to demonstrate your topic. You may wish to read chapter 12, in which visual aids such as the chalkboard, posters, movies, slides, opaque and overhead projections, living models and physical objects, handouts, and you (as a visual aid) are discussed. Which items will be most useful for your topic? Do not rely on those visual aids that are the simplest to construct or the most obvious; instead, use those items that best illustrate your topic. The following list has some titles of speeches that were highly effective speeches of demonstration.

1. The Latest in Fall Fashions.
2. How to Fillet a Fish.
3. Using Mnemonic Devices to Aid Memory.
4. Trimming the Thighs with Exercise.
5. Making Electricity.
6. Building Big Biceps.
7. Uses for Computer Graphics.
8. Comparing Luxury Cars.
9. Selecting Shoes for Serious Walking.
10. Learning the Martial Arts.
11. Comparative Architecture: New Theatres and Old.
12. How to Care for Your Compact Discs.
13. Making Vietnamese Food.
14. Where to Visit in Washington, D.C.
15. The Best Ads for the Year.

Following is a speech of demonstration. Notice in the speech that the speaker has to spend less time and effort describing the origins of her credibility because she shows the audience her credibility throughout the speech. The photos are provided to help you visualize what Donna was doing as the speech progressed.

Back Walkovers in Gymnastics[16]
Donna Griffith

How many of you have heard of Nadia Comaneci? How many of you have heard of Kurt Thomas? How many of you have seen gymnastics on television? How many of you have been to a gymnastics meet or exhibition? What you see in elite-level gymnastics are usually very different moves such as double-back somersaults or back-layout somersaults on the balance beam, among other things. Well, it takes a gymnast a long time to learn moves such as those. A gymnast has to learn strength, flexibility, coordination, and courage before she could even attempt a move such as a back-layout on the balance beam. I would like to show you some of the work that goes into learning gymnastics. It looks easy, but even the simplest skills require a lot of work. For example, I will use a back walkover, which is a basic skill, and show you how it is learned. I will show you what muscles need to be stretched, what flexibility is required, the preliminary moves, the back walkover itself, related moves, and then I will tell you how these skills are used in gymnastics.

Before you attempt anything in gymnastics, you must warm up. Make sure your clothes don't inhibit movement; leotards, shorts, tee shirts, and sweats are some of the best things to wear. In gymnastics, you use almost every set of muscles in your body, so it's important to stretch all of them. I always begin by stretching my arms and shoulders. Try arm circles backward and forward, up and down, and side to side. Then swing your arms around, pivoting at the waist; these are called windmills. To stretch your shoulders, grasp your hands behind you, turn your wrists out, and pull up. As you pull upward, lean forward and let the weight of your arms stretch your shoulders while you begin stretching your legs. Toe touches are really important, but it's also important that you pull gently to each leg; don't bounce because that isn't stretching at all. Next are butterflies. Sit on the floor with your feet together and your knees apart. Grab your ankles, push your knees down with your elbows, and pull down to the ground. Straddle stretches are important for flexibility. Straddle as far as you can, but make sure your knees and toes are pointing up and out. Pull down to each leg, then to the center, making sure to pull slowly. This next stretch is what I call hamstring stretches. Keep one leg straight

on the floor while lying down and pull the other leg straight up and toward your head as far as you can. Do this for both legs. You can stretch your back by walking your hands down a wall or by lying on the floor and pushing up into a bridge.

There are some preliminary moves that you must be able to do before you even attempt a back walkover. You should be able to do the splits in at least one direction: right, left, or center. Flexibility is important to this move. Bridges are important. When you "bridge up," be sure to push simultaneously with your hands and feet. Some people don't, and they can't get up. You should try lifting one leg at a time, and then one hand at a time, off the ground.

After a bridge, you should be able to do a backbend. A lot of people say they can do a backbend, and they'll go down, but they can't come up. Well, it's not a backbend unless you can begin and end standing. So begin standing with your arms overhead. Keep your weight on your feet while you're arching backwards and gradually shift some weight to your hands. Push off the floor with your hands and come back to a stand.

Cartwheels are important because they teach you what it feels like to be upside down and supporting yourself on your hands. After cartwheels and backbends, you should master the front limber. It's a lot like a backbend, but it also involves a handstand. Begin standing, arms overhead, and kick into a handstand. Arch over, but don't throw your weight over, or you'll fall. Push up and end standing.

Now we're ready to do back walkovers. I consider form very important. Arms and legs should be straight, toes pointed whenever they're not on the floor, and legs split as much as possible. Begin standing, arms overhead. Keep your head up and look for the floor as you arch backwards. Extend one leg out (I'm left handed, so I use my left leg) with the toe pointed. Arch over, keeping your weight on your supporting leg while your lead leg moves higher. Look for the floor. As your hands touch the floor and your lead leg rises, kick off the floor with your supporting leg. Keep your arms straight so you don't smash your face. Step out and end standing. A more difficult back walkover begins with the lead leg off the floor.

There are other moves you can learn that are similar to back walkovers. A front walkover is a lot like a limber, except you step out of it. A front tensica combines a cartwheel with a front walkover, and it goes hand-hand-foot-foot. A back limber begins like a back walkover, but you bring your legs together in the air and down on the floor together. There are also back tensicas, which are back walkovers with one hand going down at a time, and back handsprings, which involve an arching jump backwards to your hands and a spring off to your feet.

Back walkovers are used in lower-level gymnastics as a part of a tumbling pass. You can see them in high school and lower-level meets. In higher levels, back walkovers are used as an artistic element in floor exercise and as connecting elements in beam routines. While a back walkover on the beam may be a major element in a high school routine, many elite gymnasts use it to begin a tumbling pass on the beam. A gymnast such as Nadia may begin with a back walkover, do two back handsprings, then dismount with a double twist from the beam.

I hope you now understand some of the work that goes into gymnastics. I showed you some of the flexibility required, some different moves and how they are done, and what back walkovers are used for in gymnastics. Gymnastics is meant to look easy, but it, in many ways, requires more strength and coordination than sports such as basketball and football. The gymnasts you see on television are probably stronger in proportion to their weight and size than any other athlete. So, the next time you watch gymnastics, instead of just being amazed, you hopefully can appreciate the work it takes to be a gymnast, and you may also recognize some of the moves I've shown you.

Following is an example of an entire informative speech. Composed by Laurie Sheridan, this speech won first place in local, divisional, and tri-state contests before it became the first runner-up in a national Future Farmers of America contest. Ms. Sheridan first started developing the speech as a sophomore in high school. She participated in the national contest as a first-year student at Ohio University. Ms. Sheridan is currently the State Vice-President of FFA's Ohio Association. The sidenotes are provided to indicate organization and content of this contest-winning speech.

Speech of Information

Biotechnology: Benefits for Our Future[17]
Laurie Sheridan

How many people in this audience feel that they know what biotechnology is and how it can be applied to food production, nonfood products, and our environment? Raise your hands. Ten years ago, biotechnology sounded like a frightening science fiction scenario: cell fusers and gene splicers producing plants never before seen on earth, laboratory-designed animals, and obedient microbes. At that time, the agricultural sector could see little significance in the advantages biotechnology would give to food production. Even today many of us have no real concept of what biotechnology is or what it can do for us.

Invites Audience Participation

Gains Audience Interest and Attention by Introducing a Term— Biotechnology—That Few Are Likely to Know

Relates Topic to Audience

Today I want to tell you about biotechnology: what it is, how it works, and how it will provide food and products for us in years to come. My interest in biotechnology came from my own experience in agriculture, from interviews with experts in biotechnology, and from my own research on the subject.

We will examine this interesting subject together by examining the positive impact of biotechnology on food production, on useful products, and on our environment.

What is biotechnology? It can be defined as the natural use of biological systems to create substances and products too complex and expensive to make by traditional chemical means.[1]

First, let us discuss the production of higher quality food products. Biotechnology can drastically improve agriculture by influencing economic conditions and producing higher quality products. Dr. Thomas Wagner, Director of the Edison Center of Biotechnology at Ohio University, believes that our focus should be on controlling aspects of production such as growth rates, growth efficiencies, and disease resistance. By controlling production, he says that farmers will improve plants and animals, increase production efficiency, and lower production costs. Improved products will increase profits to a more reasonable level by providing totally new, high-profit-margin agricultural products.[2]

A good example to illustrate the advantages of biotechnology is the market pig enterprise at Embryogen, Inc. Jeff Hoover, a technician at Embryogen, gave me a tour of the facilities. While I was there, I was able to compare litter mates harboring the expression growth hormone gene with those that were not. The difference was amazing! Litter mates harboring the gene are 30% more feed efficient and have up to 80% less back fat than their untreated siblings.[3] This difference not only improves the quality of agricultural products, but also decreases labor for meat processors and provides consumers with more meat for their money.

Now that the positive impact of biotechnology on the quality of agricultural products is evident, let us examine the benefits of producing nonedible products through biotechnology.

According to Dr. Floyd Schanbacher, a scientist at the Ohio Agricultural Research and Development Center, "Agriculture has traditionally focused on marketing conventional agricultural products. However, biotechnology will create a closer alignment of agriculture to such industries as biomedicine, pharmaceuticals, and nutrition."[4] Edible products will be used as nonedible items, including corn for synthetic plastics and fibers and soybean oils for fuel.

Dr. Clague Hodgson, a molecular biologist at OARDC, says: "The intent is to get away from overproduction and develop new and useful products."[5] New and beneficial products are flowing out of laboratories. According to Jeff Gibbs, attorney for the American Biotechnology Association, "More than three hundred nonedible products have been approved by the Food and Drug Administration and are on the market."[6] Examples are human insulin marketed by Eli Lilly, a human growth hormone for treating disorders in children, new agents for the treatment of cancer, and medical diagnostic kits for homes manufactured by Diagnostic Hybrids.[7] Imagine the new opportunities these products will provide for agriculture and for consumers!

As you can see, American farmers can—through biotechnology—expand their markets by creating nonedible agricultural items, and there is business support to make it happen!

Finally, let us discuss the harmful effects some current agricultural practices have on our environment and how biotechnology can alleviate these practices.

At present, there is great concern about environmental pollution from the application of fertilizers and chemicals. In fact, a survey in the February 1988 issue of *Farm Journal* reported that ". . . of all the groundwater consumed by humans, 75% of it is contaminated."[8] D. H. Sander, an agronomist at the University of Nebraska, states "that the excessive use of chemicals and fertilizers lowers agriculture's competitiveness and at the same time pollutes our environment."[9]

Historically, attempts to reduce environmental problems have included methods such as crop rotation and drainage systems. But biotechnology offers an alternative plan which is more productive and, at the same time, decreases ecological dangers.

For example, marigolds have natural toxicity to some insects. By transferring to tomato plants the DNA from marigolds with codes for a substance that is toxic to caterpillars, the need to use certain insecticides on tomatoes can be eliminated.[10] With these advances in biotechnology, the question becomes: Why should farmers continue using harmful chemicals when they can produce disease-resistant plants and animals with biotechnology?

In the last decade, public awareness of environmental concerns has increased dramatically. However, action is needed! Dr. Charles Benbrook, Director of the National Board on Agriculture, is currently lobbying the Congress and governmental regulators with the message that biotechnology is a key to improving ecological conditions.[11] His message urgently needs the support of the entire agricultural sector.

Quotes Two More Authorities in Support of Second Main Point

Specific Examples

Provides Transition between Second and Third Main Points

Signals Impending Ending

States Third Main Point

Gives Oral Footnote and Direct Quote from Written Source and an Expert

Provides Subordinate Idea

Provides Specific Example Comparing Traditional and Biotechnical Methods

Argues from Authority

As I have illustrated, environmental problems caused by agricultural practices can be reduced with the use of biotechnology. Presently, technology isn't the only issue: product quality, profitability, and ecology also play significant roles in this process. With biotechnology the agricultural picture can once again be a bright and profitable one. Biotechnology can answer challenges facing our society by focusing on the production of higher quality edible and nonedible agricultural products, and by altering environmental imbalances.

How many of you now feel that you have a better understanding of biotechnology? Raise your hands. Biotechnology is not science fiction nor is it something that we should fear. Instead, your increased knowledge of what it is, how it works, and what it can produce may help you look forward to our challenging future with biotechnology.

Ends with Summary of Three Main Points

Invites Audience Participation

Brings Conclusion Back to the Idea Early in Introduction

Rewards Audience with Promise of a Brighter Future

Summary

In this chapter you learned that the purposes of informative speeches are to generate a desire for information on the part of the audience, to seek audience understanding of the information, and to invite audience retention and application of the information in the speech. Among the important points concerning the purposes of informative speaking, you learned that audiences comprehend generalizations and main ideas better than details; audiences comprehend simple words and concrete ideas better than big words and abstractions; a sense of anticipation can encourage listening and understanding; and audience participation increases comprehension.

Two rhetorical principles function in informative speaking. The first is that the speaker should explicitly state the relationship between himself or herself and the topic. The second is that the audience needs to know its relationship to the topic. These principles can be observed by describing your qualifications to discuss the topic and by demonstrating how the audience will find this information useful.

You learned five principles of learning related to the informative speech. They are (1) build on the known, (2) use humor and wit, (3) use presentational aids, (4) organize your information, and (5) reward your listeners.

Finally, you learned about four different types of informative speeches: the speech of definition, the speech of description, the speech of explanation, and the speech of demonstration. The speech of definition is based on explaining the meaning of a word or a few words. The speech of description relies upon your ability to offer precise, accurate, and concrete language; to demonstrate a sufficient vocabulary; to use appropriate words; and to offer definitions. The speech of explanation is one in which you tell how something works, why it occurred, or how it should be evaluated. The speech of demonstration includes some object that is actually seen by the audience. Following is a checklist that you can use to assess your own informal speech and the speeches delivered by others.

A Checklist for the Informative Speech

_____ 1. Have you created a desire for information?
_____ 2. Have you helped your audience understand your information?
_____ 3. Have you helped your audience remember information?
_____ 4. Can the audience apply the information?
_____ 5. Have you revealed your relationship to the topic?
_____ 6. Have you related the topic to your audience?
_____ 7. Have you employed wit and humor when appropriate?
_____ 8. Have you built new information on old information?
_____ 9. Have you used presentational aids when necessary?
_____ 10. Have you organized your message effectively?
_____ 11. Have you included rewards for the audience?
_____ 12. Have you reviewed earlier chapters for ideas on how to improve this informative speech?

1
Applying a Rhetorical Principle: The Speaker

Think of three topics about which you could give a three-minute speech to inform. List the topics in the blanks at the left. In the blanks at the right explain how you relate to the topic in ways that might increase your credibility with the audience.

Topics   **Your Relationship to Topic**

1. _____   _____
                               _____
2. _____   _____
                               _____
3. _____   _____
                               _____

2
Applying a Rhetorical Principle: The Audience

In the topic blank below, name one topic that you did not use in the previous exercise and explain in the blanks following how you would relate that topic to your own class in an informative speech.

Topic: _____

The audience's relationship to topic:

_____
_____
_____
_____

3
Applying Principles of Learning

Write down a topic for an informative speech that you have not used in previous application exercises. Explain in the spaces provided how you could apply each of the principles of learning to that topic.

Topic: _____

One way that I could relate this topic to what the audience already knows is _____

_____

One way that I could relate wit to wisdom in an informative speech on this topic is by

_____

One way that I could use several channels to get my message across on this topic is by _____

_____

_____

One way that I could organize my speech to help the audience learn my information is by _____

_____

One way that I could provide reinforcement to my audience for listening to my informative speech on this topic is by _____

_____

▼▼

Application Assignments

1
The Speech of Explanation

Deliver a four-to-six-minute speech in which you explain how something works, why something occurred, or how something should be evaluated. You are encouraged to rely on sources of information like encyclopedias, textbooks, newspapers, magazines, and professional journals. Chapter 6 cites other sources that might be helpful as you prepare this assignment. You will be evaluated on how well your audience understands what you are explaining. The information on audience analysis presented in chapter 4 may be useful as you consider the most successful manner in which to present your information. Consider information with which your audience is already familiar and demonstrate relationships between the known and the new information that you are offering. Consider how you can translate unfamiliar terms into known quantities. Try to determine how you can motivate your audience to be interested in what you are attempting to explain.

2
The Speech of Demonstration

Write an outline for a speech of demonstration that is to be about four to six minutes in length. Include in your outline a title, a purpose statement, an introduction, a body, and a conclusion. On the left-hand side of the sheet, specify the visual aids that will be used and the purpose of each visual aid. Examine your outline to determine if the visual aids are really necessary for understanding or if they are merely "props;" try to insure that no additional visual aids are necessary for the audience to understand your message. You will be evaluated on your ability to identify creative and appropriate visual aids for your topic, and on your ability to use visual aids when they are necessary and useful for understanding.

▼▼▼

Vocabulary

behavioral response   One objective of a speech to inform is to see if the audience shows some kind of physical reaction to the speech.

desire for information   A need the speaker creates in an audience so they are motivated to learn from the speech.

principles of learning   Principles governing audience understanding by building on the known, using humor or wit, using presentational aids, organizing information, and rewarding listeners.

reward   A psychological or physical reinforcement to increase an audience's response to information given in a speech.

rhetorical principles   Two principles of public speaking that focus on the relationship between the speaker and the topic, and on the relationship between the audience and the topic.

subordination   Showing that one piece of information is less important than or merely supports another.

▼▼▼

Endnotes

1. Charles R. Petrie, Jr., "Informative Speaking: A Summary and Bibliography of Related Research," *Speech Monographs* 30 (1963):79–91.
2. Petrie, p. 80.
3. Carole Ernest, "Listening Comprehension as a Function of Type of Material and Rate of Presentation," *Speech Monographs* 35 (1968):154–58. See also John A. Baird, "The Effects of Speech Summaries upon Audience Comprehension of Expository Speeches of Varying Quality and Complexity," *Central States Speech Journal* 25 (1974):119–27.
4. Petrie, p. 84.
5. Elena P. Zayas-Baya, "Instructional Media in the Total Language Picture," *International Journal of Instructional Media* 5 (1977–78):145–50.
6. R. Ehrensberger, "An Experimental Study of the Relative Effectiveness of Certain Forms of Emphasis in Public Speaking," *Speech Monographs* 12 (1945):94–111.
7. Ehrensberger, pp. 94–111.
8. Kenneth Andersen and Theodore Clevenger, Jr., "A Summary of Experimental Research in Ethos," *Speech Monographs* 30 (1963):59–78.
9. "Household Insecticides," *Consumer Reports* 44 (1979):362–67.
10. Ehrensberger, pp. 94–111.
11. The information in paragraph one is from Leonard Larsen, "America's Willie Hortons now George Bush's problem," *The Athens Messenger,* 5 January 1989, 4.
12. Based on a paper submitted by Robert Fott in Fundamentals of Human Communication, Ohio University. The paper contained the following bibliography entries: Dixon, Andrew L. "The Long Goodbye," *Supervisory Management* 27 (January 1982), 26–29; Embrey, Mody, and Noe. "Exit Interview: A Tool For

Personnel Development," *The Personnel Administrator* (May 1979), 43–48; and "Exit Interviews of Departing Employees Can Provide Valuable Management Information," *Practical Accountant* 14 (June 1981):65–69.

13. From a speech of definition delivered in Fundamentals of Public Speaking, Iowa State University.

14. From a speech of description delivered in Fundamentals of Public Speaking, Iowa State University.

15. From a speech of explanation in Communication and Persuasion, School of Interpersonal Communication, Ohio University. The speech contained the following endnotes: [1] Wentworth and Hoover, "Students with Diabetes," *Today's Education* (March 1981), 42; [2] Wentworth and Hoover, 42; [3] Covelli, Peter J. "New Hope for Diabetics," *Time* (March 8, 1981), 63; [4] Wentworth and Hoover, *Today's Education,* 43; [5] Wentworth and Hoover, 43; [6] Wentworth and Hoover, 44; [7] Wilkins and Odayle, "Sugar Sensor, Measuring Glucose Concentrations in the Body," *Science News* (September 5, 1981), 154; [8] Covelli, *Time,* 62; [9] Covelli, 64.

16. From a speech delivered in Public Speaking, School of Interpersonal Communication, Ohio University.

17. Laurie Sheridan's speech contained the following endnotes: [1] Personal interview with Dr. Thomas Wagner, Director of the Edison Center of Biotechnology, Ohio University, February 17, 1988; [2] Wagner; [3] Personal interview with Mr. Jeff Hoover, technician at Embryogen, April 1, 1988; [4] Tom Storey, "Animal Biotechnology—Super Options," *Ohio 21,* I (1987): 15.; [5] Storey, p. 15; [6] Telephone interview with Mr. Jeff Gibbs, Attorney for the American Biotechnology Association, April 11, 1988; [7] U.S. Congress, Office of Technology Assessment, *Biotechnology Firms and Products,* January 1986; [8] Suzanne Halas Steel, "Taking Fertilizer to Task," *Farm Journal,* February 1988: 8–9; [9] Steel, pp. 8–9; [10] Dr. Jasper S. Lee, *Biotechnology: Science at Work in Agricultural Industry,* U.S. Department of Agriculture, May 1988, p. 4; [11] Laura Sands and Marcia Zarley Taylor, "People to Watch in '88," *Farm Journal,* January 1988, 20.

Persuasive Speaking

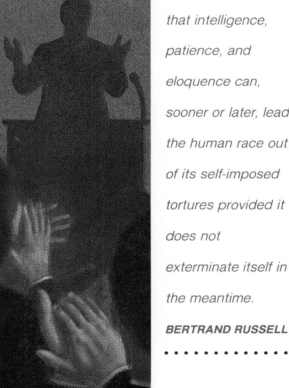

. . . I am convinced that intelligence, patience, and eloquence can, sooner or later, lead the human race out of its self-imposed tortures provided it does not exterminate itself in the meantime.

BERTRAND RUSSELL

Introduction

The persuasive speech provides an opportunity to build on everything you have learned so far about public speaking. The kinds of speeches that you learned about in the chapter on informative speaking—definition, description, and explanation—are used in persuasive speaking as well.

In this chapter you will learn some of the characteristics of persuasive speaking, some principles of persuasion, the use of various kinds of appeals, and some types of persuasive speeches.

What Is Persuasive Speaking?

First, let us compare informative and persuasive speaking. Perhaps no speech is completely informative or completely persuasive, but the following chart might help highlight the characteristics of the two kinds of speeches.

	Informative speech	Persuasive speech
Speaker's intent	to increase knowledge	to change mind or action
Message's purpose	to define, describe, explain, compare, etc.	to shape, reinforce, or change audience responses
Listener's effect	to know more than before, to advance what is known	to feel or think differently, to behave or act differently than before
Audience's choice	to willingly learn new knowledge	to change behavior without coercion

Persuasive speaking is a message delivered to an audience by a speaker who intends to influence the audience's choice by shaping, reinforcing, or changing their responses toward an idea, issue, concept, or product.

Three Purposes of Persuasive Speaking

Central to the definition of persuasive speaking are the three **purposes:** to shape, reinforce, and change responses in an audience.[1]

Shaping Audience Responses

Shaping responses means that the persuasive speaker tries to move the audience toward some predetermined goal. A parent shapes a child's behavior to encourage the child to walk: sitting up draws cheers, standing up brings encouragement, and the first step is picture-taking time. Similarly, the persuasive speaker shapes responses in the audience by moving the audience toward a predetermined goal.

Public speakers often encourage audiences to continue believing as they do now.

For instance, let us say the speaker wants the audience to have a more positive attitude toward the disposal of nuclear waste from power plants. Most people do not want a nuclear waste dump in their state much less their back yard. So the persuasive speaker must shape the audience's responses by first demonstrating the marvelous potential of nuclear energy to generate the power necessary for our life-style. Next, the speaker might shape the audience by asking them to explore alternatives to nuclear power, most of which are even more expensive or too dirty to contemplate. Shaping, then, is moving an audience closer and closer to the speaker's solution by presenting ideas in palatable doses.

Reinforcing responses is a second purpose of persuasive speaking. Reinforcing means rewarding the audience for sustaining their present beliefs, attitudes, and values. Wallace Fotheringham called this "continuance,"[2] keeping an audience doing what they already do.

Reinforcing Audience Responses

Political speakers try to keep audiences loyal to a certain party and a particular candidate. Religious speakers try to encourage faithfulness to a certain doctrine and to a particular organized group. Educators try to persuade a sometimes reluctant clientele that knowing how to read, write, and speak, as well as having a wide knowledge about many disciplines, is the mark of an educated person. All are trying to persuade people to continue voting, believing, and gaining education as in the past.

Changing Audience Responses

A third purpose of persuasive speaking is **changing** responses, altering an audience's behavior toward a product, concept, or idea. Often, the persuasive speaker pursuing this purpose asks the audience to start or stop some behavior: start exercising, stop smoking, start studying, stop eating unhealthy foods, or start drinking fruit juice instead of alcohol.

Changing responses in an audience is a tough assignment. People tend to behave the way they have in the past, but the persuasive speaker who adopts this purpose is asking the audience to behave differently. Changes that alter well-established habits come hard for most people.

Historically, shaping has been associated with learning; reinforcing has been largely ignored as a persuasive purpose; and changing has been the main focus of persuasive speaking for two thousand years.

What Is Being Influenced?

A public speaker needs to keep in mind the goal of persuasion. What is it that you are trying to shape, reinforce, or change in an audience? Usually what you are trying to influence are the audience's beliefs, attitudes, values, and behavior.

Beliefs

Daryl Bem says that **beliefs** may be taken for granted (an object exists even when we are not looking at it), or based on our senses (I can see that he is fat), or based on authority (the Bible says the poor shall always be with us).[3] We can have many beliefs based on a single attitude, and people with the same attitude might have rather different beliefs.

For example, my attitude that all people are created equal might be based on authority: the legal system says so; on peers: my friends hold the same belief; and on experience: the people I have known seem to have the same basic intelligence and skills. Another person who believes all people are created equal might base that attitude on religious beliefs (authority), parental teachings (authority), and wide reading on the subject. Both persons have the same attitude but support it with different beliefs.

Attitudes

Attitudes, according to Martin Fishbein, "are learned predispositions to respond to an object or class of objects in a favorable or unfavorable way."[4] In other words, we learn attitudes; we are not born with them. And they are our generalized likes or dislikes. Bem calls them likes or dislikes toward people, ideas, policies, or situations.[5] So your general dislike of people who smoke, your pro-life stance on abortion, your distaste for the Internal Revenue Service, and your love of parties are all learned attitudes.

Values

Values tend to run deeper than either beliefs or attitudes because they are even more basic. Bem calls them "a primitive preference for or a positive attitude toward certain end states of existence (like equality, salvation, self-fulfillment, or freedom) or certain broad modes of conduct (like courage, honesty, friendship,

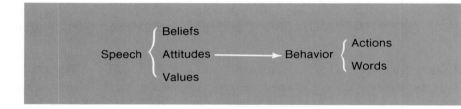

Figure 14.1 A persuasive speech affects audience values, attitudes, and beliefs in order to elicit certain words or actions (behavior).

or chastity)."[6] Your reluctance to report a friend for an illegal act is based on a basic value that friends do not tell on each other; your reporting of a friend might be based on the value that no one is above the law. In either case your behavior is based on a value.

Finally, **behavior** means simply that the persuasive speaker tries to change audience behavior. Sometimes the behavioral change is obvious: vote for a certain candidate, buy a certain product, go to a certain place or try a certain exercise. Sometimes the behavioral change is less obvious: read more about modern warfare, listen to more talk about taxation, or tell people about the welfare state. Sometimes the behavioral change is almost imperceptible: an audience member becomes slightly less Republican and votes for a bond issue in the secrecy of the voting booth; an audience member answers questions from a pollster just a little differently than she would have before she heard your speech; or an audience member earns somewhat better grades because of your motivational speech about study habits. In all of these cases behavioral change took place as a result of a speech.

The public speaker often meddles in the cognitive domain, in the mind of the audience, tinkering with this belief, that attitude, or this value. But we never know if that tinkering had any effect except through the audience's behavior. It is what they say and what they do, their behavior, that tells us what they must think.

Behavior

. . . .

Principles of Persuasion

1. Consistency persuades
2. Small changes persuade
3. Benefits persuade
4. Fulfilling needs persuades
5. Gradual approaches persuade

Principles of Persuasion

. . . .

Consistency Persuades

The first principle of persuasion is that audiences are more likely to change their behavior if the suggested change is consistent with their present beliefs, attitudes, and values.

People who have given money for a cause (a behavior) are the likely contributors to that and other related causes in the future. People who value competition (a value) are the most likely candidates to enter into another competition. People who want to segregate old people in communities of their own (a belief) are the most likely to promote bond issues that provide separate housing for the aged. Finally, people who dislike immigrants (an attitude) are likely to discourage immigrants from moving into their neighborhood.

Fortunately for public speakers, people tend to be relatively consistent. They will do in the future what they did in the past. The public speaker uses this notion of **consistency** by linking persuasive proposals to those old consistencies. Some examples of appeals based on consistency are:

> The members of this audience were among the first in their neighborhoods to buy home computers, VCRs, and centralized home security systems. Now you can be among the first to own a laser disk sound system. I know that you are basically conservative folks who do not spend money without deep thought and careful scrutiny. That is why you will find this new sound system so appealing: it is expensive, but will outlast every appliance in your house; it is small, but more powerful than any previous system; and it is new, but designed to bring to your ears with great clarity all the songs that you like to hear.

The public speaker shapes, reinforces, and changes by showing how the promoted activity is consistent with the audience's past behavior.

Small Changes Persuade

The second principle of persuasion is that audiences are more likely to alter their behavior if the suggested change will require small rather than large changes in their behavior. A common error of beginning speakers is that they ask for too much change too soon for too little reason. Audiences are reluctant to change, and any changes they do make are likely to be small ones. Nonetheless, the successful persuasive speaker determines what small changes an audience would be willing to accept consistent with the persuasive purpose.

What if you, as a persuader, are faced with an audience of overweight Americans who are loath to exercise and resistant to reduced eating? Your temptation might be to ask for too much too soon: quit eating so much and start losing weight. The message would likely fall on unreceptive ears, because it is both inconsistent with present behavior and asking for too much change too soon. You could limit your persuasive message by encouraging the audience to give up specific foods, or a specific food that is part of their problem. However, an even better example

of a small change consistent with the audience's present behavior would be to have them switch from regular to dietetic ice cream. An audience that would reject a weight-loss program might be more willing simply to switch from one form of food to another, because that change would be minimally upsetting to their present life patterns.

Are there any qualifications or limitations on this second principle of persuasion? One factor that needs to be considered in deciding how much to ask of an audience is commitment level. Studies in social judgment show that highly committed persons, people who believe most intensely or strongly about an issue, are highly resistant to any positions on the issue except their own or ones very close to it. To such an audience, reinforcement would be welcome, shaping would be a challenge, and change would be very difficult indeed. On the other hand, audience members who do not feel strongly about an issue are susceptible to larger changes than are those who already have established positions to which they are committed.

To state the principle more concretely: a speaker addressing a religious rally of persons who abhor drinking, dancing, and smoking can get warm acceptance for a persuasive message that reinforces or rewards those ideas; he would be greeted with cautious skepticism with a speech attempting to shape any responses different from those already established; and he would be met with outright rejection if he requested changes in behavior that run counter to those already embraced. On the other hand, a heterogeneous audience of persons uncommitted on the issue of regular exercise would be susceptible to considerable response shaping, and an audience of the already committed would receive reinforcement and would at least consider adopting some small changes in behavior. The successful persuader is skilled at discerning which small changes, consistent with the persuasive purpose, can be asked of an audience.

Benefits Persuade

The third principle of persuasion is that audiences are more likely to change their behavior if the suggested change will benefit them more than it will cost them. **Cost-benefit analysis,** for example, is considered every time we buy something: "Do I want this new jacket even though it means I must spend $50.00 plus tax? The benefits are that I will be warm and will look nice. The cost is that I will not be able to get my shoes resoled or buy a new watch." The persuader frequently demonstrates to the audience that the benefits are worth the cost.

A student who sold vacuum cleaners told of a fellow sales representative who donned white gloves and a surgical mask when he looked at the customer's old vacuum cleaner. By the time he had inspected the brush and changed the bag, he was filthy. He would then demonstrate that the old vacuum threw dust all over the house as it dragged across the carpet. By the end of his sales pitch, the sales representative was going to try to convince the customer that the old vacuum was not only ineffective, but also increased the amount of dirt flying around the house. The cost of the new vacuum would, according to this salesman, be worth the benefit of owning a cleaning machine that picked up dirt instead of spreading it around. Remember that you need to reveal to your audience the benefits that make your proposal worth the cost.

How can you use cost-benefit analysis in your classroom speech? Consider the costs to the audience of doing as you ask. What are the costs in money, time, commitment, energy, skill, or talent? Consider one of the most common requests in student speeches: write to your representative or senator. Many student speakers make that request without considering the probability that nobody in class has ever written to a senator or representative. Even if the speaker includes an address, the letter writing will take commitment, time, and even a little money. Few students are willing to pay those costs. On the other hand, if the speaker comes to class with an already written letter and simply asks for signatures from the class, then the cost is a few seconds of time, and the speaker is more likely to gain audience cooperation. Whenever you deliver a persuasive speech, consider the costs and how you can reduce them so the audience will feel they are worth your proposed benefits.

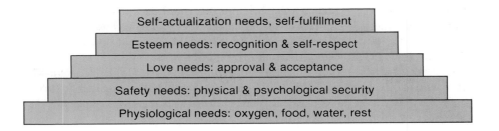

The fourth principle of persuasion is that audiences are more likely to change their behavior if the change meets their needs. Abraham Maslow has an often-quoted **hierarchy of needs**[7] depicted above.

Fulfilling Needs Persuades

Maslow's pyramid makes sense. As a human being you do need all of the items in the hierarchy, though many people never get very far above the second level and few think they have achieved complete self-fulfillment.

You can use Maslow's hierarchy in your public speeches. Are you in a place where the air and water are so bad that they threaten public health? If so, speeches on those issues are about the basic physiological needs. Do the people in your audience have decent places to live? If not, then speeches about space and psychological health are appropriate. Is everyone in your audience happy with his or her relationships? If not, then speeches about approval and acceptance are in order.

You can analyze your audience for specific needs. Do they need money? Jobs? Day care? Do they need help in dealing with government bureaucracies? Do they need better living conditions? Do they need to learn how to study, how to handle children, or how to live with spouses? Check out your own audience and determine what they need because a speech that meets the audience's needs is likely to be successful.

Gradual approaches work best when the audience is likely to be unreceptive to your message. With a friendly audience you can ask them to do what you already know they are likely to accept and then simply give them reinforcement and a good rationale for doing so. But many persuasive speeches ask for audience changes that they may not wholeheartedly endorse just because you say they should.

Gradual Approaches Persuade

Do not ask a hostile audience for too much too soon. Persuading a reluctant audience is a kind of seduction in which the audience is more likely to cooperate after courtship than after an abrupt proposition. Start with common ground to show the audience that you share their basic humanity. Move from arguments and evidence that they will find quite acceptable to that which they find harder to accept.

Asking for too much change too fast can result in a hostile audience.

One of the authors watched a Democratic governor face a highly Republican audience of radio and television owners and managers. The governor disarmed his potentially hostile audience by beginning with a story about how he sent his young son to school that morning. The story was amusing, but more importantly it showed that the governor—like most of the people in the audience—had the same kinds of things going on in his life that they had in their own. This common ground set the stage for the rest of the speech, in which he gently pushed the audience toward his position on the issues.

Similarly, in a persuasive speech do not start by saying, "I want you to donate your eyes to the eye bank." Instead, start gently with "safe" information about how many people have been saved from blindness by cornea transplants. Mention that the program is sponsored by the local Lion's Club. Reveal how many other people in the community, students in particular, have signed papers to allow their eyes to be used to help another person. Only after this careful courtship do you reveal that you have pledge cards for them to sign if they have compassion for their fellow human beings. The behavioral change—the signing of a commitment card—is the end result of a gradual approach.

Remember, as you prepare your persuasive speech, that audiences are more likely to change their behavior if the suggested change is consistent with their present beliefs, attitudes, and values; if it requires small rather than large changes in their lives; if it benefits them more than it costs them; if it meets their needs; and if it is a culmination of acceptable ideas. With these principles to apply in your persuasive speeches, you can move to the matter of content in the persuasive speech.

Reasoning in Persuasive Speaking

How can you convince an audience that your idea meets their needs? How can you demonstrate the benefits of your plan? How can you show that your idea is consistent with the audience's present beliefs, attitudes, and values? One of the two primary methods of persuading an audience is through reasoning—through the use of arguments with reasons, evidence, and inferences. To begin to understand reasoning, you will need to know the difference between inductive and deductive reasoning, two of the categories into which reasoning can be divided.[8]

As an overview of reasoning, you can start with the idea that inductive reasoning starts with a generalization and demonstrates its validity with various types of evidence. In deductive reasoning, you proceed to a conclusion from a major and minor premise. Let us look at these two kinds of reasoning in more detail.

Inductive Reasoning

Inductive reasoning consists of reasons, usually in the form of evidence, that lead to a generalization. The following example illustrates the form of inductive reasoning:

Professor X gave me a D in history.
Professor X gave Fs to two of my friends in the same course.
Professor X posted a grade distribution with many Ds and Fs.

Professor X boasts about his rigorous grading standards. Therefore,
Professor X is a hard grader [generalization].

Inductive reasoning, then, provides evidence that gives you an "inferential leap"
to the generalization. Inductive reasoning requires an inference because a generalization is drawn that is probably, but not unquestionably, true—based on the
evidence.

In the example, the **generalization** that Professor X is a hard grader remains
only a probability, even with the evidence presented. What if both you and your
friends are poor history students, and the posted distribution was for a "bone-
head" history course open only to students with poor academic records? You need
to remember that in inductive reasoning, the persuader gathers evidence that
leads to a *probable* generalization, but that generalization can always be questioned by reinterpretation of old evidence or the introduction of contrary evidence.

Deductive reasoning is a second way to apply logic to your argument. In inductive
reasoning you have a generalization supported by or induced from the evidence;
in deductive reasoning you have a **conclusion** deduced from a major and a minor
premise. Instead of resulting in a probability, as inductive reasoning does, the
deductive argument results in a conclusion that necessarily follows from the two
premises. A deductive argument looks like this:

> Major premise: All insects have six legs;
> Minor premise: ants are insects;
> Conclusion: therefore, ants have six legs.

Deductive
Reasoning

Notice that if the premises are true, then the conclusion must necessarily be true
also, because in a sense the two premises are the same thing as the conclusion.

In conversation and even in most speeches, a deductive argument usually does
not sound or look quite as formal as it appears above. In fact, the argument cited
above would more likely appear in a speech like this: "Since all insects have six
legs, ants must too." The reasoning is still deductive, except that the minor premise
is implied rather than openly stated. This can make deductive arguments difficult

to analyze—or even detect—in actual speeches. For this reason, it is necessary to listen closely to the reasoning in speeches, in order to determine what has been implied—or *seemed* to be implied, but actually wasn't—in addition to what has been stated openly.

On the other hand, if you feel you have particularly strong deductive arguments in your own speech, you should take the time to state them clearly and completely. Well-reasoned deductive arguments can have great persuasive power because once the audience has accepted the validity of the premises, *the conclusion is inescapable*. Mathematical proofs commonly take the form of deductive arguments, and the reasoning in your own speech should have all the clarity and impact of such proofs: if A equals B, and if B equals C, then A equals C.

You can apply several "tests" to correctly identify inductive and deductive reasoning. One test is to observe if the argument moves from the general to the particular ("All adolescents have skin problems; therefore, since Amanda is an adolescent, she must have skin problems"). If so, the argument is probably deductive. A second test is to see if the argument moves from a big category to a small or individual one ("All people have fears; so our enemies must have fears also"). If so, the argument is probably deductive. A third test is to observe if the argument moves from a small group or collection of individuals to a large one ("Randy drinks beer, Cindy drinks beer, and Rod drinks beer; so they must be alcoholics"). If so, then the argument is probably inductive.[9]

Try application exercise 3 to test your own skill at identifying inductive and deductive reasoning.

Evaluating Reasoning	There are at least four ways to evaluate your own reasoning and that of other speakers. One way is to ask critical questions about the use of evidence. A second way is to invite inspection of your own sources of evidence. A third way is to learn how to recognize common fallacies. And a fourth way is to systematically analyze your detailed outline.

Chapter 8 on support material included questions to ask about testimony, statistics, examples, comparisons, and analogies. You might want to review those questions that refer to specific kinds of support material and consider some of these more general questions:

1. Is your evidence consistent with other known evidence? An example is the current controversy over insurance rates. Cities, counties, and even transit authorities are facing rates that they cannot afford to pay. The federal government claims that those high rates are partly because of all the lawsuits, a claim that they back with evidence. The lawyers counter with their evidence that the actual number of lawsuits involving insurance have increased only with the increase in population. The point is that the amount of evidence you have that consistently supports your position can help you persuade an audience. At this point in the lawyer-government-insurance controversy none of the combatants have really won the public's endorsement with their evidence.

2. Is there any evidence to the contrary? When you try to reason with evidence, you must always be aware of any evidence that does not support your cause. An opponent can do much damage to your arguments and your credibility if he or she can find contrary evidence that you did not mention. Usually, you are better off mentioning any conflicting evidence, especially if you can argue against it in your presentation.

3. Does your generalization go beyond your evidence? Speakers always face the danger of overstating what their evidence shows. A small study that shows grade inflation is treated like a universitywide problem. Evidence of a local problem becomes a national problem in the speech. Always be careful that you do not go beyond what your evidence demonstrates.

4. Is your evidence believable to the audience? In persuasive speaking you need to provide only enough evidence to have the audience believe and act as you wish. More than that is too much, less than that is too little. A large amount of evidence that the audience finds unacceptable will not persuade them; a small amount that the audience finds acceptable will be sufficient to persuade.

Asking critical questions is just one way that the speaker as persuader can evaluate evidence and reasoning. Another method is to invite your listeners to check on your evidence themselves. The speaker does this through oral footnotes to indicate where he or she found the information, evidence, or idea.

One research study indicated that an authority-based claim, in which you state who said what, may slightly improve your own credibility. Also, using a claim made by an authority slightly improved the speaker's chance of changing the audience's attitude.[10] Standard classroom practice, the rules of scholarship, and the ethics of persuasive speaking all support the idea that the persuasive speaker should reveal the sources of information to the audience.

A third means of evaluating your own reasoning and that of others is to learn how to recognize **fallacies,** violations of the rules of inference.[11] There is not room or time enough to enumerate all of the common fallacies here, so you may wish to consult a book on argumentation or debate where more fallacies are discussed. For now, we will look at five fallacies that will serve as examples of the many fallacies described in the literature.

• •

Common Fallacies

1. Hasty generalization
2. Post hoc, ergo propter hoc
3. Cross-ranking
4. Equivocation
5. Argument from analogy

• •

Basketball players cannot be classified by using many bases of comparison at once.

The hasty generalization violates the rules of inference by drawing a generalization based on too little evidence. Example: I have in the past employed two white, male workers. Both proved to be poor employees. Therefore, I have vowed never again to hire a white, male employee. Problem: the sample—two persons—was too small and not random; also, the generalization does not account for the many other reasons why the employees may have been inadequate.

The post hoc, ergo propter hoc ("after this; therefore, because of this") fallacy confuses correlation with causation. Just because one thing happens *after* another does not necessarily mean that it was *caused* by it. Example: I found that I was pregnant right after our trip; therefore, going on a trip must cause pregnancy. Problem: the trip may have correlated (occurred at the same time) with the onset of pregnancy, but the trip is not necessarily the cause.

The cross-ranking fallacy violates the rules of inference by using more than one basis of comparison at the same time. Example: I want to classify the basketball players in the NBA into (a) tall players, (b) black players, and (c) high-scoring players and then compare their performances. Problem: height, color, and skill are three different bases of comparison; so a tall, black, high-scoring player fits in all three categories and in a sense is merely being compared with himself.

The equivocation fallacy means that a word is used in several different ways to make it appear more relevant than it is. Example: Johnny is a juvenile delinquent for talking to his mother that way. Problem: the term *juvenile delinquent* is a legal term for underaged children who commit serious crimes; verbal abuse to one's mother is not such a crime.

The argument from analogy fallacy means that an analogy compares two unlike things, asserts that they have something in common, but then goes too far by suggesting that still another characteristic is common to both. Example: Both England and the United States have democratic governments, both have laws that spring from "common law," and both have problems with crime. England has fewer deaths from police bullets because their police, the bobbies, do not carry guns. Therefore, we should disarm our police to reduce the problem of police killing citizens. An argument from analogy necessarily omits important differences (fewer English criminals are armed), making the argument from analogy a weak form of argument.

A fourth way to evaluate your own reasoning in a persuasive speech is a systematic analysis of your detailed outline. Major arguments should appear as main points in the outline, and each argument should be followed by the supporting materials. Analysis of your outline should allow you to determine both the quantity and the quality of the evidence and the probable acceptance by the audience.

Critically questioning, verifying sources, identifying fallacies, and analyzing the detailed outline are all methods of assessing your own evidence, arguments, and reasoning.

Appeals to the Emotions

So far in this chapter, you have considered reasoning and logical appeals. However, you need to recognize that reasoning is not the only means of securing change in an audience's mind or actions. As one writer put it:

> The creature man is best persuaded
> When heart, not mind, is inundated;
> Affect is what drives the will;
> Rationality keeps it still.[12]

Among the multitude of ways that a persuader can persuade, the use of reason has the highest regard. Appeals to the audience's emotions, on the other hand, are often regarded as a less reputable means of persuading. **Emotional appeals** are in this book not because we encourage their unqualified use, but because we hear them and occasionally use them.

Monroe Beardsley, in his book *Thinking Straight*,[13] provides over 300 pages on how reasoning and logic apply in everyday discourse. Some of the appeals he discusses are seen as unacceptable or downright unethical in public speaking or debate over issues. Learn to recognize these appeals to be an enlightened critic of public speeches. After examining a sampling of some of these illegitimate emotional appeals, we will look at some that you should know, because they do have a place in public speaking.

. . . .

Unacceptable Emotional Appeals

1. Pity
2. Flattery
3. Provocation
4. Deception
5. Distraction
6. Prejudice

. . . .

We will quickly examine the unacceptable emotional appeals because they need only to be recognized, not practiced. These appeals are "unacceptable" in public speaking because they short-circuit the reasoning process. They try to persuade an audience to do something for the wrong reasons.

Your convictions can be a persuasive appeal.

Pity is an unacceptable emotional appeal because it attempts to persuade an audience to do something because of misplaced anguish. An example is the candidate who tries to secure votes for himself because he is poor and needs the money. You should vote for a candidate whose qualities will advance your community, your state, or your nation, but you should not vote for someone simply because he is pitiable.

Flattery is an equally unacceptable reason for submitting to someone's persuasive purpose. Although flattery of an individual or an audience can be enticing, its problem as an appeal is that seductive attempts to stroke an audience's collective ego do not play to real qualifications but to an exaggerated bit of puffery. "You are such a wonderful audience," "People as terrific as you must find this product very tempting," or "This audience is the best we have had in our entire tour" are all examples of appeals that invite further scrutiny.

Provocation is an attempt to incite an audience to action, usually by making the audience angry over some issue. Provocation is the stuff of which lynch mobs, gang fights, and wars are made. When people are riled about an issue anyway, then provoking them to anger is something almost any fool can do. The difficult task is turning an angry crowd to any constructive activity.

Deception is an attempt to convince an audience to do something for the wrong reasons. They are "deceived" because they do not know the real reasons for the speaker's persuasive attempt. The speaker gives an apparently objective speech about the merits of personal property insurance and recommends one broker over all others—without revealing that the recommended broker is his brother-in-law.

Distraction is an attempt to circumvent reasoning by throwing audience attention toward some unrelated aspect of the issue. In a hot public debate about the issue of rezoning a residential area for commercial use, one speaker points out that the developer who is asking for the variance was once arrested for alleged possession of marijuana. The speaker hopes to distract attention away from the zoning issue and throw it instead on the credibility of the developer.

Prejudice is another unacceptable emotional appeal that raises an audience's hackles over age, race, creed, color, or sexual preference. People can be prejudiced about almost anything. But the speaker who uses prejudice as an appeal tries to use it to divert attention from the issue itself and motivate the audience to dislike people who might be involved. The tough part about solving problems and settling issues is doing so without resorting to base appeals.

Let us look next at emotional appeals justifiable in public speaking.

• •

Acceptable Emotional Appeals

1. Idealism
2. Transcendence
3. Justified fear
4. Determination
5. Conviction
6. Dramatic example

• •

Among the acceptable emotional appeals is idealism, the communication of humanity's lofty possibilities, however rare their reality in practice. Martin Luther King, Jr., was an idealist who believed that human rights could be achieved for all people through peaceful resistance to laws, policies, and practices that treated some people as second-class citizens. Appeals to idealism are loaded with emotional content, but they are seen as appealing to our best qualities.

Transcendence is an emotional appeal that says differences can be overcome (transcended) by looking at greater and more basic commonalities among people. We do not look at what blacks, Hispanics, or poor people need; we look instead to what human beings need to exist in the richest country in the world. Gandhi is an example of a person who believed that India could overcome its ethnic and religious rivalries to forge a nation. Here again the speaker who seeks to transcend is appealing to humanity's finer qualities.

Some people would classify **fear appeals** as unacceptable because they short-circuit reasoning and encourage alarm. But justified fear refers to fear appeals in situations where we should truly be afraid, where a real threat exists to life

and property. Although some researchers have found that milder fear appeals work better than stronger ones,[14] others have found that stronger appeals work better than mild ones.[15] The most solid conclusion from the research is that reassurance is an important part of any fear appeals. That is, if you are going to scare someone, you had better also tell them how to avoid or overcome the fear.[16] Otherwise, you might succeed in scaring them so much that they repress the message to avoid it.

Speakers who are working on long-term causes have to rely on an emotional appeal called sheer determination, a drive to bring about change or reform regardless of obstacles. Determination is not rational; it is a hard-headed, single-minded will to carry a cause to its completion. Caesar Chavez exhibited such determination in his attempts to organize laborers. Speakers who urge audiences to complete a task no matter how much sacrifice or time it takes are using determination as their appeal.

Conviction is your depth of belief, your certainty in the truth, righteousness, and virtue of your cause. Union leaders have strong convictions about unions, corporate executive officers have strong convictions about free enterprise, and students often have convictions about education. Convictions have an emotional component that is unmistakable in the words and actions of the true believers. A person with convictions usually communicates those convictions to an audience.

The last of the legitimate emotional appeals is the dramatic example, the narrative or story that illustrates a message. In the Bible, dramatic examples are called parables; in children's stories they are called fables; and in speeches they are called dramatic examples or stories. Sometimes one actual example can give life to your statistics about drunken driving. The dramatic example plays more to the audience's emotions than to their rationality, but ordinarily it is not seen as disreputable to use dramatic examples in a sermon, a broadcast, or a public speech.

Presenting Sides and Citing Sources

After you have developed an argument that meets the tests of evidence and the requirement of believability—and now that you are at least familiar with the basic emotional appeals—what are you supposed to do? This section answers these questions: When should you present only arguments in favor of your case? When should you present both sides of an issue? What does the educational level of your audience have to do with presenting a one-sided or two-sided treatment of the issue? Why should you be careful not to omit important arguments in your presentation? And what other factors should you keep in mind as you put together your persuasive speech?

First, when should you present a **one-sided approach**—that is, only arguments and evidence in favor of your position on an issue? Research seems to indicate that pro-arguments and evidence are more effective when the audience already agrees with your position; in fact, a two-sided approach appears to work less well for such an audience. A **two-sided approach** tends to work better when the audience is basically opposed to your point of view. An educated audience, like your classmates, are also usually more favorably disposed to a two-sided approach, while less-educated persons tend to favor only a one-sided presentation with supporting arguments. Why should you be careful to include relevant arguments that the audience knows? The absence of a relevant argument is more noticeable to an audience in a two-sided approach than in a one-sided approach with supporting arguments only.[17] Finally, if your audience is likely to hear arguments against your position from others, you can reduce the impact of those counterarguments by mentioning them openly in your own persuasive speech.[18]

Types of Persuasive Speeches

The main distinction between the informative and the persuasive speech is its purpose: the informative speech attempts to increase what the audience knows; the persuasive speech attempts to change what an audience does by shaping, reinforcing, or altering its behavior. The six types of persuasive speeches that we will examine here are the speech of investigation, the speech of reasons, the speech of opposition, the speech of policy, the speech of values, and the speech of action.

A speech of investigation could be predominantly informative or mainly persuasive, but its distinguishing characteristic is that it is heavily based on investigation. We place it in the chapter on persuasive speaking because it is so difficult for students, after investigating a topic, to remain neutral about the topic. Instead, the more we know about a topic the more we tend to form our own opinion about it and the more we want others to adopt our opinion on the issue. So, a speech of investigation can be neutral and objective (i.e., informative) or it can be persuasive.

The Speech of Investigation

Some speech titles for a persuasive speech of investigation follow.

1. Should This State Change the Drinking Age?
2. What Is Behind the New Zoning Policies?
3. Hunger on the Home Front: Our City's Embarrassing Problem.
4. Background on Conflict in the Middle East.
5. Who Are Our Politicians?
6. Why Judges Cannot Afford to Serve.
7. The Best Jobs for the Future.
8. Problems with the Space Program.
9. The Story behind Military Pensions.

10. Plagiarism on Campus: How Big an Issue?
11. Why Drugs Are Dangerous.
12. What Does a Neilsen Rating Mean?
13. Should You Buy Stocks?
14. The New Tax Laws and You.
15. What Is Happening to Unions?

The speech of investigation illustrated here was based on personal experience that gave the speaker the incentive for exploring the issue of a national drinking age.

RAISING THE DRINKING AGE NATIONALLY TO TWENTY-ONE[19]
Diane Rettos

Legislators and concerned citizens have recently turned their attention to the issue of raising the national legal age for alcohol consumption to twenty-one. The reasoning behind this move is to lower alcohol-related traffic fatalities and reduce alcohol abuse among the youth of America. This speech will reveal why I am concerned with this issue and with what I was able to discover about it through my own investigation.

My interest in the issue of the legal drinking age was first aroused when I was in high school. Our local bar had a Sunday night event which attracted nearly everyone in the eighteen-to-twenty-five-year-old set and anyone else who could find a fake ID. Customers paid $3.00 at the door and then drank as much 3.2% draft beer as they wanted.

On the Sunday night of the 4th of July weekend the summer I graduated from high school, my best friend died after the car in which she was riding plunged twenty-five feet over a cliff and landed on its top. Stacey's neck was broken; she died in the arms of the police officer who pulled her from the wrecked car. The twenty-year-old driver was going 65 miles per hour on a 35-mile-per-hour curve in the road. His perception had been distorted by $3.00 worth of 3.2% beer. My friend was dead at age seventeen.

This experience devastated me. I had nightmares about the accident for many months; I still cannot forget the senselessness responsible for her death. When the recent interest in the drinking age surfaced, I decided to do some research on alcohol-related traffic accidents among the eighteen-to-twenty-year-olds in states with different legal drinking ages. The facts are startling.

First let me provide some background information. The legal drinking age issue became widely publicized in the early 1970s. In 1971 the legal voting age was lowered from twenty-one to eighteen and at least eighteen states subsequently lowered their legal drinking age to eighteen. Two states in particular—Michigan and

Massachusetts—then became very concerned when they experienced an alarming increase in alcohol-related accidents involving eighteen-to-twenty-year-olds.

After Michigan lowered its legal drinking age in 1972, a study conducted by the University of Michigan's Highway Safety Research Institute found a 17% increase in traffic accidents involving eighteen-to-twenty-year-olds and alcohol. According to the Michigan Department of State Police, within six months after the law was passed on January 1, 1972, there was a 100% increase in alcohol-related accidents involving eighteen-to-twenty-year-olds compared to the same period in 1971.[1] Massachusetts reported that alcohol-related traffic fatalities involving teenagers nearly tripled after the drinking age was lowered in 1973.[2]

As a result of these types of studies, states began raising their drinking ages. Their statistics show the positive results. A follow-up study in Michigan after the drinking age was raised from eighteen to twenty-one showed a significant drop in accidents involving alcohol and eighteen-to-twenty-year-old drivers. Officials in Maine reported that after their drinking age was raised from eighteen to twenty in 1977, there was a ". . . 30% drop in arrests of 17- and 18-year-olds for drunken driving. . . ."[3] One fact that helps validate these studies is that there was no change in accidents involving twenty-one-to-forty-five-year-old drivers, which suggests a direct correlation between the raised drinking age and the reduction of accidents with eighteen-to-twenty-year-old drivers.

Another reason behind raising the legal drinking age nationally is an effort to combat growing alcohol abuse among young people. Under present law in many states an eighteen-year-old high school senior can buy alcohol; too often that person will share the alcohol with younger friends. According to Ron Baily, Superintendant of Schools in Farmington, Maine, after the legal age for drinking was raised in 1977 from eighteen to twenty, the "drinking in schools isn't as flagrant as it was."[4] He says the illegality of drinking makes it easier to curtail the problem and that many students refuse to drink when it is illegal.

A national law raising the drinking age to twenty-one would eliminate the problem of young people driving to another state where the drinking age is lower. Some states have already developed regional cooperation on the drinking age issue. In New England, for example, Maine and Massachusetts raised their drinking age to twenty, and the governors of neighboring states are beginning to express interest in the idea.

My research on the issue of the legal drinking age included the search for evidence on keeping the drinking age at eighteen. However, the evidence on this side of the issue is less compelling. Vermont, for instance, reported no significant increase in alcohol-related accidents when they lowered the drinking age to eighteen. However, Dr. Richard Douglass, who conducted a study for the University of Michigan's Highway Safety Research Institute, produced a graph that showed an increase of twenty deaths the year after Vermont lowered its drinking age.[5] It is possible that the state of Vermont found twenty deaths statistically insignificant, but probably the family and friends of the twenty dead persons would feel otherwise.

A frequently cited argument concerning the legal drinking age is the one that says if a person is old enough to vote, marry, and defend our country at eighteen, then that person is old enough to decide what and how much to drink. But facts and statistics indicate that substantial numbers of eighteen-to-twenty-year-olds have not made responsible decisions about drinking in the past. As Bertram H. Holland, Executive Secretary-Treasurer of the Massachusetts Seconday School Administrators Association, stated in an interview in *U.S. News & World Report*," . . . is drinking before the age of 19, 20, or 21 a constitutionally protected right, or is it a privilege? . . . What we're dealing with here is a practical problem."[6]

My investigation into the issue of legal drinking age leads me to believe that college-age students should take a serious interest in this problem that affects us more than any other group. We should be the ones who find the facts and publicize them to others. The resulting changes in the laws could save our lives.

The Speech of Reasons

The primary persuasive purpose of the speech of reasons is to change the audience's mind on an issue using reasoning to shape their responses to it. This speech presents logic, evidence, inferences, generalizations, and conclusions to convince the audience to respond favorably to a specific position on an issue. It might result in a measurable shift of opinion, which one could record on a questionnaire or determine from audience responses showing that the issue is now seen differently. People who already believe as the speaker advocates hear a speech that reinforces their responses on the issue. They might register their agreement on the evaluation form or in the question-and-answer period. However, the majority of persons in the audience should not already agree with the position; otherwise, it would simply be a speech to reinforce rather than to shape an audience's responses.

As you approach your assignment, one of your first problems will be to select a topic. You can brainstorm or draw on your education and experience to find a suitable topic for you and for your audience. To give you a few ideas for speeches that are designed to shape the audience's responses, the following list is provided.

The police work with children to shape their attitudes toward law enforcement.

1. The Drinking Age Should Be Raised to Twenty-Five.
2. Tuition Should Be Raised.
3. Computer Courses Should Be Required in College.
4. Hearing Loss: A Reason to Avoid Live Bands.
5. Why Speaking and Writing Should be Required in College Courses.
6. Reading Newspapers: A Lost Art among College Students.
7. Why College Youth Should Oppose Social Security.
8. A Regular Program of Exercise Can Harm You.
9. Why Students Should Avoid Law and Medicine.
10. Five Reasons Why You Should Not Be a Business Major.

One characteristic that all ten topics have in common is that the majority of students in the audience probably would not agree. If they were to agree, then the topic is probably inappropriate for this assignment. Use the list to generate some ideas of your own on topics for the assignment illustrated here.

The speech of reasons attempts to shape an audience's responses by presenting arguments and evidence—reasoning—to induce change in the audience. The student speech presented here assumes that many college students talk themselves out of an exercise program and tries to overcome that problem by examining the students' rationale and by providing reasons for change.

AEROBICS[20]
Mark Dupont

"The way I look at it, my heart is only going to beat a certain number of times, and I'm not going to waste some of my valuable heartbeats on aerobics."

"Well, I just can't afford aerobic exercise. I mean, it just takes too long. I've got to study and go to work, and I have an eight o'clock every morning. I just don't have the time."

"Hey, I'm only eighteen. My heart and lungs are in great shape. I don't need aerobics; that's for old people, and I'm nowhere near thirty yet."

Why should we care about aerobic exercise? We're either too young, can't afford it, or don't want to "waste those valuable heartbeats." Too young? Autopsies done on American soldiers killed in the Vietnam War, young men whose average age was 22.1 years, revealed that 55% of them showed evidence of arteriosclerosis, a hardening of the arteries. Maybe we're not so young.

Can't afford aerobics? Well, a program of aerobics does demand that we make time in our busy schedules to exercise regularly, but the time we devote to our bodies is an inexpensive alternative to spiraling medical costs we might have to face because of an unhealthy heart, circulatory system, and lungs. Insurance companies are now recognizing this fact in the form of discounts to policyholders who participate in exercise programs like aerobics. Maybe we can afford it after all.

But what about those heartbeats? Well, there is no evidence that the number of times our hearts will beat is limited. What there is evidence of is that by strengthening the heart and improving the lungs and blood vessels, aerobic exercise can improve your health and perhaps increase your life span. Maybe it's time we learn something more about aerobics.

In 1968, when Dr. Kenneth Cooper published his book, *Aerobics,* he introduced to America an exercise program which has become so popular that aerobics is well on its way to becoming a household word. And as America becomes more interested in physical fitness and preventive medicine, more of us are being urged to participate in aerobic exercise. Ultimately, the decision on whether to do so is up to each of us. But to make such a decision, we need to have a general knowledge of what aerobics is.

Today, I'd like to acquaint you with what I call the three Ps of aerobics—its purpose, its program, and its profit, which I have learned through research on exercise. What you do with this knowledge is up to you, but knowing the purpose, the program, and the profit of aerobics will enable you to make a well-informed judgment of it and make you familiar with a program millions of Americans have made a part of their lives.

But first, a definition of *aerobics*. The word aerobic means "requiring air or oxygen." Aerobic exercises, or aerobics, are those that demand a long-term, relatively moderate use of oxygen. Unlike such anaerobic exercises as weightlifting which rely on oxygen stored in the muscles and create sporadic high/low demands on the heart and lungs, aerobic exercises increase heart and breathing rates to a steady, moderate level. Herein lies the purpose of aerobics: to strengthen the cardiovascular-pulmonary system—the heart, blood vessels, and lungs—through exercise which demands long-term moderate use of oxygen.[1]

The program to accomplish this end is basically simple. The choice of what exercise you will perform is up to you. A wide range of exercise or sports, from walking to baseball, rope-skipping to stair-climbing, are considered aerobic because of their long-term, moderate oxygen requirements. But their benefits differ. As you can see from this chart [student shows visual aid], running ranks higher than tennis in improving flexibility.[2] Based on their overall effects on the cardiovascular-pulmonary system, running, swimming, bicycling, and walking (in that order) rank highest among the aerobic exercises.

For people over thirty-five, the first step in a program of aerobics should be a consultation with a doctor who can administer a stress test. Following this is the twelve-minute test which everyone should take. This test simply determines how far you can run, walk, swim, or cycle in twelve minutes, giving you a gauge of your overall fitness. The results are categorized from very poor to superior, depending on age and sex. From this point you begin to exercise from three to six times per week by following a program of progress given in charts in Dr. Cooper's latest book, *The Aerobics Way*. Under Dr. Cooper's system, points are given for the amount of weekly exercise. You begin by seeking a certain number of points per week gradually by—in the case of running—running farther, longer, or more times per week. Once into the program full swing, men should be earning thirty points per week; women should be earning twenty-four points per week. At this level of activity, steady progress will be made toward more efficient heart, blood vessels, and lungs.

This brings us to the profit of aerobics. While not all of the benefits are known, the book *Rating the Exercises* summarizes the benefits nicely: "your lungs will process more air with less effort; your heart will grow stronger and pump more blood with each beat; the number and size of the blood vessels carrying blood to the body tissues will be increased; tone of the blood vessels and muscles will be improved; and your total blood volume will increase."[3]

Physical fitness is the theme of many speeches.

Thus, a simple program of aerobics, made a permanent part of your lifestyle, will strengthen the cardiovascular-pulmonary system through regular exercise which requires long-term, moderate use of oxygen. And because your heart, lungs, and blood vessels are at work whether you're awake or asleep, running or sitting, giving a speech or listening to one, every aspect of your life is affected. So not only do you create a better body through aerobics, but a better life as well, and perhaps a longer one.

The Speech of Opposition

A third type of persuasive speech, the speech of opposition, is one in which you oppose ideas that are commonly believed but seldom if ever disputed. These are the "sacred cows," things so commonly and widely believed or practiced that we do not even think about why we believe or practice them.

A good example of a speech of opposition was the student speech about why we should not brush our teeth. The belief that we should brush after every meal is so entrenched in most people's thinking that we suffer guilt when we do not brush our teeth. This student argued that with people living into their 90s, the practice of brushing three or four times per day is not so smart. She argued that the abrasive elements in toothpaste that remove tartar also wear off enamel. Her pitch was that we would be better off finishing our meals with salads and fruit, like apples, natural tooth cleaners, instead of relying so heavily on commercial toothpaste and brushing.

"Sacred cows" do not have to be universal. They may be beliefs that are common only in the audience you are addressing—as long as that group has a relatively unquestioning perspective on the issue. For instance, bankers rarely see much need for reform in their own practices; neither do educators. Both bankers and educators have their "sacred cows."

The list below might give you some ideas for a speech of opposition.

1. The Case for Nuclear War.
2. Why Fight Extinction of Rare Animals and Birds?
3. Some Major Reforms Needed in Higher Education.
4. Why the Government Should Operate the Steel, Gas, and Oil Industries.
5. Speech Anxiety: the Case against Public Speaking.
6. Negative Aspects of Organized Religion in America.
7. Eliminating the Traditional Family.
8. Why America Should Ban Automobiles.
9. How to Wean Yourself from Your Television.
10. Why Reading and Writing Are Unnecessary Today.

The purpose of the speech of opposition is to help the speaker and the audience recognize that there are usually reasonable arguments on both sides of issues that go undiscussed. The speech of opposition encourages skills in analysis of argument, researching for additional evidence, and selecting arguments that an audience will find persuasive.

What exactly are you to do in rebutting someone else's ideas? A careful look at the section on reasoning in this chapter suggests these important questions: Did the speaker reveal the source of evidence through oral footnotes? Were those sources expert, objective, and legitimate? Did the generalization go beyond the evidence? Did the reasons and the evidence lead to the generalization? Was there any unmentioned contradictory evidence? In addition to these general inquiries about someone else's position on an issue, you may want to keep alert for any fallacies in your opponent's speech.

In the speech of opposition, the speaker uses argument and evidence to oppose a commonly held idea or an idea presented by another speaker. Notice how the speech "Let's Let Men Cry" begins by arousing the interest of both men and women and then proceeds to forecast the topic and to relate the speaker to the topic. The speech attempts to shape the audience's attitudes by arguing for a change in the way men behave in our society.

LET'S LET MEN CRY[21]
Dorothy M. Takacs

Throughout all time, there have been many distinct differences between males and females. Some of these are more obvious than others. One difference that is very evident is the fact that males do not display emotion as women do. For some reason, in the beginning of time, someone decided that women should be free to express sadness, fear, anxiety, and concern. Men, although experiencing these very same emotions, were told that they must be suppressed. Except under extreme circumstances, men are not supposed to cry, show fear, or feel sadness, even though they experience these emotions just as women do.

Our society has made it difficult for men. Forcing men, or anyone for that matter, to suppress feelings and emotions leads to several problems and concerns. Society, making men feel that they must act and be "macho," has done all of us a great wrong. From the time of birth, males are taught to act a certain way. The time has now come for this to stop. Society must allow men to become and express whatever they wish. Men, like women, should be given the freedom to express their emotions whenever they deem it necessary.

I have been interested in this topic for a long time and have done extensive reading on it. I believe now that I have enough evidence to convince you of the need for change. In the next few minutes, I would like to present some reasons why I think men have been treated unfairly by society. I will tell you how rewards and punishments have shaped their behaviors and of the negative outcomes of their behaviors, such as greater amounts of stress and lack of certain interpersonal skills. I will give you some facts and opinions to make each of you aware of this problem and encourage you to take the proper steps to insure that this male "myth" is not perpetuated.

To begin, we must first address the problem itself. An article in *McCall's* magazine pinpoints the problem by stating that although biology has something to do with it, we now have evidence that most of the differences between male and female behavior are learned. They are the product of how we are raised and socialized. One of the most important and evident of these learned differences is the way in which men and women deal with their feelings.[1] The typical boy is encouraged from early childhood to "act like a man." Research has revealed that boy babies are picked up less promptly and are held less often when they cry when compared to girl babies. Male children are often spoken to more harshly than their female counterparts when exhibiting similar behavior. A boy who is treated in this manner learns early to suppress feelings of anxiety, fear, or pain. That very suppression may discourage the expression of other feelings as the boy matures, such as love, joy, and excitement.[2] As you can see, the suppression process begins at a very early age and can lead to serious effects in later life.

While women are often rewarded for behavior such as crying, men are almost always punished in some way. This punishment can be physical or emotional. For example, when a man and a woman have an argument and the woman begins to cry, the man usually gives in. The very act of his giving in to her behavior is a reward to her because it either ends or postpones the fight. When a man shows his emotions, he is usually punished by a significant other who shows disapproval of the action. When the man displays behavior identical to that of the woman, the responses and rewards are very different.

This difference between males and females is so ingrained in our society and in our minds that, despite all of the intentions, desires, and efforts to do away with it, men who do venture out to give free rein to their feelings may be met with rejection from women and from other men who see this behavior as a lack of masculinity.[3] Although females claim that they want their men to be more sensitive and emotional, they tend to avoid males who exhibit those behaviors, seeing them as too feminine.

McCall's magazine reported a recent study in which males and females of similar age groups were asked to rank their values in order from greatest to least importance. Among the highest ranking were companionship, love, satisfying work, rewarding sexual and emotional relationships, spiritual sustenance, financial security, and the right to make personal decisions. Comparing men and women, these values were ranked equally. Authors Lasswell and Lobsenz conclude, "If men so clearly share the same goals as women, it seems likely that they will ultimately refuse to be trapped by the myths that perpetuate men as strong, silent types, untouched by fear, sadness, or uncertainty."[4] If males exhibit the same feelings as females, and research shows that they do, why are they not given the same choice and opportunity as females to let their emotions show?

Females have another advantage over males because they are free to allow themselves to exhibit emotion. Females are more able to discern the emotions of others because they have full use of both hemispheres of the brain, according to research. Males, on the other hand, use primarily the right half of their brains. The left half of the brain is responsible for the "verbal codes" we experience, such as anger, happiness, and sadness. The right half is responsible for the "imagery codes" such as vocal tones and visual images. In discerning the emotions of others, females have the advantage over males because of their ability to utilize both halves of their brains.[5] According to *Psychology Today,* "Since emotions are largely a part of the right hemisphere and men are discouraged from acknowledging their emotions, they may not build connections between hemispheres as women do."[6] Hence, because males are taught not to show emotions, they may be limiting themselves when it comes to relationships and understanding others.

Probably *the* most important reason for men to modify their behavior concerning expression of their emotions is stress. Many feel that there is a strong correlation between suppression of emotions and stress. The mere "bottling-up" of one's feelings can bring on the symptoms of stress. Although stress is a part of everyone's life, great amounts of stress can lead to exhaustion, illness, accidents, nervous breakdowns, and even heart attacks.[7] It seems obvious that if one has the opportunity to let out emotions, less stress will occur, and the individual will feel better.

Males have come a long way since earlier "macho" image days. According to an article in *Newsweek,* "Men are becoming more and more aware of how pointless and painful it can be to keep their emotions veiled."[8] Since this myth is beginning to change in our own lifetime, it is up to us to perpetuate the trend that it is okay for men to show their feelings. It is okay for men to cry. We all need to be aware of this as we bring up our own children, as we confront those males who are trying to break custom and show their emotions, and as we try to help those males who cannot cope with this drastic change. We need to teach our males proper skills and rewards rather than to punish their emotional behavior. This appeal goes out to both males and females. We all must strive for accomplishment of this goal.

To sum up what has been said: males are only hurting themselves when they continue to participate in the "macho" myth. Men can hurt their relationships with others, their perceptions of others, and can hurt themselves physically and psychologically. There is no good argument which supports the cultural "given" that males are not to show emotion; there are only arguments against it. We all have an obligation to the males in our lives and to the children of the future. Let us all be aware of the male myth, and let us all do our best to stop it from continuing.

Thank you.

The Speech of Policy

This fourth type of persuasive speech encourages the audience to adopt the speaker's position on a statement of policy. The entire speech focuses on why the audience should favor a change in the **status quo,** a Latin expression for the way things are at present. If current law says that people under twenty-one years of age are in violation if they drink alcoholic beverages (the *status quo*), then this statement would be appropriate for a persuasive speech on policy: "The state should allow people who are eighteen years or older to drink alcoholic beverages."

The persuasive speech of policy recommends a change in permissible behavior, a change in what should or should not be done. Other examples of appropriate topics for this type of persuasive speech are:

1. People Who Work in Childcare Centers Should Be Subjected to Deep Background Checks on Their Character, Possible Legal Offenses, and Psychological Makeup.
2. Colleges Should Provide Textbooks for Students.
3. Physical Education Should Be Required in the College Curriculum.
4. Smoking Should Be Prohibited in All Public Buildings.
5. Chemical Weapons Should Be Prohibited Internationally.
6. State Taxes on Liquor and Tobacco Should Be Repealed.
7. The United States Should Require All Citizens to Serve in the Armed Forces.
8. Students Should Be Required to Pay for the School Paper.
9. Physicians Should Be Required to Reveal to Patients the Effects of Prescribed Drugs.
10. Food Companies Should Be Prohibited from Using Palm Oil and Coconut Oil in Their Products.

The main goal of a persuasive policy speech is to gain audience acceptance of the proposed policy. You are expected to reach this goal by revealing (1) what is wrong with the current policy, (2) exactly how you proposed to change the current policy, and (3) how the new policy will work in practice. The easiest way to organize your policy speech is to use this three-part division.

First, you should explain what is wrong with the *status quo*. Let us say that you decide to deliver a persuasive speech about number seven on the previous list: "The United States Should Require All Citizens to Serve in the Armed Forces." You can begin by giving some reasons why current practice is inadequate. Some possibilities:

United States security depends on a strong defense, but a voluntary system (the *status quo*) keeps the armed forces as small as the number who volunteer.

A voluntary armed force invites the least, rather than the best, qualified to serve.

Many college students are not mature enough to start college at seventeen or eighteen years of age.

Next, you could explain exactly how you propose to change the current policy. Perhaps like this:

All high school graduates (or drop-outs who are eighteen) would be expected to serve for two years in the armed forces.

Rich or poor, intelligent or not, majority or minority, the armed forces would consist of a cross-section of American society.

Nearly every college student would be twenty-years-old or older, which could result in more mature and qualified students.

Finally, you could show how your policy would work in practice:

This country would have a large number of able-bodied citizens who could be called up at any time in defense of their country.

Thousands more citizens would learn skills and discipline that would be useful for a lifetime of work or for additional education.

Our system of selection would be non-discriminatory because all people would be expected to serve.

Another speaker could deliver a speech of opposition showing the high cost of such a policy, the problem of training the unmotivated, and the logistical problems of implementing such a policy; but you could still achieve your immediate goal of making the audience consider an alternative to current practice.

The following speech about airport security is an example of a persuasive policy speech.

Preventing Sky Death[22]
Leon Abbellera

I don't speak English so good. I'd rather say this speech in Spanish because I could say it faster and better, but I do have something that I am very worried about which I want to say to you.

A few weeks ago Flight 103 blew up and killed 258 people. Thirty-five were students from Syracuse University. Their dying makes me afraid because I, like some of you, have relatives and friends in other countries. Mine are in the Phillipines, a place that is hard to get to any way except by air. Even if you are from the U.S., you probably do travel by plane and you may be afraid of traveling by plane like I am.

I think the airlines have to start a new policy to make us safer. I think that all airlines need to start doing more than having passengers walk through a metal detector. I think airlines need to check all individuals and all baggage to stop sky death.

The blowing up of Flight 103, a terrible thing which has happened before and could happen again, is a reason to change what airlines do. I am going to be afraid to fly home, and you are going to worry on every flight if airlines do not do more to stop terrorists from making us all feel unsafe.

According to this week's *Newsweek,* the explosion might have been caused by a bomb.[1] I know something about bombs because I have seen how they worked back home when my own country was going through trouble. Another article in *Newsweek* about airport security talks about an "invisible" bomb made of plastic explosive. I know from reading about bombs that they can be small; they can be made of things that do not show in X-rays; dogs, people, and machines cannot smell them; and they can be put in the plane's luggage area without much trouble. The first plastic bomb blew up a Pam Am flight way back in 1982. It killed a 16-year-old Japanese kid and injured fifteen passengers on the way to Tokyo. Another was found unexploded in Rio de Janeiro. It was only twelve inches long, three inches wide, and one-fourth of an inch thick.[2]

My idea for solving this problem is to have all baggage and all individuals checked for guns and explosives. Now terrorists have plastic guns and explosives that can only be found with the eyes. Unless security people look for these things, all of us will be unsafe. You might think: Leon's plan is bad because I will have to go the airport two hours early for every flight. I say, what is two hours compared to forever being dead?

Anyway, people who fly short distances don't carry much luggage. Only people on long flights to other countries carry many pieces of baggage. So most people would not have to spend lots of time at the airport.

Another thing that you wouldn't like is being searched all over your body at the airport. I don't like that idea much myself, but my idea does not mean that everyone would have to take off all clothes at the airport. I think it would be enough if male security people would "pat down" male passengers and female security officers would "frisk" women passengers. Unless I am wrong, that would be enough to keep terrorists from taking a risk of getting caught.

Billie Vincent, who was FAA security director, does not think that airports are doing enough to detect new explosives like C-4 or Semtex, a plastic explosive.[3] I don't either. I think my idea will work. I think I will feel more safe if everyone and everything is checked with the eyes. I think you will feel more safe too. And you will not end up with the same bad thing that happened to the passengers on Flight 103.

The fifth type of persuasive speech is the speech of values, a speech which examines controversial issues about which there is no universal agreement because there is no right answer. Or perhaps many people think they have the right answer, but there is not one answer upon which all may agree. The speech of values focuses on a value judgment.

The Speech of Values

Some examples of speeches of values appear below. Notice that each of them invite the speaker to prove that the idea is right or wrong, moral or immoral, ethical or unethical.

1. Honoraria from Special Interest Groups to Members of Congress Are Inconsistent with the Idea that Senators and Representatives Are Supposed to Provide Legislation for All the People.
2. Anti-Abortionists Are Unethical.
3. "Mississippi Burning" Is the Best Picture of the Year.
4. Long-Distance Truckers Who Use Drugs Threaten the Lives of Other Drivers on Our Highways.
5. When High School Administrators Suppress a Story in the School Paper, They Violate the Students' First Amendment Rights.
6. Criminals Have More Rights than Victims.
7. Sexual Harrassment Is One of The Biggest Problems in the Workplace.
8. As the Richest Nation on Earth, We Should Treat Our Poor and Impoverished Better Than Do Other Countries.
9. Basketball Is a More Important Sport than Football.
10. The California State University System Treats its Students Better than the University of California System.
11. Childcare Workers Deserve Higher Pay.
12. Right-Wing Extremists Are Threatening Our Liberty.
13. The Democratic Party Is in a State of Decline.
14. Women Are Capable of Front-Line Fighting in Time of War.
15. Statesville, North Carolina, Is an Ideal Place for a Business Location.

Speeches of values tend to talk about an issue without explicitly calling for action. They also tend to have plenty of facts on both sides of the issue. They differ from speeches of investigation because they center on a value judgment, they differ from the speech of policy because they do not recommend a policy, and they differ from the speech of action because they do not specify exactly what the audience is supposed to do about the controversy.

The speech of values can be organized many ways, but one of the easiest is the criteria/application design. This two-part organization speaks first about the standards of judgment and then about how the subject of the speech meets the standards. Let us say, for example, that you are a student at Mitchell Community College and you choose number fifteen from the previous list.

You might start your speech by stating what makes an ideal business location: "An ideal place for business is a community that (1) is located on a major interstate highway, (2) has rail or trucking warehouses for distribution of products, and (3) has a relatively large number of people available to work and to buy."

The second part of your speech would be devoted to stating how Statesville meets those criteria, perhaps with a quote from an official of the chamber of commerce or a businessperson who already resides in Statesville.

Another variation of this kind of speech is one in which the standards are implied or in which the speaker explains each criterion and how it applies during the speech. Here is an example of a speech of values to help you envision this type of speech:

Chemical Weapons Are Inhumane[23]
Anita Shaw

Weapons already exist that can make you cry, vomit, blister, choke, and bleed. Some affect your nervous system. Others give you fever and give you diseases that you can spread to others. All of them are inhumane.

As many of you know, I am a chemistry major. Lately, I have become more and more concerned about a problem faced by people in my major: would I work for a company that made chemical weapons? Your interest in this subject may be less direct, but maybe you will listen because chemical weapons can affect you too. Accidents at chemical plants have already killed people and their intentional use in warfare has already been tried with success.

Probably no weapon is humane, that is, respects human life. But chemical weapons are especially terrible because (1) their targets hit everyone in an area without control, (2) because they cause not just death, but untold suffering and impairment, and (3) because they can be concocted by anyone, including an undergraduate chemistry major.

Let us look first at how chemical warfare is uncontrolled. My father served in Vietnam where Agent Orange was used. Agent Orange is a chemical that kills plants. The idea was to wipe out the foilage so the enemy could be seen. At that time, no one seemed to know that it also caused damage to humans, but it did. Agent Orange killed plants and it later impaired and killed humans. It was sprayed by planes all over the tropical forests of Southeast Asia.

The chemical warfare that spreads disease to kill enemies is even worse because its intent is to kill people, not just military personnel, but kids, mothers, old folks—everyone. The disease goes wherever it is spread, not just at the airbase, the military complex, or the factory at which it is aimed. Yes, chemical and biological warfare are uncontrolled ways to kill large numbers of humans.

Second, chemical warfare is not just used to kill, it is often designed to cause extreme suffering as well as death. Mustard gas, used way back in World War I, causes blisters and burns that kill or maim. Nerve gas, the most common chemical agent stockpiled around the world, is developed to kill by interfering with the nervous system. According to the January 16, 1989, *Newsweek,* a choking gas called phosgene "caused 80% of the fatalities during World War I."[1]

Just so you don't think this method of killing is one that was used only in the past, you should know that Iraq won its war against Iran in 1988 largely by using chemical warfare and purposefully destroyed many of its own Kurdish minority the same way. Those who lived had burns that apparently came from a mixture of mustard gas and hydrogen cyanide, according to the article.[2] So chemical warfare is not only uncontrolled, it is deliberately used to incapacitate its victims by hurting them badly or making them sick.

A third reason why chemical warfare is inhumane is that these dangerous chemicals are cheap and easy to make. I know enough about chemistry already to make a chemical weapon, and I am only a junior in college. The ingredients for most chemical weapons can be made out of the same chemicals that are already used for pesticides. Early in 1989 Lybian leader Omar Kaddafi was accused of building a very large factory for the purpose of making chemical weapons. In an article entitled "Showdown With Libya," *Newsweek* showed satellite pictures of the plant and George Bush called chemical warfare the "poor man's atomic bomb."[3]

Unfortunately, any country can convert a plant that normally makes something as innocent as toilet cleaner, bug spray, and crop dust into a plant that produces nerve gas, liquid acids and bases, and toxic dust that can kill humans, slowly or quickly. The ingredients are inexpensive, easy to find, and buy. And it does not take a Ph.D. in chemical engineering to produce the stuff. Soon we might find ourselves with an even more serious problem than we thought we faced with nuclear weapons because they take advanced technology, specialized ingredients, and lots of education to develop.

I still don't know what I would do if I were an employee of some big pharmaceutical, petroleum, or pesticide company that produced products for killing instead of convenience. But I do know already that chemical warfare is uncontrolled, is designed to maximize suffering, and is cheap and easy. And I do know that the new outbreak of chemical warfare in the world has given me—and you—a lot to think about.

The Speech of Action

This sixth type of persuasive speech is a culmination of all that you have learned about public speaking. You can and should use the defining, describing, explaining, and demonstrating that you learned in the informative speech. You should reinforce the responses of those who already believe as you do, shape the responses of those whose perceptions you wish to alter, and change the responses of those who do not believe as you do. The most important aspect of the speech of action is that its purpose is to induce an overt change in the audience, to get a response to your speech.

The speech of action should use the principles of persuasion. It should (1) suggest change that is consistent with present beliefs, attitudes, and values; (2) suggest change that will require small rather than large changes in their lives; (3) suggest changes that will benefit the audience more than it will cost them; (4) suggest changes that meet the audience's needs; and (5) approach the change gradually in the speech.

Because the speech of action is successful only if the audience is actually moved to action, the speech can use a mixture of rational and emotional appeals. You may wish to show the audience that you share their concern because of what you have in common with them; you may wish to use fear appeals with reassurance; or you may wish to include narrations or stories that give your speech dramatic impact. Avoid the use of arguments and evidence or emotional appeals that are unacceptable such as appeals to hate, prejudice, sexism, or racism. Use of these types of emotional appeals can result in a *boomerang effect* in which the audience dislikes you and/or your topic more after the speech than they did before.

The speech of action allows you to express your own feelings and opinions based on your own experience, but the best speeches of this type rely heavily on expert testimony, careful reasoning, and the use of good evidence that meets the tests of quality and believability. A review of inductive and deductive reasoning and the tests of evidence and generalization is in order.

Two research findings are relevant to the speech of action. The first research finding is that a highly credible speaker can ask for more change in an audience— and get it—than can a speaker who is perceived as low or moderate in credibility.[24] The speech of action is likely to be one of the last that you deliver in your public speaking class. By now you should know more about your credibility with your classmates. If you sense that you are perceived as highly credible by your classmates, then perhaps you can ask for more change from your audience and get it. The second research finding relevant to the speech of action is that the speaker who explicitly asks for an audience's overt response is more likely to get it than will the speaker who only hints, implies, or suggests that the audience take some action.[25] You can improve your chance of gaining audience compliance by asking for the specific action.

In speeches of action, consider building your speech toward a request for action, rather than stating the action you seek at the beginning of the speech. In most of the other types of speeches considered in this text, you have been encouraged to be as clear as possible about your purpose by stating it in the introduction. Indeed, that works well in an informative speech, where the objective is clarity. However, asking an audience to do something, without proper preparation, can result in failure in a speech of action. For example, a speech that begins with "I want you to donate your body to science," could be met with revulsion, but a speech that builds a sound case for that goal by reviewing its humanitarian purpose can lead the audience to accept the idea.

A word of caution about the speech of action: do not urge your audience to do things over which they have no control. Some speakers unrealistically ask their audience to save the whales, ban the bomb, or settle international disputes. You can ask them to join groups, voice their own protests, and influence others to change public policy. You cannot get an audience to do something beyond its power.

What are some possible topics appropriate for the speech of action? The following is a brief list that you can use to help you find others.

1. Start an Exercise Program.
2. Stop Eating Meat.
3. Vote This Week.
4. Tell Others about Lobbyists.
5. Study Creatures of the Deep.
6. Learning through Public Television.
7. Avoiding Venereal Diseases.
8. Budgeting Your Time.
9. A Method of Decision-Making.
10. Preparing for the LSAT.

In the speech of action the speaker seeks some overt behavioral evidence of effect in response to the speech. In the following student speech, notice how the speaker opens with a narrative approach to capture audience attention and how the speech addresses the advantages of being an organ donor, involves the commitment of the speaker, meets the objections of the audience, and seeks audience compliance.

GIVING YOURSELF: THE ORGAN DONOR[26]
Lisa Schaffner

In 1978 Robert McFall had a fatal blood and bone marrow disease. His only chance, his only hope for survival, was a marrow transplant. Robert's cousin, David Shimp, was that hope. Shimp was a perfectly matched marrow donor. However, Shimp refused the operation that would save his cousin's life even though the bone marrow would regenerate after giving it to McFall. Shimp never consented to be a donor for his cousin. Three weeks later, McFall died.[1]

Several months ago, a young girl was very close to dying. She needed a kidney transplant from a donor close to her own age if she were to survive. Unfortunately, no donors were available. Her only hope for survival was that someone would come along quickly to be her donor. Four-year-old Michael became that strand of hope. Michael was killed in a car accident. Upon his death, his parents donated his kidney to the young girl. The organ transplant was successful, and the young girl celebrated her fourth birthday two weeks ago.

These two stories demonstrate how organ transplants can determine the life or death of another person. In the first story, Robert McFall died for lack of a willing donor. In the second story, based on an actual case, an organ transplant saved another human being's life.

Increasing numbers of people are donating their body organs to individuals or to research institutions.[2] People are joining this movement as they become increasingly aware of the desperate need of donated organs. During the last ten years, millions of Americans have unselfishly pledged their organs for transplant when they die.[3] The movement to donate body organs gained favor a decade ago when Dr. Christian Barnard performed the first heart transplant. However, even with steady support, some persons harbor misconceptions about organ donation that have resulted in a shortage of organ donors.

I believe in doing something constructive about the shortage of organ donors. About a year ago I signed a Uniform Donor Card that wills, upon my death, any of my needed organs to a person who needs them. Why did I do this? The reasons why one should become an organ donor are very clear.

First of all, medical scientists are seriously short of organ donations to save the lives of those doomed by disease or accident. The National Kidney Foundation recorded 4,600 successful transplants in 1978.[4] Unfortunately, more than 15,000 persons needed kidney transplants.[5] The result: over 10,000 individuals were doomed to die for lack of available transplants. Those 10,000 would have had a chance to live if all of the people killed in car accidents that year had been organ donors.

A second reason for becoming a donor involves your family's need for comfort. According to Dr. Currier, director of transplantation at Georgetown University Hospital, relatives are comforted with the thought that the death of their loved one represents the beginning of life for someone else.[6] Dr. VanHook of the University of Minnesota Organ Donor Program adds that the donor's family has a chance to receive something positive from a loved one's death.[7] Becoming an organ donor, then, not only allows you to save the life of another individual, but also permits your family to find some meaning and comfort in your death.

In addition to the shortage of organs for transplants and the comfort of your family, a third reason for being a donor is that upon dying you have no further need for your body parts. Therefore, the donation of your organs to someone who is living and has a need for them seems both reasonable and natural. The dying person's need for your body organs far outweigh your need for those organs upon your death.

These three reasons strongly support the idea of becoming an organ donor and for signing a donor card. However, I can see that many of you have reservations regarding the donor transplant process. You probably have valid reasons why you think you cannot be a donor. Well, let me admit that originally I had many reservations about the donor process. However, I found that my reasoning was faulty and that my reasons for refusing to become an organ donor were based on misconceptions.

For example, one misconception is that donating an organ will result in a closed-casket funeral. This notion is simply untrue. Vernon Gambill, administrator of the Tissue Bank of the Naval Medicine Research Center in Bethesda, Maryland, says that painstaking efforts take place to avoid altering the donor's appearance.[8] Gambill adds that if the appearance of the donor's body is altered, meticulous reconstructive procedures restore the donor's appearance.

A second misconception is that donating your organs after your death violates religious beliefs. Christian Science is the only American religious group that opposes the practice of organ donation.[9] In fact, according to Moses Tendler, Ph.D., an orthodox rabbi who chairs the biology department of New York's Yeshiva University, if an individual is in a position to donate an organ to save another person's life, it is obligatory to do so, even if the donor never knows the beneficiary.[10] The Lutheran Church-Missouri Synod indicated its position with a recent resolution encouraging its members to sign organ donor cards.[11]

A third misconception about organ donation centers on the idea that donors must be in perfect health. This idea is not necessarily true. All organs for transplant must be healthy; however, the entire body of the donor does not have to be in perfect physical condition. For example, a paralyzed person could donate glands, blood vessels, cartilage, parts of the inner ear, and corneas. A blind person can donate a cornea if the cornea was not the cause of blindness. An accident victim can donate any body organ that was not injured in the accident that took his or her life. Clearly, the body does not have to be in perfect health for a donation that can save someone else.

A fourth and very common misconception involving organ donation is the idea that your decision to donate body organs is irreversible. Not true. Any individual who decides not to be an organ donor can simply destroy the donor card and notify the proper officials. The decision to become an organ donor is an important one. However, once made, the decision is not permanent. The decision can be changed at any time by the person who made it in the first place.

How do you become a donor? The steps involved are simple. You merely need to fill out and carry a Uniform Donor Card. The card is available from the American Medical Association, independent donor groups, organ associations, and many hospitals. In addition, forty-seven of the fifty states now provide space on or with the driver's license that declares you as an organ donor. Ours is one of those states. An individual can easily register with the Department of Motor Vehicles upon renewing his or her license. Signatures of two witnesses are all that is required to legalize the donor card on the back side of the driver's license.

Most of you appear to be over the age limit of eighteen; but if you are not, parents may sign the consent for minor children. As a donor, you can bequeath specific organs or donate all needed organs or parts for persons who need them. You are encouraged to inform relatives and the nearest of kin regarding your decision to donate. You should make your donation known in writing to your attorney and to relatives, so that your request can be honored.

Your decision to become an organ donor is a serious one. By becoming a donor, you can help alleviate the serious organ shortage, while providing life for a person who might otherwise die. Furthermore, by donating your organs upon your death, you can help your family adjust to your death and create in them some positive feelings about your death. The decision to become an organ donor is completely up to you. Make the choice for the life of others; make the decision and the commitment to become an organ donor.

Summary

This chapter began with a definition of persuasive speaking that indicated the persuader intends to change the audience's behavior through reinforcing, shaping, and changing its responses on an issue. Five principles of persuasion were explained: (1) the role of consistency in persuasion, (2) the need to break down big proposed changes into smaller ones, (3) the necessity of showing benefits that are greater than the costs to the audience, (4) the importance of meeting audience needs in the speech, and (5) the suggestion that a gradual approach to change works better than asking for too much too early in the speech.

Next we explored inductive and deductive reasoning, the tests of evidence, and the requirement of believability. We discussed when to use a one-sided or a two-sided message, especially in relation to audiences of different educational levels. Citing sources with oral footnotes was reviewed as a means of allowing the audience to verify evidence.

Our discussion of reasoning in persuasive speeches was followed by a consideration of emotional appeals. Among the illegitimate emotional appeals were pity, flattery, provocation, deception, distraction, and prejudice. Among the legitimate emotional appeals were idealism, transcendence, justified fear, determination, conviction, and dramatic example.

Finally, we explored six basic types of persuasive speeches: (1) the speech of investigation, with its emphasis on researching the topic as a basis for a change in belief; (2) the speech of reasons, with its emphasis on shaping an audience's response through arguments and evidence; (3) the speech of opposition, with its emphasis on presenting a case against a commonly held belief or practice; (4) the speech of policy, which advocates acceptance of a change that would invite new behavior; (5) the speech of values, which explores an issue embedded in a value judgment by shaping the audience's position on the issue; and (6) the speech of action, with its mixture of rational and emotional appeals aimed at changing the audience's behavior.

▼▼

Checklist

A Checklist for the Persuasive Speech

_____ 1. Have you determined if your intent is to shape, reinforce, or change your audience's responses?

_____ 2. Have you shown how the change you are suggesting for the audience is consistent with their past behavior?

_____ 3. Have you kept your requested changes modest so that the audience does not perceive your request as too much to ask?

_____ 4. Have you demonstrated for the audience the benefits received if they do as you request?

_____ 5. Have you shown the audience ways that your request will fulfill their needs?

_____ 6. Have you approached your suggested change gradually so the audience does not perceive that you are asking for change without sufficient preparation?

_____ 7. Have you employed inductive and deductive reasoning with evidence that meets the tests?

_____ 8. Have you placed your arguments for maximum effect, consciously presented one side or two, and cited sources to verify your evidence and arguments?

_____ 9. Have you avoided fallacies and evaluated your emotional appeals for appropriateness?

_____ 10. Have you composed your speech so that it fits predominantly into the classification of investigation, reason, opposition, action, policy, or values?

Application Exercises

1
Student Hierarchy of Needs

Persuasive speeches often appeal to an audience's unmet needs. Since needs vary in different communities, colleges, classes, and individuals, you can make yourself more sensitive to audience needs by rank, ordering the five unmet needs that you believe are important to your audience.

1. _____

2. _____

3. _____

4. _____

5. _____

2
Principles of Persuasion

After reading the section on principles of persuasion, you should be able to identify cases in which they are correctly used. Examine the cases below and indicate in the margin which of the following principles is being observed:

C = consistency persuades

S = small changes persuade

B = benefits persuade

N = fulfilling needs persuades

G = gradual approaches persuade

_____ 1. To save my audience considerable time and effort, I am going to provide them with a form letter that they can sign and send to the administration.

_____ 2. Because I know that most of my classmates are short of cash, I am going to tell them how to make some quick money with on-campus jobs.

_____ 3. I plan to wait until the very end of the speech to tell the audience that the organization I want them to join will require two hours of driving per week.

_____ 4. My audience of international students already believes in the values of learning public speaking; so I think they will respond favorably to my recommendation for a course in voice and articulation.

_____ 5. I really want my audience to believe in Jesus Christ the way I do, but I'll try today to simply get them to consider going to church while they are in college.

Answers

1-B, 2-N, 3-G, 4-C, 5-S.

3
Inductive and Deductive Reasoning

Using the "tests" described previously and the descriptions of inductive and deductive reasoning, identify each of the following arguments, with **I** for inductive or **D** for deductive, by placing the appropriate letter in the blank on the left.

_____ 1. Sam, Fred, and Joan are all rich; therefore, most people in this community must be rich.

_____ 2. College students always cause mischief; so Andy must be a college student.

_____ 3. Other states have raised the drinking age to reduce accidents; therefore, this state should raise the drinking age also.

_____ 4. Americans practice freedom of speech; so those students in the public speaking class must be Americans.

_____ 5. Every time I drink milk I break out with hives; so I must have an allergy.

Answers
1-I, 2-D, 3-I, 4-D, 5-I.

▼▼

Application Assignments

The Speech of Investigation

Deliver a speech in which you research a controversial issue for facts that lead to a conclusion. Use arguments and evidence from your reading and listening. Be sure to use oral footnotes to indicate when you use ideas, arguments, and evidence from sources. This can be a speech of reinforcement for those in the audience who believe as you do, or a shaping speech for others.

The Speech of Reasons

Deliver a speech in which you shape the audience's responses by using arguments and evidence supporting a conclusion that invites the audience to change its mind on an issue (shaping). The emphasis in the speech of investigation was on research, on finding facts and evidence; the emphasis in the speech of reasons is reasoning, the marshaling of facts and evidence through skillful argument to change the audience's perception of the issue.

The Speech of Opposition

Deliver a speech in which you attack a "sacred cow," a widely-held idea that is accepted uncritically. Use analysis, evidence, inference, and argument to bring about doubt in the minds of the audience. When you are finished with your speech, the idea should no longer be a "sacred cow," but should look more like an "ordinary cow."

The Speech of Policy

Deliver a speech in which you advocate a policy that would change the *status quo,* a change in current behavior. Explain to the audience what is wrong with current policy, exactly how you would change it, and how your new policy would work in practice. The goal is to gain audience acceptance for your proposed policy.

The Speech of Values

Deliver a speech in which you examine a controversial issue of propriety, morals, taste, or ethics that is based on a value judgment. Your task is to measure your position on the issue against criteria or standards that could more generally apply to the issue. Your goal is to persuade your audience to think about the issue and to move toward favoring your position on it.

The Speech of Action

Deliver a speech in which you use a mix of reason and emotion to secure behavioral change in the audience. The idea behind this speech is to invite overt action from the audience, not just a change of mind.

▼▼

Vocabulary

attitude   A tendency to like or dislike something or somebody; a learned predisposition to respond favorably or unfavorably toward something.

behavior   The actions the persuasive speaker seeks to change, such as the way a person votes, buys, talks, eats, exercises, etc.

belief   Based on attitudes, beliefs are our hypotheses about the nature of things and what we should do about them; e.g., I might have the belief that good works will lead to salvation (value).

changing   One of the three behavioral purposes of persuasive speaking, in which the audience alters overt behavior as a result of a persuasive message.

conclusion   The logical deduction in deductive reasoning, a conclusion is true if its major and minor premises are true and correctly arranged (valid).

consistency   The idea that people are more likely to be persuaded by that which is in line with or consistent with what they already believe and do.

cost-benefit analysis   The idea that an audience is more likely to do as the persuader suggests if its costs in time, money, or effort are lower than the expected benefits of advantages.

deductive reasoning   A kind of reasoning that employs a major and minor premise that necessarily leads to a conclusion.

emotional appeals   Attempts to persuade an audience by using human emotions (love, hate, fear, prejudice, and so on) to secure change. These appeals are discredited when they distract from the issue at hand.

fallacies   Violations of the rules of inference, such as hasty generalizations, equivocation, or cross-ranking.

fear appeals   Emotional appeals that threaten you or your loved ones; linked with reassurance, they tend to work better than they would if you did not indicate to the audience a way to escape the threat.

generalization   The inferred result of inductive reasoning, this broad statement is a probability that encompasses the evidence presented to support it.

hierarchy of needs   A rank-ordered list of physical and psychological requirements needed to keep body and mind healthy. It forms the basis of making persuasive appeals.

inductive reasoning   A kind of reasoning which employs evidence leading to a generalization that is probably true.

one-sided approach A situation in which the audience is provided with only the "pro" arguments and evidence on an issue; appears more persuasive with less-educated audiences and with those already committed to the position being advocated.

purpose The purpose of a persuasive speech is to change the audience in some way by shaping, reinforcing, or altering its responses concerning some idea or issue.

reinforcing One of the three behavioral purposes of persuasive speaking, in which the audience perceives reward for its present behavior, ideas, or beliefs; reinforcing encourages the audience to persist in its present mode.

shaping One of the three behavioral purposes of persuasive speaking, in which the audience learns from the speaker to change perceptions about an issue or idea.

status quo A Latin term that refers to the way things are at present; the current situation.

two-sided approach A situation in which the audience is provided with both the pro and the con sides of an issue; an approach that appears more persuasive with educated audiences and with persons hostile to the proposed position on the issue.

value A primitive preference for or positive attitude toward a state of existence (justice, freedom, fulfillment) or broad mode of conduct (bravery, integrity, friendship); relatively resistant to change through persuasive messages.

▼▼▼

Endnotes

1. Gerald R. Miller, "On Being Persuaded: Some Basic Distinctions," in Michael E. Roloff and Gerald R. Miller, *Persuasion: New Directions in Theory and Research* (Beverly Hills, Calif.: Sage Publications, 1980), 16–26.
2. Wallace Fotheringham, *Perspectives on Persuasion.* (Boston: Allyn & Bacon, 1966), 33.
3. Daryl Bem, *Beliefs, Attitudes and Human Affairs* (Belmont, Calif.: Brooks/Cole, 1970), 4–7.
4. Martin Fishbein, seminar lecture on attitude change conducted at the University of Illinois, Spring 1965, and quoted in Gary Cronkhite, *Persuasion: Speech and Behavioral Change* (Indianapolis: Bobbs-Merrill, 1969), 64.
5. Bem, p. 14.
6. Bem, p. 16.
7. A. H. Maslow, "A Theory of Human Motivation," *Psychological Review* 50 (1943):370–96.
8. Monroe C. Beardsley, *Thinking Straight: Principles of Reasoning for Readers and Writers* (Englewood Cliffs, N.J.: Prentice-Hall, 1956), 28.
9. Beardsley, p. 31.
10. Jack L. Whitehead, Jr., "Effects of Authority-Based Assertion on Attitude and Credibility," *Speech Monographs* 38 (1971):311–15.
11. Beardsley, p. 29.
12. From Marvin Karlins and Herbert Abelson, *Persuasion: How Opinions and Attitudes are Changed,* 35. Copyright © 1970 by Springer Publishing Company, Inc., New York. Used by permission.
13. Beardsley, pp. 283–91. Only a few of the categories used here are from Beardsley; most were developed by the authors.
14. I. Janis and S. Feshbach, "Effects of Fear-Arousing Communication," *Journal of Abnormal and Social Psychology* 48 (1953):78–92.

15. Fredric A. Powell, "The Effects of Anxiety-Arousing Messages When Related to Personal, Familial, and Impersonal Referents," *Speech Monographs* 32 (1965):102–6.
16. Frances Cope and Don Richardson, "The Effects of Reassuring Recommendations in a Fear-Arousing Speech," *Speech Monographs* 39 (1972):148–50.
17. C. I. Hovland, A. Lumsdaine, and F. D. Sheffield, *Experiments in Mass Communication* (Princeton, N.J.: Princeton University Press, 1949), 201–27.
18. A. Lumsdaine and I. Janis, "Resistance to 'Counter-Propaganda' Produced by a One-Sided Versus a Two-Sided 'Propaganda' Presentation," *Public Opinion Quarterly* (1953): 311–18.
19. From a speech composed in Communication and Persuasion, School of Interpersonal Communication, Ohio University. Endnotes for the speech: [1]Richard L. Douglass, "The Legal Drinking Age and Traffic Casualties: A Special Case of Changing Alcohol Availability in a Public Health Context," *Drinking and Traffic Accidents—U.S.,* ed. Henry Weschler (Lexington, Mass.: D. C. Heath and Co., 1980), 93; [2]M. Beck and P. Malamud, *Newsweek* (April 2, 1979), 38; [3]Beck and Malamud; [4]Beck and Malamud; [5]Douglass, p. 104; [6]B. Holland and B. T. Cheney, *U.S. News & World Report* (April 16, 1979), 61–62.
20. From a speech delivered in Fundamentals of Public Speaking, Iowa State University. Endnotes for the speech: [1]Kenneth H. Cooper, *The Aerobics Way* (New York: M. Evans & Company, 1977.); [2]James F. Fixx, *The Complete Book of Running* (New York: Random House, 1977); [3]Charles T. Kuntzleman, *Rating the Exercises* (New York: William Morrow, 1978).
21. From a speech delivered in Communication and Persuasion, School of Interpersonal Communication, Ohio University. Endnotes for the speech: [1]Marshia Laswell and Norman Lobsenz, "Why Men Can't Talk About Their Feelings," *McCall's* 105 (September 1978), 60–62; [2]Lasswell and Lobsenz; [3]Lasswell and Lobsenz; [4]Lasswell and Lobsenz; [5]Jack C. Horn, "Women's Ambidextrous Brains," *Psychology Today* 16 (March 1982), 23; [6]Horn; [7]Hans Selye, M.D., "How to Master Stress," *Parents Magazine* 52 (November 1977), 25–27; [8]David Gelman, "How Men are Changing," *Newsweek* (January 1978), 52.
22. The sources for the speech entitled "Preventing Sky Death" were [1]"An Explosion in the Sky," *Newsweek,* January 2, 1989, 14–19; [2]"Security: The 'Invisible' Bomb," *Newsweek,* January 2, 1989, 20; and [3]"Security: The 'Invisible' Bomb," 20.
23. The sources for the speech entitled "Chemical Weapons Are Inhumane," came from [1]"The 'Winds of Death,' " *Newsweek,* January 16, 1989, 22–25; [2]"The 'Winds of Death,' " 24; and [3]"Showdown With Libya," *Newsweek,* January 16, 1989, 16–17.
24. C. Hovland and H. Pritzker, "Extent of Opinion Change as a Function of the Amount of Change Advocated," *Journal of Abnormal and Social Psychology* 54 (1957):257–61.
25. Karlins and Abelson, pp. 11–14. See also W. Weiss and S. Steenbock, "The Influence on Communication Effectiveness of Explicitly Urging Action and Policy Consequences," *Journal of Experimental Social Psychology* 1 (1965):396–406.
26. From a speech delivered in Communication and Persuasion, School of Interpersonal Communication, Ohio University. Endnotes for the speech: [1]"Do You Own Your Body?" *The Futurist* 15 (December 1981), 73; [2]"How Can You 'Will' Parts of Your Body?" *U.S. News & World Report* 85 (December 18, 1978), 72; [3]"How Can You 'Will' Parts of Your Body?"; [4]"How Can You 'Will' Parts of Your Body?"; [5]"How Can You 'Will' Parts of Your Body?"; [6]"How Can You 'Will' Parts of Your Body?"; [7]"Easing Shortage of Organs," *USA Today* 110 (October 1981), 16; [8]"Can You Be a Donor?" *Health* 14 (April 1982), 43; [9]"Can You Be a Donor?" 56; [10]"Can You Be a Donor?"; [11]"Can You Be a Donor?".

Credits

Photographs
Photo research by
Doris Nigg

Chapter 10
Page 191: © Jean-Claude Lejeune; **page 194:** © James Shaffer.

Chapter 11
Page 201: © Nancy Anne Dawe; **page 203:** © James Shaffer; **page 207:** © Nancy Anne Dawe; **page 213:** © James Shaffer; **page 215:** © Nancy Anne Dawe; **page 217:** © James Shaffer.

Chapter 12
Page 236: © Comstock; **page 242:** © Comstock; **page 243:** © Richard Anderson; **page 246:** © James Shaffer; **page 251:** © Amwest.

Chapter 13
Page 258: © Camerique/H. Armstrong Roberts; **page 265:** © James Shaffer; **pages 279, 280:** all, © Mark Rightmire.

Chapter 14
Page 291: UPI/Bettmann Newsphotos; **page 298:** © Alan Carey/The Image Works, Inc.; **page 302:** AP/Wide World Photos; **page 303:** © H. Armstrong Roberts; **page 305:** © James Shaffer; **page 307:** UPI/Bettmann Newsphotos; **page 309:** © James Shaffer; **page 313:** © James Shaffer; **page 321:** © Mark Antman/The Image Works, Inc.; **page 328:** © Michael Geissinger/Comstock.

Illustrations

Chapter 6
Page 112, figure 6.5: Rolin Graphics.

Chapter 8
Page 155, figures 8.2, 8.3: Rolin Graphics.

Chapter 10
Page 180: Rolin Graphics; **page 183:** Rolin Graphics.

Chapter 11
Page 209: Rolin Graphics.

Chapter 12
Page 231, figures 12.1, 12.2: Rolin Graphics; **page 232, figure 12.3:** Rolin Graphics; **page 234, figure 12.4:** Rolin Graphics; **page 235, figures 12.5, 12.6:** Rolin Graphics; **page 239, figure 12.9:** Rolin Graphics; **page 240, figure 12.10:** Rolin Graphics; **page 247, figures 12.11, 12.12, 12.13:** Rolin Graphics; **page 249, figure 12.14:** Rolin Graphics.

Chapter 13
Page 269, figure 13.1: Rolin Graphics; **page 270, figure 13.2:** Rolin Graphics.

Index